SNAKEBIT

LESLIE ANTHONY

Snakebit

CONFESSIONS OF
A HERPETOLOGIST

GREYSTONE BOOKS

D&M PUBLISHERS INC.
Vancouver/Toronto/Berkeley

11 12 13 14 15   5 4 3 2 1

Greystone Books
An imprint of D&M Publishers Inc.
2323 Quebec Street, Suite 201
Vancouver BC Canada V5T 4S7
www.greystonebooks.com

Cataloguing data available from Library and Archives Canada
ISBN 978-1-55365-236-6 (cloth)
ISBN 978-1-55365-527-5 (pbk.)
ISBN 978-1-926685-39-7 (ebook)

Editing by Nancy Flight
Copy editing by Iva Cheung
Cover design by Peter Cocking
Text design by Naomi MacDougall
Cover photo © Martin Harvey/Digital Vision/Getty Images
Printed and bound in Canada by Friesens
Printed on acid-free, 100% post-consumer paper
Distributed in the U.S. by Publishers Group West

We gratefully acknowledge the financial support of the Canada
Council for the Arts, the British Columbia Arts Council, the
Province of British Columbia through the Book Publishing Tax
Credit, and the Government of Canada through the Canada
Book Fund for our publishing activities.

For Leslie and Ralf, who put up with it all. Sort of.

*OPRAH CLAUSE: Anything herein to do with science is factual; anything to do with people is as close to true as the subjectivity of experience and unconscious temptation to exaggerate will permit... or that anything this bizarre could actually be.

MURKY

I'm chestwader-clad, stooped
'midst the harbinger cries
of a thousand vernal vanguards
and every muskeg-suction step
throws a turbid wake of decomposition
and swirling methane rot
into the soaring anuran chorus
from reeds they scream and cluck
the Mormon Tabernacle Frogs
pig-eyed, unblinking, clamoring
distended with an urge to mate
swarming in my headlamp to
place jellied-egg hors d'oeuvres
on cattail crackers
under vocal-sac watchful
amphibian grins

    this morning, I asked a woman to marry me
    from a phone booth on an all too unfamiliar road
    urged on by buckets of salamanders
    and the hormone surge that comes
    after winter's impoundment 'neath a ton of snow

meanwhile, my slippery friends
at the beaver pond
grind onward in the rain
lured by blind instinct
to the water's welcome edge
muddy doormat, murky concierge
house of destiny

    —Leslie Anthony

CONTENTS

ACKNOWLEDGMENTS

· · ·

MANY HAVE ASSISTED me, inspired me, or kept me from being killed over the years. This is no small debt, so I hope I don't forget any of them.

Early on I had many unwitting accomplices: my brothers, Vincent, Michael, and Chris; Laurie, Jimmy, Tommy, and Gregory Walsh; my turtle-mad friend Mike Campbell; and camp counselor Marty. For enduring various university dramas, both indoors and out, I have Lisa Anderson, Wendy Bush, and Linda Nyilus to thank. Diligent laboratory help at the Royal Ontario Museum came from ever-smiling Marj "the assistant" Burnett and at the University of Toronto from Cheryl Smith and her amazing flow cytometer. In Whistler I've been grateful for time in the bush with Bob Brett, Connor McGillion, and Elke Wind, as well as the indulgences of Caroline Carnerie, Lillian Clark, Mike Douglas, Paul Morrison, and Auli Parviainen; Mary and the girls at Starbucks Creekside kept me awake for well over a year. Musical kudos to The Shins and Wilco for similar stimulation.

Key field help on scientific and journalistic assignments came from Levon Aghasyan, Scott Alexander, Alex Fishbein, Michelle Fulford, Myles Garland, Christopher Hart, Lesley-Ann

Hawthorn, Danny Jacques, Alexandre Malkhasyan, Mr. Mosquito, and, for one especially long and cherished spring that would predispose her to never touching another salamander, Caleigh Garland.

None of this would have been even remotely tolerable without the fun-loving, hard-working grad students I have played guitar, drunk beer, or collected with (often all three): Raoul Bain, Joel Bonin, Jeff Brown, Michael Caldwell, Paul Chippindale, Tom Drysdale, Ian Dworkin, Hugh Griffith, Hinrich Kaiser, Greg Klassen, Hans Larsson, Amy Lathrop, Barb Mabel, Nick Mandrak, Fernando Marques, Randy Mooi, Timothy Sharbel, Tanya Trepanier, and Clifford Zeyl.

A toast of camaraderie and heartfelt thanks to the many inspirational professional herpetologists I have interacted and/or published with over the years. To start, although he doesn't appear in the narrative, I owe more than he imagines to the inimitable and iconic doyen of Canadian herpetology, Francis R. Cook of the National Museum, for his hovering, fatherly presence in the nation's capital, generous encouragements, historical perspectives, keen eye for the minutiae of variability where others saw only homogeneity, books, papers, preternatural shock of gray hair, and constant demonstration of scholarly—albeit often glacial—patience that included thoughtfully answering a handwritten letter from an aspiring young herpetologist. Shout-outs also to Aram Aghasyan, Ilya Darevsky, John Gilhen, the late Stan Gorham, David M. Green, Patrick Gregory, Michael J. Lannoo, Lawrence M. Licht, Ross D. MacCulloch, the late David J. Morafka, Nikolai Orlov, Martin Ouellet, William B. Preston, the late Mike Rankin, Mike Sarell, and Richard Wassersug.

While I'm digging for accomplices, I may as well throw in a few vertebrate paleontologists: I learned much on this front from Michael W. Caldwell, Robert L. Carroll, and Thomas S. Parsons.

Although everyone listed above has given me something of intellectual, emotional, and, let's face it, comic value, there are a few whom I consider true mentors: Dave Barton, Geoff Powers, and J.C.H. Carter at the University of Waterloo; Jim Bogart at the University of Guelph; Dan Brooks (though he probably doesn't know it) at the University of Toronto; and especially, at both that institution and the Royal Ontario Museum, the inimitable and beloved (certainly by me) Robert W. Murphy, whose fractious tutelage, underrated genius, intellectual largesse, and sheer personal generosity have forged in me an unequivocal admiration and friendship.

I have also benefited from working on herp-related articles at magazines such as *AirLines, Cottage Life, Equinox, explore,* and *Seasons,* parts and permutations of which are sprinkled throughout the present work. I am particularly thankful for the editorial guidance of Alan Morantz and James Little. While we're in the realm of people being patient with me, let me state my overwhelming debt to the caretaker and editor of this volume, Nancy Flight, and my agent, Ashton Westwood.

Finally, I thank my long-suffering daughter, Myles Emily Garland—dragged along since birth to look for critters on occasions too numerous to count—for her unvoiced support and occasional interest (you take what you can get with teenagers), and Jory Lee Mullen, siren of my personal swamp at this writing, for much appreciated research, moral support, and the kind of wide-eyed wonder at the natural world we all should enjoy.

A TALISMAN IN THE SNOW

IN THE END, the *kyy käärme* were exactly where Teemu had said they would be.

When Vuokko and I stepped off the lift, partway up Ylläs Mountain, near the terminus of the long, sloping bench that delivered skiers from dense taiga to treeline to tundra, I clicked out of my skis and scanned the bonsai islands poking from the surrounding sea of snow.

The most promising spots quickly proved disappointing: a warm shelf of small boulders draped in juniper and Labrador tea held only dead leaves; a sere, sandy ridge constellated with lichen-coated rubble was too exposed; a sunny tangle of Lapland's quintessential Dwarf Birch was picketed by cool, rapidly moving shadows.

Clearly I would have no facile discovery, and superficial searching of the type used to locate the glint of lost car keys on a groomed lawn wouldn't cut it in messy ground cover. But I knew that. I also knew that what I was trying to find was supremely adapted to *not* being found.

From the human standpoint, the exercise was an amusing little contest that pitted visual acuity against concealment and logic against camouflage, driven by a hard-wired hunting instinct that would end with a photo instead of a kill and a meal. My advantage was intellectual understanding, whereas my unreasoning adversaries had only a low-watt instinct for survival—albeit backed by some fairly high-voltage weaponry.

Vuokko stood by, amused at my zeal, horrified by my temerity, likely regretful she'd kicked the whole thing off. (Her skis were still affixed—prudently, I imagined she imagined—in case of the need for a quick getaway.) I was more excited than I'd been in years. After all, how often do you find yourself in the Arctic with a meter of snow on the ground, girded by the invincibility of Gore-Tex and ski boots, with a chance to hunt for poisonous snakes?

THE TRIP HADN'T begun so auspiciously. I'd journeyed to Finnish Lapland to work on a ski story for an international travel magazine. Not exactly a pedestrian pursuit, but it *was* work and very much the bread-and-butter I'd made a career from. In my mind, I was an intrepid adventure-travel writer with a penchant for exotic winter destinations, a cultural plumber of the White Planet. My friends, however, considered my calling a permanent vacation. Even my daughter struggled with the concept. "I'm not sure," I'd once overheard her say of my job to a friend. "He goes skiing with weird people in weird places and writes about it."

Her comment contained a certain quotient of truth: here I was, after all, in the waning days of April, traipsing through an ungodly expanse of frozen bog with a troop of fun- and vodka-loving Finns, several hundred kilometers north of the Arctic Circle.

My official escort at Ylläs, Vuokko was milk blonde, of course, and framed her luminous blue orbs with stylish, cat's-eye glasses. She spoke an excellent, albeit nasal, version of the

King's English and was both smart and wickedly funny. Her humor was as flat and dry as the crispbread adorning every table in the land, and, combined with the Finnish art of understatement, she could deadpan with the best. After several hours in her company I'd yet to figure out when she was serious.

Toward the end of our first day, we rode a chairlift up the south side of Ylläs. Blazing spring sun warmed the forest below, stirring a strong potpourri of evergreen and moss. I imagined a car deodorizer called Vernal Bliss.

"I love skiing this time of year," Vuokko sighed, inhaling deeply and leaning back. Then, after a moment's hesitation. "Well, except for all the..."

And here she paused to make a wiggling motion with her arm, as if it would help conjure the correct term, a word she then triumphantly spat through a broadening grin, "... snakes."

"Yeah, I know what you mean," I offered, certain she was dramatizing the hazards of sloppy spring snow or fallen branches. "I've been tripped up a few times today, too."

"No, no," she laughed. "Snakes. *Kyy käärme.* You know—the kind that bite you and make you sick." She laughed even harder and made a Monty Python–like stabbing motion near her mouth with two crooked fingers.

Now a thinking person had any number of reasons to dismiss this idea—latitude, snowpack, Vuokko's general wisecracking, and the impending national three-day drunk known as *Vappu* that people were clearly already practicing for. The one that made the most sense, however, was Vuokko's potential familiarity with a peculiar English phrase I knew all too well: snow snake.

Whimsical epithet for an invisible scapegoat, the term is frequently invoked by snow-sport enthusiasts to excuse their own ineptitude—a phantom whose absurdity is its very reason for existence. When someone trips up or unceremoniously plants face-first in the snow for no discernible reason, companions commonly dismiss it with colloquial utterances like "Uh-oh, snow snakes gotcha" or "Musta been the snow snakes."

The snow snake was once native only to North America; however, modern mobility, the global march of English, and perhaps even text messaging have allowed the mythical creature to disperse, expanding its range to the point where it's now referenced by ski cognoscenti in even the farthest-flung locales. Vuokko, dearest, surely *this* is what you meant?

Apparently not.

She was insistent: venomous snakes appeared around several of Lapland's ski hills every spring and were numerous. She would show me tomorrow, she promised.

"It's not so much that I'm *afraid* of the snakes," she'd bubbled. "I only worry about running *over* them. Ha!"

The absurdity was much on my mind that evening. Snakes slithering over snow? Possible? A joke? Or merely the bad translation I suspected? (After all, linguists perpetually debated the origins and structure of Finnish, a sui generis among languages.) But whether Vuokko's revelation was true seemed to matter less than the degree to which I desired it to be.

THE SKI RESORT of Ylläs is draped over a massive, treeless boil of wind-hammered basalt, a geological zit rising from the taut skin of surrounding forest. For much of its November-to-May season, the hill is a bastion of Arctic frigidity, but it was sunny and warm again when I rendezvoused with Vuokko.

"Everybody is talking about the snakes today," she glowed.

Her friend Teemu, the mountain manager, confirmed a rash of reports; to prove it, he put out a call on his radio.

"We had one here, crossing the track," crackled a lift operator.

"I've just seen five in one place," radioed a maintenance worker making his rounds on snowmobile.

In fact, Teemu said, first thing that morning a large snake had dashed down the T-bar line, scattering skiers like bowling pins. This news conjured a most fantastic picture for a place where wildlife encounters usually involved Reindeer, Arctic Fox, or drunks.

"Check between Tower 7 and Tower 9," he advised in what now seemed surrealism of the highest order. "There are always a few in that area."

So that was where we'd headed. And here a confession is due: I actually knew a lot about snakes—perhaps too much. Like any critical mass of knowledge, this one came with an abiding fascination with all there was yet to know on the subject. The current intrigue had me entertaining this emergent other, an academic id in need of gratification.

As we rode the T-bar, Vuokko's chatter drifted in one ear and out the other. I was too busy eyeing up a low ridge of glacier-plowed rubble ahead as a likely place for a den or hibernaculum—the communal sanctuary in which snakes commonly wait out winter.

Sure enough, the formation neatly straddled the track just below Tower 8. Here we stepped off the T-bar; I kicked off my boards and looked over the few patches of exposed ground. Nothing.

And then that subtle cognitive shift. Like booting up a computer program. In a mental menu bar, under "Locate," was a pull-down checklist: south-facing aspect, wind-sheltered microhabitat, thermal inertia, route of retreat. This itinerary quickly singled out a mossy depression several meters away, where a tangle of ground-hugging blueberry was warmed by radiant heat from two large trees and buttressed by their roots. I took but a single step toward it before freezing in stride.

In the hollow, as if placed on instruction, lay two camou-flaged coils adeptly playing to the contrasts of sun and shadow. Plate-sized pinwheels in charcoal, slate, and chocolate. Reaching, limbless and silent, for the waxing sun of summer, a mere hand's width from the waning snows of winter. Geometric. Captivating. Beautiful.

ALTHOUGH I'D NEVER actually seen one, this snake could be only one thing—the mildly venomous European Adder, *Vipera berus*, a species whose generalized habits, hardiness, and adaptability made it the world's most widespread reptile, ranging from the United Kingdom to the Russian Far East and China, south to the Alps and Central Asian steppe, and, as it was aptly demonstrating, north to the continental Arctic.

The species' ubiquity in northern climes also explained its heavy presence in Norse mythology—Europe's most fertile screed of post–Ice Age animism—which held that the "World Ash" Yggdrasil, a tree supporting the nine cosmological worlds of top-god Odin, was guarded at its roots by a great serpent, Jormungander, frequently depicted in illustrations as the lowly European Adder. The scene before me provided an eerily genuine example of life imitating art in the service of some heavy ancient beliefs.

Crouching, I crept closer to the snakes, observing the subtle full-body inflations effected by every breath. Their coils rose and fell like slow bellows, each exhalation resembling a mute sigh of resignation. How did it feel to draw fresh air for the first time in eight months? To emerge each spring to spend but a few dozen desperate weeks battling anew with the rigors of the north?

One thing every organism needed to survive up here was a well-honed thermoregulatory behavior and morphology that took advantage of every erg of environmental heat. Thus the snakes' bodies were both dark and stout, heat-absorbing and heat-conserving traits, respectively. To cope with the short Arctic growing season, females would judiciously store sperm from infrequent matings and bear a handful of live, largish young every two or three years when the food supply, at least some of which could be foraged for under cover, was especially abundant. Viperworld, Arctic edition.

There had been a time when things like snakes coiling under trees had been my primary focus, for I'd been immersed in the scientific milieu of herpetology—the study of reptiles and their amphibian cousins—for many years. A distant past that erupted happily into consciousness in serendipitous moments such as these. This time, however, it had arrived with a pang of sadness and confusion.

I put the hash of strange feelings aside and bent to the task of photography; a discovery like this couldn't go uncaptured (that hunting instinct again). The cold-blooded snakes were lethargic enough for me to carefully pick up the larger of the two and admire it more closely, in the eternal dialectic of the herpetologist—forever checking the locked, unblinking stare of lidless eyes against his or her own faltering humanity, comparing each new color or pattern to a mental trove of organic art.

A viper's vertical pupils are vaguely evil looking, and scales above the eyes form small ridges to effect a stern but benign scowl, like a skeptical teacher. The characteristic dark zigzag down an adder's back looks to have been inspired by the decorations of ancient pottery, but very likely the converse was true. I handed Vuokko my camera and cradled the animal on my arm for a portrait.

Vuokko leaned in and snapped the shot, then turned on her skis and set off to join friends while I gently lowered the snake back to its blueberry cradle. But warmed and emboldened by handling, instead of coiling back into the brush, it bolted. Out over the snow and down the path of least resistance—Vuokko's tracks. I did her the supreme favor of not calling attention to the surreal sight of the trailing serpent as she slid onto Ylläs's main run.

I'D COME TO Finland to write about skiing, but a deeper self had emerged, like a clump of brown tundra melting out of a white landscape. A pair of diligent, unassuming creatures milking what sparse heat they could from an unforgiving earth had conjured some uncertain emotion in me but also a comforting certainty—a feeling of connectedness and a knowledge that the reason I was even here was somehow related to these animals.

Was this gift from Odin a true epiphany? Or something I'd secretly known all along? Although I'd long oscillated between two very different worlds, they had never collided quite like this before. If reptiles and amphibians had been such an important part of my life's equation, I suddenly wanted to know why. And why, in some sense, I'd released them.

Pieces to this puzzle were scattered across the globe, in the hands of dozens of people, hanging like price tags from a thousand memories, associations, and experiences. I would have to gather them one by one and carefully sort and fit them together—partly through recollection, partly by returning to those storied places, partly by making new journeys. I'd see cool things. Connect with old friends. Discover new animals. Have an adventure or two.

The prospect sounded fab save for one small thing: it scared the living shit out of me.

INTO THE SWAMP

And he says: "Snakes along the railroad tracks."

JONI MITCHELL, "Don Juan's Reckless Daughter"

I SPENT THE first four years of my life in the northern suburb of Willowdale, Ontario, a postwar enclave capping the mushrooming city of Toronto in a pastoral flush of remnant farmland, streets lined with stately hardwoods, and an abundance of eponymous willow—so many that when the trees' white, fluffy seeds coated the ground each May, the place looked as though giants had had a pillow fight. In the late '50s Willowdale was a suburban idyll with nature still writ large enough to read.

In a time when few thought to park kids in front of a television for safekeeping, I was pastured in the backyard several hours a day while Mom tended my infant brothers—a fitting first step down reptile road, since a range of herpetologists' biographies show exile to be a surprisingly common theme.

A tiny square of suburban turf was my first opportunity for natural exploration, and alone on those ersatz moors I ruled a kingdom of observation that included the relentless industry of ants constructing sandy, pyramidal entrances to their nests one grain at a time; the stealthy, zebra-striped jumping spiders that hovered on red-brick walls like Warhol paintings and made popcorn plays for alighting flies; the perpetual tumble of butterflies mating above mustard-yellow forsythia; and mute lessons in camouflage offered by Monarch caterpillars in umbrage on marigold stems. I also smuggled worms, beetles, millipedes, and the soil that bore them into the house to foul laundry and gum up the washer.

If the ground-level flea circus of a backyard is biology's elementary school, what quirk of curriculum steers you to want to trade in the stuff of other people's nightmares? Not that you have time to entertain the question, but *How did I get here?* seems forever relevant when a snake is dangling from your hand by its teeth.

Evidence points to an early affinity for nature's myriad sideshows. "I can't remember a time when I wasn't fascinated by animals," writes venom specialist Sherman Minton Jr., in his charming autobiography, *Life, Love, and Reptiles*, "particularly the ones that most people feared or disliked. Creatures like the big dragonflies . . . and praying mantis . . . [that were] regarded with suspicion."[1]

An eerie symmetry exists between his sentiments and what I've gleaned from a host of peers. And I, too, was obsessed with dragonflies and mantises, neatly pinning out the former in display boxes and keeping the latter as free-roaming pest control in various university residences.

The notion of a common crucible is suggestive: although the joint fathers of evolution, Charles Darwin and Alfred Russel Wallace, conceived of natural selection independently, both enjoyed histories of childhood beetle collecting followed by psychotically detailed observations on tropical island archipelagos. You typically imagine scientific kinship as based on a formal body of shared knowledge—dictates dredged from similar textbooks in a thousand different lecture halls—but apparently a constellation of similar *experiences* might likewise prescribe biological destiny.

In my case, the freakish convergence went further: herpetologists on this continent seemed most frequently to turn out where the competing human ecologies of development and abandonment met; India's snake charmers may have hailed largely from rural outposts, but North America's mostly came from the 'burbs.

Minton leads with a familiar chant in describing his early years in an Indiana suburb: "To the north and west . . . were miles of hilly country covered with woods and small farms, and threaded by little rocky creeks . . . The [school bus] stops were in patches of woods where I often saw snakes and lizards while waiting . . ." On weekends Minton's mother packed him a lunch and sent him off to "trudge the footpaths and gravel roads" with only a warning to be careful of venomous snakes (which pretty much guaranteed he'd look for them).[2] Preteen Sherman had leave to explore to his heart's content in the Indiana wilds, but given the projection powers of little boys, he may as well have been in the Amazon.

THE DON RIVER is no Amazon, but the bramble-clogged valleys surrounding the muddy watercourse that bisected suburban North Toronto were *my* jungle.

When we moved there in the early 1960s, Don Mills was making waves as Canada's first "planned community." A paragon of urban organization, the 'hood most would come to know from planning textbooks was, more so than Willowdale, an urban-rural quilt of undeveloped lots, grown-over pasture and orchard, and deep, dark ravines where tiny streams bubbled toward the coffee-colored Don. Green tendrils penetrated the concrete mosaic of curling streets from an edging forest that continued northward, we imagined, to Hudson Bay.

For the first few years, at least, we did feel as if we dwelt on the edge of something approximating wilderness. A parade of displaced deer, fox, raccoon, skunk, rabbit, and birdlife was welcomed by cheering throngs of children weaned on a steady diet of anthropomorphized storybook animals, which were, paradoxically, despised by the books' suppliers—battle-hardened parents fighting the incursions tooth and nail. After all, they'd spent their life savings on neat little houses with manicured grounds that a bevy of bewildered wildlife was now chewing up.

But the march was a heaven-sent plague for me, as I crouched against the cold metal of slick-sided window wells scooping out toads that tumbled in with welcome regularity; watched the Murray sisters run screaming down the sidewalk with mason jars of braceletlike Ringneck Snakes (*Diadophis punctatus*) plucked from a backyard woodpile; hung speechless over the handlebars of my bike, eyeing a tiny auburn DeKay's Snake (*Storeria dekayi dekayi*) coiled on a roll of cedar snow fencing; and in an almost mystical event, sighted my first Northern Leopard Frog (*Rana pipiens*), a doomed creature sitting stoically in a shaft of light by the only remaining puddle in a rapidly vanishing ravine.

Beyond histories of wide-eyed observation, herpetologists also shared the inevitable switch to active purloiner. My brothers and I were frequently bundled off to parks and conservation areas where we could run wild while my parents read books and ate boiled eggs. When it was time to leave, they'd pry us soaking and reeking from the creek or brush, along with a bounty of crayfish, water bugs, frogs, and salamanders. Animals invariably roamed the car on the ride home; our laundry was invariably more foul.

For us, the cliché of a grasshopper in a jar was an inelegant experiment in desire. Not desire to *possess* the organism but desire to possess *knowledge* of it. Like most kids, we hung on to things because we were unable to discriminate between the two. Instead of suggesting that more might be gleaned by tipping the jar's contents back into the soup of the wild, Dad simply indulged our fascination with these animals he largely viewed as fishhook fodder, and our garage brimmed with dying animals we had no idea how to care for. Once loosed from within, it seemed, and in the absence of any mentoring, the collector simply collected.

IN THE SUMMER of my sixth year I was once again in exile. This time it was several weeks of day-camp. I have only the dewiest, most translucent memories of watery juice, soggy cookies, forced sing-songs, faux campfires, insipid games, dyed feathers, and braided plastic bracelets—the latter an inexplicable central focus of daily tenure at Camp Mil-da-la-ca. One memory, however, still burns bright as the day it happened.

Mil-da-la-ca was wedged between the motor madness of the newly opened Don Valley Parkway and the base of the valley's western slope. The forest ended where the slope leveled onto a grassy bend of former farmland punctuated by a few crabapple trees. On a self-imposed furlough from braceletmaking one steaming day, I found myself angling toward the cauliflower shade of a large, twisted apple tree spreading its branches in the center of camp. At the edge of the shadow thrown by the aging arbor, something moved sharply in the periphery of my vision. I halted to look, but whatever it was had stopped, vanishing completely.

When I took another step it moved again, but all I caught were blades of grass bending right and left. Again it disappeared when I stopped; I held still, scanning the ground, unaware that the key to crypsis was the very immobility I was encouraging.

Without knowing it, I'd taken the first steps in a dance that would repeat itself a thousand times before I reached puberty; an Arthur Miller School of Stealth that would become so deeply ingrained in my neural patterning that forever the snap of a twig, crackle of a leaf, or unmistakable susurration of something sliding through grass would stop me in my tracks.

Also without knowing it, I was learning a valuable lesson from an invisible teacher, precisely *because* the teacher was invisible. The questions my naïve senses struggled mightily to answer in those few seconds opened up a dialogue with nature that would blossom into a lifelong conversation. The defining turn onto the long and winding road to the Finnish vipers started under an apple tree.

At the time, however, the conversation was flagging. I could not decipher the visual puzzle; anything that got through spoke only to my lower brainstem (amusingly known as the "reptilian brain"), which understood only one thing: if I moved toward whatever was hidden in the grass, it would almost certainly reappear. I took a step. A black band sprang from the grass and raced toward the tree. With all the lobotomized bravado of a little boy, I dove for it.

IT'S UNCOMFORTABLY STEAMY when I land in Toronto one recent June, and thunderstorms are predicted before things cool overnight. The quintessential Ontario summer day— oppressively hot under vaporous, undetermined skies. In town on business, I've concocted a secondary mission to parse the childhood haunts that figured in the bitmap of my natural awakening. Basically, I want to look for snakes.

Descending on the old neighborhood, trying to remember which snake was found where, I recall a recent conversation with a friend who was also once a proto-herpetologist.

"That was *all* my sisters and I did as kids," she'd enthused of her time growing up in Stratford, Ontario. "You have no idea what kind of snake freaks we were."

And although this revelation may have seemed unusual in a society steeped both in the early vilifying of snakes to children and certain assumptions about girls, it had certainly sounded familiar. "There was a quarry where we used to find a lot of snakes," she'd told me. "A certain *kind* of rock we knew was good, and a few that almost always had a snake or two under them."

The reference to habitat and habitus neatly fit my own experience, as did her posse of sibling accomplices and the counterintuitive notion that human activity often created favored hunting sites.

Disturbed areas, in fact, are excellent places for snakes. Not because the animals *enjoy* disturbance but because such places are environmental caricatures where key features and conditions of natural habitat are exaggerated, feeding into the opportunistic bent of certain species. Quarries and gravel pits, for instance, host shallow, ephemeral ponds that attract breeding frogs and toads, whose multitudinous progeny then serve up easy pickings for predators like gartersnakes, which fortuitously find ample cover in the rock-strewn surroundings. An old quarry is often like a marsh-in-a-box.

The most fortuitous disruption for the budding herpetologist, however, is a railway, which slices determinedly into urbania and efficiently funnels the countryside in its wake. The closest railway to our house was a perilous and strictly forbidden journey—one my brothers and I nevertheless made regularly—across a busy four-lane street to an industrial park. On long summer evenings we would dutifully return home at dusk on our banana-seat bikes, paint buckets chock-full of squirming snakes swinging from high-handled angel bars. Surreptitiously unloading this booty into the backyard was part of a campaign to seed our own population; we didn't realize that we were merely feeding local cats and crows.

And so it's to "the Factories" (as we'd lamely called it) I head.

I'm unsurprised but disappointed to see that the Factories remained a toxic saddlebag on the sanitized suburban mule. Industrial garbage and barrels of oozing, unknown chemicals abut the resilient greenery that creeps along the railroad right-of-way, demonstrating just how adept nature is at filling even the most noxious vacuum. Paradoxically, it is a place where snakes find foothold (so to speak). Wading into a tangle of leg-abrading Scotch Thistle, Queen Anne's Lace, and sawgrass, I stare tentatively at the mess before me. And I see Marty.

Another preteen day-camp had included a nature hut run by the eighteen-year-old budding herpetologist. He had a few exotic species like the chill, pink-striped Rosy Boa (*Lichanura trivirgata*) that wound through the grubby fingers of virtually every camper and a large python that we crowded into the hut to watch constrict and swallow its weekly rabbit (some kids cried at this brutality—all the better for the social standing of those who sat stoically through it). But mostly he showcased banks of aquaria with local frogs, toads, snakes, and turtles.

While campers *oohed* and *aahed* their way from species to species, I would stand obnoxiously behind, spouting information cribbed from a weekly raft of library books. Piqued by my keenness, Marty took me under his wing, and we made a date to go snake hunting. The tall, swarthy counselor showed up at my house one Saturday in his Ray-Bans and sockless, low-cut deck shoes. Over a couple of beers he assured my parents we'd play it safe. We tore off in his white convertible, and I slid across red, seatbelt-free upholstery as he careened around corners with a Pepsodent smile.

I'd proudly directed Marty to the Factories, where we'd spent hours catching and releasing small snakes that abounded beneath railway ties, paint-can lids and chunks of linoleum. Several rats took runs at us when we'd uncovered them by mistake; one made it halfway up Marty's calf before he kicked it away. Though bemused by my lowbrow haunts, Marty kept mum; he understood that for all its baseness, this was the natural world in microcosm. The paradox was that much of this "nature" was effectively unnatural, composed largely of nonindigenous plants and animals unfazed by creosote, solvents, or PCBs.

Gazing over the familiar bricolage of broken pallets, garbage, and truck tires—little changed from that day with Marty— evokes a certain earthy fondness. Just not enough fondness to want to touch anything.

ALTHOUGH IT BORE another of childhood's unflaggingly dull names, "the Pond" was a place of constant discovery and attending marvels. A remnant oxbow thrown off by one of the Don's precolonial meanderings, it had been fully sequestered by the crook of a wooded slope and a raised rail bed.

I park on a side street atop the valley wall and backtrack along a busy avenue to the juncture of a bridge over the railway and the slope we'd walked down as kids. At the guardrail signaling the beginning of the bridge, where a mute path descends to the tracks, a movement catches my attention. A large Eastern Garter-snake (*Thamnophis sirtalis sirtalis*) is twisting through the tall grass.

Seconds later it's calmly wrapping itself around my hands, drawing dry, keeled scales across the front of one finger, then the back of another. Its tongue flicks rapidly, a sophisticated olfactory organ conducting a parts-per-billion molecular assessment of this odd interruption while it searches for a way back to the ground. Not alarmed enough to bite, it still sees fit to squeeze off a dose of the infamously foul combination of anal-gland musk, feces, and uric acid most snakes wield as a calling card.

As a kid, this odor was always with me; you could scrub three times with anything and still detect it. It had a knack for settling into fabric, a fetid Scratch 'n' Sniff reactivated by even a hint of water. Snake pong is a perpetual hazard of the trade that ranges from mildly unpleasant to vomit inducing. Like many herpetologists, I developed a sick fondness for it.

The snake is lumpy with young. Feeling gently along its length, I count at least twelve well-developed embryos. The majority of snakes are oviparous, or egg-bearing, but like many other northern species (e.g., the Finnish vipers), garter-snakes are viviparous, or live-bearing. This adaptation—which has evolved over thirty different times in snakes—in this case serves a demand for safe, rapid gestation at extreme latitudes or elevations where seasons are short and resources scarce. Being retained internally, with various degrees of placental involvement, protects the embryos from the vicissitudes of weather (and/or predation) that egg laying might expose them to, and the rate of embryonic development can be enhanced when elevated body temperatures are actively sustained through behavioral thermoregulation. I know all of this because my career in midwifery began with my first pet snake.

We'd been playing combat in a field near my house on an August evening, and a couple of us had taken cover in a small dugout. I'd pulled up the piece of cardboard I found behind me to have something to kneel on, exposing a somnolent garter-snake that had only recently curled in after a day of foraging. Hunting had been successful, I'd reasoned, because the animal, already large at around sixty centimeters, was further distended around the midsection, where pale white skin showed between stretched scale rows.

It was the largest snake any of us had ever seen and the first I'd caught close enough to home to consider keeping. We dubbed it Hercules after the mythological Greek superhero (though our version was the protagonist in an exceptionally cheesy television cartoon of the day). We traipsed excitedly home, the unexpected prize wrapped around my shit-stained arm.

Bowing to a pressing chorus, our father agreed to let us keep the snake. We put it in the garage in an empty beer case, over which was affixed a metal screen set in a wooden frame. Two hours later, while we slept, Dad discovered the snake in the middle of the garage. He scooped it back into the box with a rake and weighted the screen down with a rock. That worked for a few days. Long enough for Hercules to birth twenty-some wriggling babies before she and most of her progeny disappeared again—permanently.

I became adept at identifying pregnant snakes; and for years the magic postvacation words "You can bring *one* home" invariably spurred a replay of the Hercules scenario. Never recognizing that I knew all too well what I was doing (or that you could even *tell* the difference between male and female snakes), my naïve parents simply crossed their fingers and hoped their house wouldn't again become an ophidian orphanage.

The miracle of bargaining for one snake that magically transformed into many was fortuitous to say the least, and I happily supervised neonatal wards where duties included helping babies exit the membranous coating they arrived in and providing them with their first meal of a small earthworm. I reveled in the way they walked tiny jaws around the worm with the same programmed verve as a newborn mammal seeking out a teat, so ravenously that two snakes often met in the middle of a worm, one trying to swallow the other. Yessireebob, a box of baby snakes could provide hours of distraction and education; even the most squeamish kid found their antics both cute and fascinating. Some adults, too.

In *Tales from the Golden Age of Rattlesnake Hunting*, Donald G. Wheeler, unrepentant paterfamilias to a clan that hunted snakes to the verge of extinction for fun and the occasional zoo, rightly observes that snakes are akin to Houdini—marvels at finding ways to disappear. "If there is the slightest question whether or not a snake could fit through an existing crack or find a tiny opening, you can be sure it will do just that," he says.[3] I witnessed this constantly over the years, marveling not so much at how snakes found ways to get loose as at how neither amateur nor pro learned to prevent it. North American news organs make fascinating fodder of this faculty. Winter 2007 saw reports not only of the usual escaped boas but also of a deadly cobra that eluded captors for months in a major metropolis.

My best escape story took place in the backyard when my brothers and I built a large plywood enclosure, a meter and a bit square, using the chintzy tools we got every Christmas. Its edges were anything but straight, seams ill-fitting and irregular, and tiny finishing nails inadequate—the whole tilting madly to one side like a parallelogram. Still, it seemed secure enough to pour in a couple dozen gartersnakes that arrived home from the cottage in socks and pockets. We did this on a Sunday afternoon, throwing in enough grass to cover the wooden bottom and give the snakes something to hide in. Monday morning our Italian gardeners arrived to cut the lawn, trim the hedges, and weed the flowerbeds. We trundled off to school without a thought.

Mom got the call around noon. She arrived home to find one gardener, Gino, sitting on the curb, attended to by the others. He was dressed in a white undershirt that clung to his beach-ball belly, and the dark skin of his forehead was beaded with a belligerent sweat that reappeared each time it was wiped away. His breath was tight and labored. He stared straight ahead as if he'd seen a ghost. It wasn't a heart attack but something damn close. The other gardeners looked fearful and angry, shouting and gesturing as they threw their equipment into the truck.

The box. Cracks that seemed impossibly thin to us were gates swung wide to an elastic, shape-shifting snake. Plywood that looked smooth to the human eye was a rough, ladderlike surface any determined serpent could find purchase on. The box was so poorly built that if a lawnmower so much as bumped it, its pathetic moorings would have twisted loose completely. In any case, the snakes had all been loosed.

The first was seen in a flowerbed, the next in the rock garden. The noise of a large lawnmower Gino was pushing across the yard had drowned out the excited shouts when he noticed strange things flying from it. Suddenly his overalls were splattered with blood and guts. Writhing bodies and tails were everywhere. Severed heads flicked tongues from disembodied mouths, the random last firings of primitive, interrupted nerves. Snakes bolted everywhere through the grass.

Gino froze in terror until the others, wielding rakes and shovels, hacked every living snake to death and quieted the twitching parts. They'd then led Gino out of Hades, stepping gingerly around snake bits, crossing themselves and wondering why such horror had been visited upon them.

It was the last time we ever had gardeners.

The next day our proper English housekeeper, sitting on the couch having a cup of tea, discovered the Smooth Green Snake (*Opheodrys vernalis*) that had been missing for a week. In her lap.

ABOVE THE POND, I lower the snake back to the grass, where it flows quickly from my hand. As I make my way down the embankment, the advertised rain arrives in big summer dollops, warm as tears at first, then a cold shower drumming my back; I'm soaked to the skin before I can duck under the bridge to wait it out.

From the graffiti-emblazoned concrete ramp where I shiver, the Pond's surface is dimpled gunmetal. Its circumference and level seem greater than I recall—the sole icon on my itinerary that looms larger than in my childhood. Dead, stripped trees stand farther from shore, tilting from watery moorings like abandoned dock pilings; the gently sloping north side, once a grassy, frog-friendly draw, is now dense cattail backed by equally dense alder; the steep eastern embankment is an impenetrable knot of sumac, burdock, and raspberry, the only trails through it tunnels burrowed by Muskrats; even a short peninsula, key feature of the old pond's geometry, is submerged.

It was into the cover and vantage of the peninsula that we'd slipped as kids to scan for Eastern Painted Turtles (*Chrysemys picta picta*), spooking the sunning, slick-backed creatures from logs, watching for their heads to pop up in the duckweed. If you frightened them again, they'd swim for the bottom, and you could wade out to pluck them from the murk, squinting nose-to-water to make out the red-etched margins of their olive shells protruding from the dark, anoxic mud. The peninsula was also the site of my version of Hemingway's *The Old Man and the Sea*.

IN THE '60S urban ponds were dumping grounds for shopping carts, appliances, and a creative assortment of other big-ticket junk. About two meters from the peninsula's northern edge, a rusted car hood lay on the bottom, and one day I'd been surprised by a strange and fulsome face peering from beneath its edge. Was it a Muskrat? Catfish? When the head protruded further and I leaned out for a closer look, I knew. There was no mistaking the snorkel nose, gold-flecked eyes, and pebbled, saurian neck of a Common Snapping Turtle (*Chelydra serpentina*).

We'd clustered around excitedly: now *this* was a find. Although we'd had to head home, planning for the beast's capture began immediately. My brothers and friends would ring the car hood so that when it was lifted, the turtle had nowhere to go; then I would make the grab. From a book, I learned the key to handling a snapper was to lift it from behind and never present yourself to its front; it's toothless like other turtles, but possesses a razor-sharp beak and preternaturally strong jaws that can, convention goes, snap a broomhandle. Snappers have extremely fast reflexes and shockingly stretchy necks, meaning they can also reach backward or sideways to inflict a painful bite. This last bit I kept to myself.

Later that week we trudged back and sat quietly on the peninsula watching the hood. Soon enough, a massive head snaked out, paused briefly, then with a lightning, twisting stab, inhaled a pair of mating sticklebacks hovering just above the bottom. This caused us all to jump back and briefly reconsider the mission— the turtle looked larger than we remembered. Somehow we convinced ourselves to go ahead and tenuously slid down the bank into the water, mid-thigh on the scrawny legs of most. We all wore long pants, running shoes, and canvas gardening gloves. I'd stuffed hockey shin guards down the legs of my jeans.

Nervously circling, we took up position. The others reached down to grip the metal while I stood tentatively where the turtle's head had appeared. The idea was to flip the hood away from me, blocking the turtle's escape to deep water and allowing time to see which way it was facing. *One, two, three!* Up came the hood . . . and a swirling cloud of muck that obscured everything. Something approximating the size and weight of a cinder block bumped my leg; I screamed, the guys dropped the hood, and we all flew from the water.

By the time we returned for another attempt, the turtle was a legend named Kola. The new plan was to scare the monster into clear water and grab it; I needed only to see the long, stegosauruslike tail to lift it by. We again waded into the turbid, reeking water and positioned ourselves around the hood. Two boys prodded under the metal with sticks while I stood poised. At first nothing happened, and we wondered if the turtle was even there. Then, directly in front of me, a massive, sawtoothed tail appeared. Kola was backing out.

With no real idea what kind of an animal was attached to a twenty-centimeter cylinder straight out of *Jurassic Park,* I reached down, wrapped both hands around it, and pulled. The back end of ten kilos of angry snapper floated up at me. Wide-eyed as Alfalfa in a *Spanky and Our Gang* episode, I faced the moment of reckoning for every nascent herpetologist: when the difference between a benign picture-book image and the real thing becomes frighteningly apparent.

Ahead of my hands, the serrated edge of a scarred and time-worn carapace trailed strings of green algae, the perfect pond-bottom disguise. Leeches curled like commas on fat flesh bulging around madly churning legs where they met the surprisingly insubstantial plastron (the much-reduced lower shell; snappers can't fully withdraw their limbs like other turtles, having taken an evolutionary stance that the best defense is a good offense). In the creature's sheer size I saw how truly foolish this enterprise probably was, but there was no turning back. Holding on for dear life as the gang splashed madly for the bank, I dragged Kola toward shore, sinking deeply into the mud as the turtle paddled hard in the opposite direction, gaining extra purchase by occasionally hooking something solid with its heavy, curved claws.

The turtle should have prevailed. Yet even though I gave up a shoe to the muddy bottom, my first true adrenaline rush came with requisite bursts of superhuman strength, and I managed to wrestle the animal onto land. Here it really went berserk, clawing frantically, lunging—to everyone else's horror—in every direction with its long, serpentine neck (the trait honored in its scientific name), and, of course, snapping madly.

The common snapper, which can live for over sixty years and grow to over twenty-five kilos, resembles a tank on land and moves with the same mechanical determination. It is among the largest predators in its aquatic niche. Capable of sucking down a duckling or torpedoing a trout, between its favored sit-and-wait ambushes the armor-plated leviathan slowly patrols the bottom for dead and dying organisms. A distant relative, the Alligator Snapping Turtle (*Macrochelys temminckii*), North America's largest freshwater turtle at over one hundred kilos, takes the sedentary lifestyle to an extreme; it sits mouth agape, wiggling its wormlike, flesh-colored tongue in a bid to lure fish its way. The enormous success of this ploy speaks volumes about why fish—and, by association, ichthyologists—are considered lower forms of life.

Kola finally ran out of cold-blooded steam. Triumphant, we took turns warily hoisting the animal for victory photos with the Instamatic camera I'd brought. (I recently looked at these photos—you can see the drama etched in the grimaces on our tiny, tilted, out-of-focus faces.) Then, out of respect for a battle well fought—and because we could neither lug it home nor convince our parents to let us keep it—we let Kola splash back into the pond.

STILL CHUCKLING OVER our epic, I walk south, following the tracks along the valley's curve as I'd so often done, flipping every piece of cover I come across. Finally, tucked into a browning mat of dry, wiry grass under a discarded railway tie, I find a small DeKay's Snake (*Storeria dekayi dekayi*), an animal that was often more abundant in our local safaris than even the prolific garter. We'd ferreted many home, pregnant ones yielding button-cute babies of slate gray with a pale yellow neck ring—tiny, improbable reptiles we charged other kids to view.

The nineteenth-century American naturalist James Ellsworth DeKay first collected the species—more properly known as the Northern Brown Snake—in New York's Central Park. The secretive beige snake with pastel-pink belly seldom exceeds the size of a ruler and is often dubbed "city snake" for its habit of turning up in urban woodpiles, gardens, and garbage heaps. Perhaps because it is small, it puts on an amusing display when threatened, flattening its body to appear larger, adopting an aggressive posture, and releasing that damnable, reeking glop from its cloaca—the common urogenital opening of all reptiles. This one is no different, momentarily flattening in my hand and smearing around a few drops of musk.

Along this stretch of track I'd also found my first Eastern Milksnake (*Lampropeltis triangulum triangulum*). Eschewing the ghetto garden fare preferred by the daintier garter and DeKay's snakes, the milksnake is a bird-, rodent-, and snake-scarfing constrictor of over a meter. Its silvery white dorsum, or back, is handsomely burnished in blotches of black-edged mahogany and redwood; its venter, or belly, is a checkerboard of black squares on white. The one I'd come across one warm September day was a fifteen-centimeter hatchling (they lay eggs), its colors vibrant and fresh, and finding it had been every bit as exciting as finding an adult (and likely less painful—they're vicious biters). I'd had no idea such largish species could be found in a city, and the discovery significantly ratcheted up the valley's exotica factor. So I'm thrilled on this day when, flipping a rock beside the tracks, it all comes swimming back.

A yearling, almost identical to that find forty years earlier, peers up, raises its tiny tail, and vibrates a warning. (Like other species, milksnakes vibrate their tails to warn off predators, the resulting buzz a frightening allusion to their venomous cousins. Biologists don't know whether *Lampropeltis* mimics rattlesnakes or if the latter's rattle is an elaboration derived from such widespread ancestral behavior in snakes.) This is the extent of the little guy's alarm, however, and it settles quickly into the warmth of my hand. As it passes itself around my finger, I feel the familiar pressure exerted by the tiny constrictor's musculature, so fundamentally different from that of the DeKay's I've just released.

The snake waterfalls between my hands like a Slinky pouring down the stairs. You can't help but be taken by its striking pattern and decorative appearance; thousands of generations of humanity have been drawn to the often exquisite beauty of snakes. There is memory and reverence here, admiration and fascination; the ethers I absorbed as a kid walking these tracks now flow eternal in my blood. As I release the snake, it gently brushes me with flickering tongue as a lover might.

By this point I've passed through a cut in the valley wall into the open and gaze over a small floodplain meadow marked by a handful of decaying crab apple trees. My eyes come to rest on one particularly gnarled apple. I'm amazed I can recognize its arthritic form.

WHEN I GRABBED the snake at Mil-da-la-ca, it had, quite justifiably, bitten me. Gripping the poor animal, I'd stared at the small horseshoe of beading blood its tiny teeth had raised between my thumb and forefinger.

I'd never seen a live snake but for some reason knew it to be harmless. I was neither hurt nor frightened and understood that the creature was instinctively fighting for its life. The sight of a snake squirming in my bleeding hand would become iconic, but in that instant it simply opened a window on three things that would ultimately propel me.

First was the naïveté of curiosity: unafraid, I'd grabbed the snake without considering the outcome; had I lived elsewhere the consequences may not have been so benign, and thus I'd learn that nature demanded caution. Second was reptilian biology: the bite was a last-ditch tactic after the snake exhausted a genetic program of more pedestrian defenses; I had simply left it no choice. Third, and most informative, was the intersection of these considerations with human behavior and attitudes: a young counselor who'd watched me pick up the snake screamed at me to drop it, then dragged me to the nurse's tent and an ensuing group freak-out; I was senselessly packed off to the nearest hospital, where my frantic mother would arrive to find I was completely fine.

No one knew what kind of snake it was. No one knew it was harmless. No one knew venomous snakes did not occur in the area. No one, in fact, knew anything. Snakes, it seemed, were a black hole for humans. And all that was missing—on all three counts—was a little knowledge.

This is where, after an awkward pause, my conversation with nature resumed. Eliciting desperation from so small a creature placed me squarely in the pantheon of natural hazards in its environment; eliciting such panic from supposedly rational adults reinforced my affinity with that same environment. It's the tipping point that many who eventually find refuge in the natural world experience. I had shifted from being "other" to being "of."

My life would take the usual serpentine twists, and I would ride more tangents than a professor of trigonometry, often angling far from what seemed the prescribed trajectory. Yet like any bona fide tangent, each flight of fancy retained a connection to the basal curve, and somehow, most often below the radar of awareness, I would always return to this Zenlike touchstone of understanding: we are one—dirt, grass, snakes, and self-conscious androids whose curiosity they arouse, whether as ham-fisted kids in Kool-Aid–stained T-shirts or studious professionals in antiseptic lab coats.

Camp Mil-da-la-ca had been prescient: in the meadow Eden, I had been Adam, and in a reversal of roles, the apple held out the devil. I had gladly taken hold.

CREEPY CRITTERS AND ANIMALS, TOO

Even the reptile people are different than the
amphibian people. They're a whole other level of weird.

STUDENT AT HER FIRST HERPETOLOGICAL CONFERENCE

THE FIRST HERPETOLOGIST I traveled anywhere with was Raymond L. Ditmars. That I covered a good part of the globe in his company by the time I was ten is a tribute to both his evocative prose and my suspicion that truth was stranger—and more interesting—than fiction.

While others my age found themselves in wild, precolonial Africa with Edgar Rice Burroughs or marooned on a South Pacific island with Robert Louis Stevenson, I was ensconced in the back rooms of the Bronx Zoo with Ditmars, sorting crates of vipers and cobras arriving from distant, exotic lands and making occasional trips to the Amazon to wrestle eight-meter anacondas from the muddy banks of uncharted rivers. Ditmars's popular books did more than satisfy a young boy's adventure bug; they also introduced a revolving door of eccentric, swaggering characters—guys (invariably, in those days) that could give Tarzan and Blackbeard a run for it.

Ditmars never portrayed himself as a snake-rasslin' superhero, but he enjoyed the reputation. As America's first great

popularizer of reptiles and someone whose job it was to interface with a reticent public, he conducted himself with a showman's air, a crime for which academics often dismissed him. But
the self-taught renaissance man also made substantial contributions to science and the public interest, an early exemplar of
someone who successfully straddled the schism between amateur and academic herpetology.

Ditmars arrived at the New York Zoological Society's newly
opened Bronx Zoo in 1899. Later, as curator of reptiles, he would
help the zoo achieve world-class status, build its collections, institute popular public programs, travel relentlessly to lecture, and
contribute to the scientific literature. His interest in snakebite and
venoms would also lead to the establishment of antivenin centers
in both the United States and Brazil. But his biggest contribution
to the zoo's fortunes was his popular films and books.

Cranking out scientific movies (silent, of course) at a time
when little such material was available, Ditmars also proved a
one-man library, producing a raft of books on zoology and his
life and travels. His first, *The Reptile Book*, published in 1907 and
updated a gazillion times, was relatively jargon free but included
as much technical detail as was known. Although by today's
postliterate standards the book might be deemed impenetrable,
it was, at the time, a breathless breakthrough. Follow-up volumes tapped into a growing public interest in these creatures—
particularly snakes—and a trio of biographical books was also
enormously successful. Save for lack of the word "bloody," Ditmars's droll, understated prose might have been cribbed from
the memoirs of a British officer stationed in some godforsaken
colonial outpost. From *Confessions of a Scientist* (1934):

> I have several times been attacked by blacksnakes when up
> on the sunny mountain ledges in the spring searching for

dens where rattlers hibernate. They have glided toward me and struck as high as my knees. One startled me by crawling on my back while I was peering under a flat rock. Another was a nuisance in following me from one spot of investigation to another. I finally got him by the neck and tossed him over the ledge, fully fifty feet. He landed on the springy tops of Sumac bushes and was not harmed.[4]

In *Contributions to the History of Herpetology* (1989), historian Kraig Adler notes that generations of professional herpetologists, including many still active today, can trace their interest to one of Ditmars's books. I was thus in good company with my flashlight under the covers as I read *Snakes of the World* (1931), likely into its fifteenth printing by the time I got my prepubescent hands on it. Outdated and largely relegated to library archives (but only $20 on eBay), *Snakes of the World* still offers a compelling and unmatched literary aesthetic:

A lithe black form is stretched upon the top of an old stone wall. The long and slender body lies in slightly suggested undulations. It appears tense and yet again soft and pliant as its outline follows the slightly uneven surface of the stones. Its hue is really blue-black and it glows with the luster of a new gun-barrel. The effect upon the average observer is threefold. The thing is startling, it is decorative, and it is wholly incongruous—this vivid form so bold in contrast to its surroundings. The head quivers slightly. If the observer's eyes are keen this is seen to be caused by the rapid darting of a forked tongue. Then the black object appears to flow over the opposite side of the wall. There is a rustling murmur among dried leaves—a hissing scrape—the sound so characteristic of a rapidly moving snake, and the thing is gone.[5]

An equally pithy account vividly detailed why the cobra, despite its capacity to kill a mongoose, invariably loses to its more agile and persistent adversary. More interesting than field anecdotes, however, were those involving beasts incarcerated at the Bronx Zoo: uncannily intelligent King Cobras (*Naja hannah* at the time, *Ophiophagus hannah* these days) that learned to know their keepers and feeding times and to drink water from a pitcher; the care and feeding of a large anaconda and her eighty young, each birthed at over a meter in length; the dramatic and terrifying near-death experience of Ditmars's colleague R. Marlin Perkins (later of television's *Mutual of Omaha's Wild Kingdom* fame, then curator of reptiles at the Saint Louis Zoo), bitten in 1928 by a Gaboon Viper (*Bitis gabonica*), a somnolent stump of outrageous forest-floor tapestry and possessor of the world's longest fangs, at five centimeters.

Despite the book's wry tales of pythons, mambas, boom-slangs, and rattlers, most remember its tremendous photo gallery—black-and-whites that added an extra monochromatic air of menace. The opening plate depicted a pair of King Cobras, the larger raised up in classic threatening stance, and a caption that began "The world's most dangerous serpent," [6] before going on to summarize why—body length, fang size, toxicity of venom, amount delivered, aggressive behavior—and to punctuate the hazard by citing the mythic animal's wide distribution.

The King Cobra's size, power, and deadliness offer a frightening and exotic litany, but Ditmars also understood that the overly attentive stare of an upright cobra could stir men far more deeply. In *The Snakebite Survivors' Club*, author and ophidiophobe Jeremy Seal embarks on a global mission to confront his personal snake demons. In the Reptile House of the London Zoo, he takes a stab at describing the cobra's considerable mystique:

[It] lay hidden among foliage and only a brief portion of its body was visible, sleek as a new tyre. Even so, what I could see of the real thing seemed to have no connection with the hooded posture that has come to be this snake's signature, a byword for a kind of absolute intent that has persuaded manufacturers of everything from cars to camera equipment, helicopters to beer, shoes to overhead projectors, golf clubs to radios and surfboards to stroboscopes, as well as millions of devotional Hindus in modern India, to entrust their products or even themselves to its dark, iconic allure.[7]

I could relate. As a first outward demonstration of my growing interest and identity, in part propelled by Ditmars's photos, I too adopted the cobra brand at a young age. I endlessly doodled it on school notebooks in Hindu-esque posture above an unnaturally symmetrical coil, incorporated it into my first juvenile attempt at a signature, and purchased it in every conceivable form—from cheesy souvenir statues with faux-ruby eyes to stickers to model cars with a cartoon cobra on the hood. What was it about this animal?

Introducing the Indian edition of *Snakes of the World*, a reviewer noted that with its "sinuous body movement and graceful slither, the snake has always charmed human beings with its manifold capabilities."[8] Meaning, I believe, that we are naturally taken by creatures that, despite being in some ways degenerate to our eyes, exude supple beauty and a capacity for the physically improbable, whether it be preternatural locomotory skills, miraculous feeding abilities, or opulent defenses. A large rattler, coiled, buzzing, and ready to strike, is an awe-inspiring sight. Yet beyond the bluster, what's most obvious is the fear inherent in an animal that has drawn itself back into a last-ditch, don't-make-me-do-it fist. The cobra's warning goes one better by transcending serpentine limitations in an anthropomorphic fashion; the unnerving upright posture and fixed gaze meet us on our own terms, interrupting the comfort of human superiority with a "Hey, you want some of this?" kind of challenge; it is a creature that is figuratively—and in some species both literally and quite accurately—willing to spit in your eye.

Popularizers like Ditmars demystified cobras to some extent, bringing an understanding of their habits and place in nature to the public fore, but humankind's fascination with these animals remains primal and pre-dates the science of biology. Then again, so does herpetology.

WHAT IS THIS thing, herpetology—a curious and illogical amalgam forged from two distinct classes of vertebrates? Moreover, *why* is this thing? To answer either requires a detour back to Classical Greece.

The etymology of the term lies in the Greek word *herpeton*, neuter of a derivative of *herpo*, which means "to creep." It turns up in the Old Testament as one of some fifty descriptors for "snake" but was also used by ace logician and classification pioneer Aristotle (384–322 BCE) for a cool new category of animals he was putting together based largely on the way they moved. Fittingly, the history of herpetology begins with maligning and misappropriation.

Aristotle was the first to recognize mammals as a cohesive group (it wasn't hard—four limbs, nipples, and hair being the criteria), but other creatures didn't similarly benefit from his astute powers of observation. Although he argued that women were also some form of lesser organism, reptiles and amphibians received maximum disrespect. Ignoring the obvious backbone distinction, Aristotle assigned anything that crept, crawled, or—as suspected for salamanders—was spontaneously generated from mud to a catch-all group called *herpetons*. Thus were erroneously allied such disparate and unrelated organisms as worms, beetles, snakes, and frogs. Invertebrate zoologists would eventually liberate their own, but snakes and frogs were in for a long ride together.

That herpetology ultimately survived as a discipline remains one of the great amusements of science, which usually prides itself on adjusting to the realities its progress uncovers. It gives herpetologists both pause and a risible kind of hubris that such a glaring error—like conflating the study of hummingbirds and bumblebees because an Aztec priest, observing their mutual fondness for nectar, thought them related—has yet to be corrected in 2,300 years of relatively informed opportunity.

Biology wouldn't emerge as a science until the late 1600s, on the heels of the invention of the microscope and other revelations. As the new discipline gathered steam, the focus was on collecting and classifying organisms. As a result, between 1750 and 1850 the number of known amphibian and reptile species each expanded by an order of magnitude over the benchmark listings of Carolus Linnaeus (1707–1778), the Swedish physician-botanist and father of modern taxonomy. In 1758 Linnaeus laid down the rules in the tenth edition of his epic tome *Systema Naturae* for how the biological name game was going to be played, when he classified all organisms then known to science using a simple binomial naming system (*Thegenus thespecies*). Though putting the lie to Aristotle's catch-all categories, it was, ironically, derived from Aristotelian logic.

Although many of his original labels persist (for example, New World standards like the Timber Rattlesnake (*Crotalus*

horridus), Linnaeus's considerable study of amphibians and reptiles did little to endear them to him. A much-cited comment
famously continued the prejudices Aristotle erected some two
millennia earlier: "These foul and loathsome animals are abhor-
rent because of their cold body, pale color, cartilaginous skel-
eton, filthy skin, fierce aspect, calculating eye, offensive smell,
harsh voice, squalid habitation, and terrible venom; and so their
Creator has not exerted his powers to make many of them."

The statement is interesting in its forceful advocacy of
amphibians as disgusting—a subjective determination at best—
and in anticipating the persistent underestimation of their vast
diversity. Far more species passed through Linnaeus's hands
than he described; to the untrained eye of the day, many looked
similar—especially after being preserved in rum for months, as
specimens arriving from Africa, Asia, and the New World were.
Linnaeus was thus handicapped both by the pervasive morphological convergence in some groups (only now being unrav-
eled by DNA sequencing) and by the better-understood, though
equally taxing, problem of cryptic habits that make many of
them hard to find. He was also burdened by the conservative
prejudices of Lutheran-state Scandinavia; Christianity had done
herpetology no favors in casting the snake—and, by unhappy
association, most reptiles and amphibians—as the Western
world's figurative whipping boy.

Related religions like Judaism and Islam have been only
slightly less harsh. Eastern belief systems like Buddhism and Hin-
duism, in contrast, are unabashed fans, painting the snake as wise,
benevolent, even revered as a deity. Many indigenous peoples
have creation myths involving reptiles and amphibians (snakes
figure most heavily), and ancient animism is rife with snake
iconography. Archaeologists hailed a startling, six-meter-long,

seventy-thousand-year-old rock carving of a python discovered in 2006 in a Botswana cave as the world's oldest object of worship, pushing this activity back an astounding thirty thousand years. Free of scriptural dogma, it seems, humanity is inclined to treat amphibians and reptiles as integral, respected parts of the natural world. And no group has committed the Aristotelian sin of lumping them together.

Throughout history, attempts to liberate amphibians from the reptilian yoke have always fallen short of full-scale revolt. Early French, German, and American anatomists argued for a separate discipline, batrachology (Batrachia being a once-popular class-level synonym for Amphibia), a movement that continues in some quarters (the Internet, de facto accelerator of many a slow-motion global discussion, has served to amp up the grassroots clamor). Given the entrenchment, infrastructure, tradition, and, let's face it, badge of honor represented by the current arrangement, a formal split is unlikely. Thus, two vertebrate solitudes whose only real relationship is the predilection of one (reptiles) to feed heartily on the other (amphibians) are doomed to share a biological lot simply because they were historically considered "lower forms" unworthy of "detailed investigation."

Investigation has, of course, consistently highlighted important differences between these two classes. Even a kindergartener can tell you that amphibians are confined primarily to moist environments because of the permeability of both their skins and egg membranes. Reptiles, they will note, are less moisture dependent, possessing scaly, waterproof skins and eggs that are protected, like those of birds, by a thick shell. Plus they bite.

Taxonomic schizophrenia nevertheless has its rewards: herpetologists can at least celebrate the richness of their field, which among zoological disciplines offers the broadest diversity of investigative opportunities in ecology, behavior, morphology, and physiology. From the humble handful of species known to Linnaeus, amphibians and reptiles now account for almost half of the world's living nonfish vertebrates. With a combined fifty to one hundred new forms described every year, over six thousand species of amphibians and some seven thousand reptiles are now recognized.

That's a whole lotta foul and loathsome.

MANY YEARS WOULD pass before I had any theoretical need to keep track of this diversity, of course, but I learned early on what such a mephitic tide looked like in practice.

The main stairwells of Toronto's Royal Ontario Museum (ROM) are symmetrical twins, turning in segments around a soaring pair of weathered totem poles fixed on either side of the building's entry rotunda and main-floor galleries. The steps are quarried from relatively resilient limestone, yet on the inside of the spiral—line of least resistance—the surface is noticeably concave, eroded by continuous passage of an irrepressible natural force: a voluminous daily flow of wide-eyed schoolkids getting their first glimpses of Chinese armor and Egyptian mummies, *Diplodocus* and dinosaur dung.

I had been one such wonder-filled sprite, racing up and down these slabs with my desk-row chums, avoiding the shepherding reach of teachers, perpetually bolting back to the reptile gallery for one last, lingering look at painted models of the world's most phantasmagorical snakes and lizards and turtles. Here, in all their garish glory, were the very animals I daydreamed endlessly about; for all its bad taxidermy and cheesy dioramas, the gallery was one step closer to the real thing.

Unless you were behind the door when the universe handed out imagination, it is impossible not to be transported in a museum, shifting from continent to continent, eon to eon.

Notions of Time's Arrow/Time's Cycle and the relative insignif-
icance of humanity offer the greatest educational watershed a
child can experience.

One of the ROM's programs was the Saturday Morning
Club, a weekly repository for kids like me with an interest in
the museum's many moldering treasures. The congregation
gathered in a large theater to listen to presentations or watch
films before breaking off into smaller, specialized groups that
reflected the museum's major archaeological and natural history themes, from Egyptology to mineralogy to entomology
to combined ichthyology and herpetology (more on this cou-
pling later). As part of this last group, I schooled through galleries, listened to lectures, asked questions, gave talks (my first
was a public-speaking disaster entitled "The Painted Turtle"),
and made behind-the-scenes visits to the bowels of the curatorial center, including a memorable descent to the collections
room of the patriarchal Department of Ichthyology and Herpetology. Here, our imaginations were ignited by a football
field–sized warehouse of tens of thousands of jars filled with
creatures gathered from everywhere on earth. For a nascent collector, the vast stores were something to aspire to—or reason to
concede defeat. In either case, they were a window into a world
vaster than we could understand, the realm for which Linnaeus
had cobbled rules and whose prescriptions, we learned, hung
before us on tiny tags looped to withering specimens afloat in
yellowed, eye-watering chemistry.

LIKE MOST REFUGEES, herpetologists are a generous lot, quick
to forgive and even quicker to include. Rather than revile Linnaeus for his religious dogma and gleeful spreading of harmful
misconception (he also wrote of reptiles: *Terribilia sunt opera Tua,*

o Domine!—Terrible are Thy works, O Lord!), scientists instead embraced him for both his classification achievements and his direct contributions to herpetology's role in the development of biology. As a celebrated dabbler, he was not alone.

Linnaeus's taxonomic oeuvre was built on a foundation laid down by one of the great scholars of the Renaissance, Swiss physician and teacher Conrad Gessner (1516–1565). Gessner's famed five-volume treatise, *Historia Animalium*, contained two herpetological volumes: *Quadrupedibus Oviparis*, covering egg-laying amphibians and four-footed reptiles, and *Serpentium Natura*, which included snakes and, in a bizarre Aristotelian bridge, scorpions (after all, both sting).

The Italian empiricist Francesco Redi (1626–1697), best known for demonstrating how maggots arose not from rotting meat but from fly eggs *laid in* rotting meat, was one of biology's earliest myth-busters and the first to bring scientific method to bear on venomous snakebite. Through experimentation (god knows how), he was able to show that people died from viper bites not because of any bewitching quality the animal possessed but because of the nasty liquid produced in sacs located on the sides of its head. He further determined that this venom had no effect if ingested; it had to be injected to cause death. One can only imagine Redi's dinner parties.

The Age of Exploration brought opportunity aplenty for the emerging science of biology and vigor to Europe's herpeto-logically minded. Jakob Theodor Klein (1685–1759), a Russian contemporary of Linnaeus's, fired the gun in 1755 by coining the term *herpetologiae*, a field of study whose earliest center of research became Paris. By the mid-1800s ground zero shifted to London as Britain's empire expanded and vast amounts of materials were deposited at the British Museum. The zoological and botanical windfall helped accelerate complementary disciplines, and a fertile combination of unbridled global exploration, advances in comparative anatomy, and the new science of geology brought another critical vine to bloom—one that ensured herpetology would not remain rooted in a garden of rubbery, preserved specimens: paleontology.

In 1809, after comparing fossils and their living relatives, the French anatomist Georges Cuvier (1796–1832) suggested the existence of an Age of Reptiles—a time, he believed, when the world was dominated by supersized lizards, relegating present forms to scrappy, pint-sized remnants of a once-great dynasty. Spectacular fossil finds in Britain confirmed Cuvier's suspicion, galvanizing scientists and inspiring gentry and commoner alike to scurry into the countryside with picks and purpose.

When Cuvier began his fossil work, it was believed that no animal species had *ever* gone extinct. By the time of his death, however, not only did Cuvier believe in extinction but he was also certain it had happened several times in successive waves, each instigated by unprecedented, large-scale catastrophe and each resulting in subsequent divine replacement with new and distinct faunas. This antievolutionary catastrophism school of thought promoted the idea of the "fixity of species" (the notion, derived from Plato and Aristotle and formalized by Linnaeus, that species were eternal and never changed) in a context of biblical "special creation" (god created every species on earth separately). In contrast, Charles Darwin pal and Scottish geo-pioneer Charles Lyell (1797–1875) championed uniformitarianism, the belief that geological processes like volcanism and erosion acted gradually over vast periods to account for changes observed in the fossil record. As we now know, certain aspects of these two ideas aren't mutually exclusive—one good meteorite strike can

provoke acute catastrophe as well as an acceleration of volcanism, tectonic rearrangement, and, at least in Hollywood, a prolonged Bruce Willis chase scene.

Uniformitarianism figured heavily in Darwin's early theo-
rizing about species transmutation (as evolution was first called),
further inciting the pious. Thus was the general ferment as herpetology barged onto the Victorian stage, brandishing ancient
giant lizards as a cause célèbre.

Cuvier's self-appointed successor was one of his students, the
eminent Swiss naturalist Louis Agassiz (1807–1873). Agassiz
would become a giant in the fields of ichthyology and herpetology
(not to mention glaciology—he's also father of the Ice Age), but he
could be a selfish, isolated character whose staunch adherence to
special creation did him no favors in a post-Darwin world.

The man who more famously picked up Cuvier's paleontology torch, British anatomist Richard Owen (1804–1892), was
also a piece of work. Charming, diplomatic, and highly produc-
tive on the one hand, he was also megalomaniacal, underhanded,
and mean-spirited on the other, not immune to assimilating
the data of others and robbing them of deserved recognition
(a prototypical scientific snake in the grass). His epochal work
on dentition—mapping characters of teeth in living and fossil
groups—was his most important contribution (fossil animals
are often described based *solely* on teeth, because these miner-
alized structures are prone to excellent preservation as well as
scattering). Owen's biggest coup was getting first crack at the
fossils Darwin dragged back on HMS *Beagle*.

Despite Owen's many transgressions, the hagiography
granted by time and accomplishment has elevated him as The
Man to many a fossil freak. The title is deserved on at least one
front: in 1842 he published an account of an enigmatic group

of giant Mesozoic land reptiles he called Dinosauria (terrible lizards). He believed that these "terrible" (i.e., awe-inspiring, in the parlance of the day) lizards provided evidence of the ultimate glory of an architect in the sky (shades of intelligent design championed by American right-wing Christians and the Bush administration).

One thing was clear: a good deal of the fossil material being pried from the ground belonged to gigantic, phantasmagorical, very extinct reptiles. Thus, herpetology inherited the most spectacular creatures ever to walk the earth. Herpetology had owned horror and fascination from day one, but with the dinosaurs came possession of something far more valuable: imagination.

The growing treasury of wonders threw up practicable questions: Why had snakes lost the legs they so clearly once possessed? Why were contemporary turtles and crocodilians virtually unchanged from ancient forms? How did a generalized ancestral amphibian resembling a large salamander become as morphologically specialized and ecologically diverse as a frog? These quandaries would largely be addressed by a new generation as biology found its footing across the pond.

North America seized herpetology's slippery reins in the late nineteenth century. Louis Agassiz had left behind fame and financial ruin to be installed at Harvard University in 1846, and here he produced the bulk of his work in herpetology, with a focus on turtles. Before his arrival, the Father of American Herpetology, John Edwards Holbrook (1794–1871), published the second edition of his lavishly illustrated *North American Herpetology* (1842), the topic's first worthy synthesis. The American West was opening up, and a concerted effort was being made to explore its geology and natural history; both living and fossil animals were shipped by the crateful to the academic institutions of the Eastern Seaboard (in Philadelphia, Joseph Leidy, dean of American paleontology, described America's first dinosaurs from this material), and urban expansion brought more intimate contact with the continent's biological diversity. These developments set the stage for the reign of America's most celebrated herpetologist, anatomist, and paleontologist, Edward Drinker Cope (1840–1897).

Known for fastidious work and staggering output, Cope produced a mountain of literature in both herpetology and ichthyology. No surprise, then, that the continent's first journal of record in herpetology was also the first journal of record in ichthyology. Published by John Treadwell Nichols (1883–1958) in 1913 and adopted by the American Society of Ichthyologists and Herpetologists (ASIH), which Nichols founded in 1916, *Copeia* honors Cope's contributions and, one assumes, his rather neat straddling of both disciplines; already a Siamese twin at birth, herpetology was officially grafted onto another sibling in North America, thanks to Cope and Nichols. I learned early that herpetologists could *never* get away from those goddamn fish.

IN THAT LONG-AGO Saturday Morning Club at the ROM, we were occasionally escorted into the field by the motley university students that mentored our junior Ichs and Herps group. These trips weren't at all like the safe and supervised school version. In decommissioned transit buses, we trundled east to the Rouge River and seined for fish and tadpoles, wearing leaky waders so oversized they brushed our chins; we headed west to scramble over the Niagara Escarpment, crawling through the cool caves riddling the fossil-pocked limestone, turning out Red-backed Salamanders (*Plethodon cinereus*) in the forest; and, on one memorable winter Saturday, we sifted into volunteer cars for a trip to the Reptile House at the Buffalo Zoo, a three-hour haul from Toronto.

I recall nothing of the destination, likely because the drive itself proved far more zoolike. While three of us sat in the back, two strangers up front, resplendent in long, unkempt hair, beards, and army coats, one with a pet Corn Snake (*Elaphe guttata*) coiled in his pocket, smoked funny-smelling cigarettes, and passed a bottle concealed in a paper bag. Several times they extended the flagon over the seat to offer a swig. It tasted like bad ginger ale, which, apparently, it was, defiled by a strange substance called rye. Although their general deportment and booze-bag fashion screamed Yonge Street wino, our hippie custodians nevertheless easily crossed the border in their beater of a car, stoned, drunk, with an illegal snake and three vomit-primed kids they didn't know. Alarm bells should have sounded, but in step with the freewheeling times, we would never have thought to mention these details to our parents, and they would never have thought to ask.

"Did you have a good trip to the zoo today, dear?"

"Yup. We saw King Cobras and an egg-eating snake and a Nile Crocodile."

"That's nice."

"Yeah, but then Bobby threw up in the car on the way home."

"Carsick?"

"No . . . I think it was something he drank."

"Oh, that's too bad dear. Dinner's ready."

Occasional slumming notwithstanding, I developed a deep reverence for the ROM and museums in general. When one day a standing invitation to work in its hallowed halls came my way, I could hardly turn it down. Who knew it would make the freak trip to Buffalo look like a bus ride to Disneyland? That day, however, was a long way off, through a minefield of scaly experience and scalier personalities.

A PET SNAKE in the pocket wasn't a new idea. At the turn of the twentieth century, where Raymond L. Ditmars entered this narrative, the convergence of print, photography, and film sparked a boom in reptile "fancying" to match the beetle-collecting craze of Victorian England. With popularization came more infamy and interest and more ways to be a herpetologist than to spend years writing great tomes filled with detailed dissection and gallery-worthy hand-drawn illustrations. You could simply collect the creatures yourself.

Reptiles and amphibians embody all the subconscious elements at play in human attraction: fascination, repulsion, desire, fear. Strange habits and a primitive look, colorful geometries and ornamental postures, ornery dispositions and death-dealing abilities add up to the perfect animal storm—an irresistible draw for would-be herpers, who, unlike bird-watchers, are not at all content to simply watch.

Amateur collecting blossomed in the roadside reptile attractions of the 1950s and '60s. People wanted to see and understand these animals, as well as those who worked with them. Thus, exhibits featured showmen who juggled harmless forms and bravely palmed some of the more dangerous animals for a hang-jaw public. Incorporating snakes into theatrics wasn't exactly a new idea, either. Carnival snake shows were old news in the colonies, having reached their zenith during the 1920s in Australia. Home to many of the world's deadliest serpents, Oz is the only continent where the harmless-to-harmful ratio is reversed; fully 75 percent of antipodean snakes are venomous—hence a history of public fascination with this glut and its heroic handlers.

In *Snakes Alive! Snake Experts and Antidote Sellers of Australia,*
author and snakeman heir apparent John Cann recounts the
bizarre and frequently tragic stories of self-styled "Professors
and Cleopatras" who brought large crowds to the country's fair-
ground circuit to watch their dangerous game: "Whatever the
reason for the attraction, two things are certain. Snakemen drew
the crowds, and it was not uncommon for a snakeman to die if
something went wrong during a performance." [9]

Stateside, the phenomenon was spectacularly manifest in
the person of Bill Haast and his world-famous Miami Serpen-
tarium. Born in New Jersey in 1910, Haast developed a penchant
for snakes at summer camp in New York State, suffering his first
two venomous bites—from a Timber Rattlesnake and Copperhead (*Agkistrodon contortrix*)—when he was just twelve years
old. But Ditmars's books kept Haast dreaming of the ophidian
bounty of the southern states. He eventually landed in Florida,
collecting in the undeveloped swampland, running moonshine
to support his habit, and opening a snake park in 1947 on the
southern outskirts of burgeoning Miami, stocking it with local
curios and deadly exotics. Like Ditmars, he regularly collected
venoms from many of his animals. In his heart-stopping routine, he caught the snakes by hand on a metal table in front of
a paying public, then had them bite a rubber-covered funnel,
through which venom flowed into a glass receptacle. His weekly
battle of wits with four-meter King Cobras on the facility's central lawn proved a huge crowd-pleaser—a pilgrimage my brothers and I pressed our parents to make the first time they took us
to Florida—after which, if he hadn't been bitten, he would sign
copies of his biography, *Cobras in His Garden.* His real claim to
fame, however, was a self-immunization program he embarked
on (known as mithridatism, the practice also has roots in the

Oz snake shows where some handlers purposely took bites to confer immunity). As of 2003, he had survived some 160 bites from a cast of the world's most toxic villains. Also like Ditmars, Haast was often pooh-poohed as a mere showman despite his considerable contributions to science in the areas of venom research and, though perhaps none too wisely, clinical understanding of snakebite. In fact, the view of amateurs from herpetology's ivory tower is often a cold-blooded one. But it has less to do with the Ditmarses and Haasts of the world than with an element plucked from the showman's tent: the freak factor.

Uncharitable though the term may be, no other way exists to describe the eccentrics lurking outside herpetology's scientific core hoping for coattail identity, meaning, or membership. The Cult of Herps. Symbologists. Occultists. A bike gang's club anaconda. A stripper's phallic boa constrictor prop. Breeders playing god, looking to create their own decorative reptilian tapestries. Searchers, emulators, obsessors, and the truly confused—caught in the mental crossfire between good and evil, between a higher calling and a lower fate; where anything and everything in life's identity roulette becomes horribly and brutally syncretic. No other biological milieu could boast a website like *cobraman.com,* on which a proselytizing, mithridatic Christian begs forgiveness for his forays into satanic occultism, repeated careless handling of deadly snakes, and many hospital stays, then signs off by offering to either sell you any venomous serpent you desire or simply have a chat about "the Savior." Unique in its susceptibility to being thus hijacked, making us all guilty by association, modern herpetology finds itself in constant struggle to wash off the taint of the damned.

Parallels appear in Susan Orlean's book *The Orchid Thief,* [10] about an amateur Florida horticulturalist and serial collector named John Laroche. After the article "Orchid Fever," on which the book is based, appeared in the *New Yorker* on January 23, 1995, Orlean received a letter from a serious gardener whose tone reflected the same professorial view that academic herpetologists hold of mere hobbyists (a title to which Laroche, unsurprisingly, could also lay claim).

The letter pointedly accuses Laroche and his ilk of being the type of perpetually lost folk who turn to horticulture partly for therapy, partly for an easy milieu in which to avoid the weight of life's true responsibilities. The writer feels that these people enter the business in a haphazard sort of way and, most often, become more notorious than famous. Furthermore, the missive opines, they tend to generally lead irregular lives, changing interests and occupations like underwear. Since they are driven mostly by impulse, their principles have no purview when it comes to their current interests. And they survive only miraculously: though they are perpetually poor, their scheming, self-serving agendas somehow always lead them to money.

They survive; indeed, they flourish. As do scientists who have the misfortune to be lumped with those who would wave a venomous snake from any of a dozen freakish pulpits. I would learn that herpetology's fraternity reaches beyond basic biology into a Pandora's box of human psychology and philosophy, its connections manifest and global, launching me not just on requisite scientific and physical travels but on myriad mental journeys as well—a search for meaning, some might say, in all the wrong places.

3

A SALAMANDER UNDER A LOG

"Are there any hybrids that occur naturally?"...

He snorted. "Well, you wouldn't, even in a fit of boredom,

decide to have sex with a gorilla, right?"

SUSAN ORLEAN, *The Orchid Thief*

M Y FIRST ENCOUNTER with a Blue-spotted Salamander was a singularly uninspiring event. Plucked from detritus under a woodpile at a rented cottage one summer, it hung limply in my fingers, blinking stupidly in the cold light of day, dirt clinging to moist gunmetal skin, making no attempt to escape.

A somber animal, it sparked little fascination in an eight-year-old who knew that Red-backed Salamanders parted company with their wriggling tails and had watched a python swallow a rabbit. So I let the blue-spot go, returning it to the muck from which it seemed to have sprung. I saw what Aristotle had been thinking.

Little did I realize that I would eventually spend the better part of a decade scrutinizing some ten thousand of the wretched things, crouching in the nighttime woods in the rain and snow each spring, tracking their automatonic migrations in a flashlight beam, getting spattered with sperm and eggs, while somewhere warm and boozy people with more sense watched hockey. Bitter? Not really. I'm just saying.

I caught my share of salamanders over the years, but for someone who'd never kept one longer than the time it took to look at it, whose pet inventory ran to a decidedly scaly stable of snakes, lizards, and turtles, salamander geneticist was indeed a strange place to end up. Still, the frog-march had seemed rather short.

During adolescence, with the advent of less swamp-tempered creatures like girls and more social activities like canoeing, climbing, and skiing, I briefly retreated from the herpetological front, content simply to know what I knew. In high school I indulged these darker interests on the side with intermittent reading, the occasional pet snake, and a fondness for *National Geographic* TV specials. It wasn't until I enrolled in a biology program at the University of Waterloo, a couple hours west of Toronto, that I dug back in, lapping up specialized courses in earth sciences, entomology, and vertebrate zoology, de facto extensions of the sandbox occupations of youth.

Inspired, I volunteered in a sea-turtle conservation program in the Caribbean, dodging barracudas and hammerhead sharks (quite harmless, really) while floating eye-to-ancient-eye with ornate Hawksbill Sea Turtles (*Eretmochelys imbricata*) over inky reefs, making underwater notes as they flapped their way through languorous, sponge-grazing lives. We rescued boat-sized Green Sea Turtles (*Chelonia mydas*) tangled in fishermen's nets and battled wild dogs away from the fresh eggs of oblivious Loggerhead Sea Turtles (*Caretta caretta*) caught in the act of laying.

Another volunteer, a craggy U.S. Navy vet named Billy Q., whose specialty had been underwater demolition, regaled me with endless horrific diving tales, each of which would have made Jacques Cousteau cringe. In one, a badly hungover Billy and another diver, charged with mining a harbor, had descended to a moderate depth during a storm. Suddenly his partner began surfacing in a panic; he didn't make it. Billy watched in helpless fascination as the faceplate of the man's diving helmet filled up with vomit and he aspirated on the spot, his flailing limbs relaxing in death, leaving him suspended in the heaving sea. "His wide-open eyes looked like they were floating on swishing puke," Billy told me. "It was sad and funny and final as hell." I wasn't sure of his point, until: "I live behind a desk now, kid, and I'd give anything to die like that. Understand?"

Got it.

But I wasn't yet a biologist reborn. Putting in time in what seemed the easiest, most preordained milieu, I returned to my studies with but one certainty: wherever I ended up, outdoor activity would be key. Perhaps I would find my way to this through biology—or perhaps not; herpetology was a hobby, but could it be a vocation? I didn't really know.

Then, as many others experience during similar drift, an unexpected event reset my course. After my sophomore year, I landed a summer job conducting a biological inventory of environmentally sensitive areas: it was the on-ramp back to the highway to hell.

The job was my first opportunity to be paid for anything biological, and although the wage made the local car wash look attractive, it was, in many ways, a dream job. To start, I moved into a nifty cornfield-hemmed farmhouse on the outskirts of Waterloo, hard against a large frog-filled marsh, within spitting distance of lakes, streams, fields, and undisturbed hardwood forest. Four of us were on the project: a botany student from nearby University of Guelph, a pair of birder/botanists from the

U of W Environmental Studies program, and me, a bona fide "zoologist" responsible for nonavian vertebrates—fish, amphibians, reptiles, and mammals. Since nobody was covering invertebrates, I took that up as well, keeping an eye open for anything unusual.

Each day we rose spectacularly early, bagged a lunch, then drove an hour or more to something that appeared as a green blot on one of our mud-stained topographic maps. At our destination—invariably in the middle of a lonely country road—we debarked in rubber boots, swathed in nets, backpacks, binoculars, notebooks, and insect repellant, the botanists lugging wooden plant-presses (little-changed since Linnaeus's time) while I slung an old newspaper bag filled with plastic containers. We'd split up, pick a meeting time and rendezvous point, and tramp off into field and forest. I would then spend an entire morning doing precisely what I'd self-trained much of my life for: laying careful, respectful siege to nature. I turned rocks and logs, peered into ponds and marshes, poked through the muck of seeps and flooded forest; I identified frogs by their calls, egg masses, and airborne trajectories as they leapt ahead into swamps and streams; I ogled distant turtles through binoculars, shell shapes easily betraying their identities; I chased all manner of snakes through high grass, rock pile, and leaf litter.

As I wandered, waded, and wallowed, my nostrils flared daily with the pungent miasma of what nineteenth-century writers termed the Chthonic Domain. Like Aristotle, other ancients had ascribed worms, amphibians, and snakes to this earthy, subterranean realm with its powers, spirits, and gods of the terra firma. It was where I belonged—a farmer working his fetid fields, reconnected and rekindled.

My work turned largely on confirming the presence of the usual cryptic suspects. One discovery that ratcheted up the area's biodiversity status, however, stood out. Returning to the cars one day, I stumbled from a sandy wood to find the group in a knot on the road, staring at the twisted, upturned body of a stout, arm-length snake. It lay in a mottled, cream-colored S, mouth agape, tongue lolling comically, seeming otherwise unscathed.

I had imagined this moment a hundred times.

"That's pretty fucking big," said a nervous botanist.

"What kind is it?" another wondered. "Did *we* run it over?"

"It's not dead," I smiled, "watch."

Leaning down I slipped a hand under the snake and flopped it over, revealing a brown-and-gray-blotched dorsum that could have belonged to any of a half-dozen North American serpents and a pointed, upturned nose that could only belong to one. It rolled right back over and resumed its possum pose. I flipped it again. It rolled over again. All you could do was laugh. It was like a person in denial.

Hognose snakes are possibly nature's greatest Shakespearean actors. Diurnal toad hunters preferring sandy areas where they can turn out prey with their shovel-like snouts, three species of *Heterodon* tour an impressive stage show throughout North America. The eastern form we were observing, *H. platyrhinos,* has the most polished act. When threatened, the snake hisses loudly, thrashes mightily, and spreads the forepart of its body like a cobra. It may then move on to a savage display of striking—with mouth closed—or proceed directly to the finale: death feigning. Why this specimen was taking final bows when no one had observed the rest of the performance was anyone's guess; had the group only noticed the snake after it had reeled off its repertoire? Or had it been confronted by a bird while crossing the road and thrown down its act just before they arrived? Either way, finding it was a thrill.

Ultraspecialized habitat makes the hognose one of Canada's rarest reptiles, all the more threatened because of its frequently misinterpreted behavior. I'd visualized it so often that to observe the defensive routine that was the stuff of textbooks on animal behavior was surreal. I'd only caught the tail end this time, but years later, collecting salamanders on Kelleys Island in Lake Erie, a small hognose coiled under an apple tree (theme?) would extemporaneously bust out a full revue, protracted enough to photograph act by act. When it finally moved off into a limestone fissure, I would stand in the crackling leaf litter of a bare spring wood, offering the hard-working snake a mock ovation. *Bravissimo!*

Death feigning, or thanatosis (you just knew it had a special name), isn't rare in the animal kingdom; it crops up in everything from insects to ducks. Though not as common as the related strategy of tonic immobility, in which an animal that's handled or attacked simply goes limp, death feigning is nevertheless thought to serve the same purpose: to up the chances of escape from a predator. But given that some predators are quite fond of carrion, it also seems risky, a fact that perhaps explains why it's always a last-ditch tactic.

The behavior has been acquired in at least three snake lineages: the hognose; the European Grass Snake (*Natrix natrix*); and the African Spitting Cobra (*Hemachatus haemachatus*). All seem to read from the same script: flip onto back, mouth agape, release accompanying foul-smelling odor that might suggest decomposition. Charming.

Speaking of death, that summer's fieldwork also involved forensics. Long before CSI made it popular, I confirmed the presence of unseen animals by examining tracks, shed skins, bones, or scat. A flipside was that I provided the crew their own little forensic lab; they merrily determined the presence of poison ivy, poison oak, burdock, bramble, stinging nettle, and an endless procession of insects simply by examining the welts, cuts, bites, and stings blooming across my legs and arms.

Technically, "inventory" meant you had only to note what you saw or found evidence of, but collecting inevitably found its way onto the manifest. Humans seldom balk at any excuse to indulge the primal collecting urge; it was certainly necessary to schlep hard-to-identify plants back to the lab. I was similarly bottling invertebrates and any Blue-spotted Salamanders I happened across; there was, apparently, a zoology professor at Guelph interested in these animals. Which is how I came to fall down the rabbit hole.

Blue-spotted Salamanders belong to the genus *Ambystoma,* or "mole salamanders," for their habit of spending much time in underground passages, including burrows left by crayfish and small mammals. They can be found close to the surface during breeding season, when they use moist conditions provided by the rains of late winter and spring to migrate to ponds, and in fall, when they exploit similar surface conditions to fatten up before descending below frostline for winter—kinda like Canadians. The blue-spots I encountered at the tail end of their breeding season in May were shipped off live to Guelph. When they were returned, neatly tagged in jars of ethanol, as I remembered from the ROM, each one's belly had been slit and the viscera removed. What was *this* gruesomeness?

The gaping intrusions were gateway to an entirely new way of understanding the natural world. Or at least *trying* to understand it, because all who worked on these animals eventually came to embrace the maddeningly appropriate adage of the extraordinary British biologist J.B.S. Haldane, who famously noted that his own suspicion was that the universe is not only queerer than we suppose, but queerer than we *can* suppose.

The simple explanation from the Guelph students was that in this area of Ontario, what we called Blue-spotted Salamanders were actually a mix of two species and their hybrids, all of which looked similar to the untrained eye. Guidebooks mentioned the issue, though more or less in painful passing, largely advising that you had no hope of determining what you were looking at. A certain Dr. James P. Bogart, however, could apparently determine what was what by ripping out their guts.

The thing I remember most about working with Jim—next to a constant stream of jokes muttered under his breath, religious Friday-afternoon draft-beer sessions with his small stable of students, and his shuffling around the lab with a pipe in one hand and some deadly chemical in the other—is his desk.

The first time I met Jim, as a Waterloo undergrad who wanted to make the commute to nearby Guelph to take his herpetology course—the only one in Canada at the time—I stood nervously in his cluttered office, hearing only half of what he said, distracted by apartment-block stacks of scientific papers on the cabinets and tables and a less-orderly mound covering his desk that looked to have been reduced by some form of erosion. I absently made note of several titles in my field of vision.

A year later I stood in the same place, discussing the possibility of becoming his grad student, peering through the same glossy canyons at precisely the same titles. Mesmerized by this suspended chaos, I again heard little of what he was saying— likely some triviality about how much funding I thought I had or that my desk would be located in the laboratory fume hood.

Over my three-year tenure, the fractal geometry of Jim's desk, like the Alberta or South Dakota badlands it resembled, shifted ever so slightly, the gentle winds of his passage obscuring some surface elements while occasionally revealing other gems and artifacts. I learned from Jim how to deduce which layer of desk sediment contained which important paper, how to mine it with minimum disruption, then later return it to its place, where it clearly fulfilled some higher geological function.

One day near the end of my master's degree I came in to find Jim's desk clean. Spotless. He sat behind it like a lost soul, sheepish and muddled by a clash of pride and loss. I wasn't sure whether he'd swept it clean and burned the lot or simply created hidden apartment blocks in various storage areas. One thing was certain: there was no way all that stuff had been filed, and I felt an immediate sense of panic. How would I find the literature required for my thesis? The monster of the library literature search—with all its Dewey decimals and dewy-eyed librarians—loomed. It was like staring death in the face.

This was the moment I think I decided it would be easier to just make stuff up, when the siren call of fiction blared louder than the stoic voice of science. When the shattered familiarity of Jim's desk had ultimately set me on course to be a writer. A scientist turned "popularizer"—a euphemism, as we all knew, for coward.

I was, in my years with Jim, constantly impressed with his ability to monitor everything in his crowded kingdom. Comprising three small rooms in a wing of the zoology building and a live-animal facility in a large annex across the street, Jim's world was a study in the limited space and do-more-with-less reality of chronic underfunding in the life sciences. But it was also what the offices and research spaces of *every* professor I'd ever known looked like: cramped and overflowing, with dangerous juxtapositions of workspace, chemicals, equipment, and reference material. Unlike other labs where—mirroring evolution itself—long periods of dust-accumulating stasis were punctuated by frantic bouts of rapid change around grant-writing deadlines, Bogart's bubbled with constant activity, most self-generated.

Whether because of monetary restriction, sheer brilliance, or, as I suspected, both, Jim was the consummate DIY workaholic. At his desk, dwarfed by the Leaning Towers of Reprints, he'd pore over vast accordions of computer paper constellated with the crumbs of a bagged lunch, checking data or working through the latest codes in the programs he was constantly writing. Next door, drying slides and slide-making paraphernalia surrounded a flaming Bunsen burner propped beside a sink where water ran constantly through a metal canister of developing film, shots of slides taken through a massive microscope abutting a green-screened library microfiche jury-rigged as a digitizer, on which was invariably projected a negative of erythrocytes (red blood cells) or chromosomes from one of many filmstrips dangling like flypaper on a string overhead.

Across the hall graduate students crouched at vanishingly small desks in a lab where carefully sliced starch gels—products of the gene-probing process of protein electrophoresis—stained with a smorgasbord of mutagenic chemicals stacked floor-to-ceiling like 3D-wallpaper floated in trays of volatile methanol-acetic acid fixative merrily vaporizing on a light table that one of us, stunned by fumes from the fixative, had forgotten to turn off. The mess spilled into the hallway, where an ancient upright refrigerator housed shelves of ice-packed gels coursing with dangerous, high-voltage electricity, separating various proteins derived from ground-up heart, muscle, spleen, or liver yanked from any number of sacrificed salamanders and frogs, whose formalin-rubberized bodies now filled Tupperware trays and pickle jar–packed shelves.

Meanwhile, live compatriots sat on death row in dozens of containers stacked willy-nilly in another refrigerator, awaiting the day when their tissues would be extracted, frozen, and crammed—along with thousands of samples donated by a coterie of Jim's foreign herp buddies—into an adjacent top-loading, ultraexpensive, ultracold freezer that wailed hellish alarm if the temperature ever crept above –60°C. Waiting in the fridge for a governor's reprieve at any given time might be bug-eyed tree frogs from Cuba, chirping coquis from the Caribbean, rugose fire-bellied toads, Amazonian forest frogs of uncertain affinity or chromosome number, and a raft of similarly vexatious hybrid salamanders.

In summertime Bogart et al. would commandeer the spacious vertebrate anatomy lab next door, loading up the dissection benches with dozens of enamel trays filled with tadpoles and salamander larvae, plus gallon jars of aerating plankton and thawing packages of boiled lettuce to feed them, guarded by carboy sentinels of deionized water and surrounded by restaurant buckets brimming with tap water that was slowly ridding itself, through hopeful oxidation, of the sanitizing, tax-supported chemistry added by the city, so that it could then be safely used in the care and cleaning of Jim's aquatic menagerie.

Day after day, month after month, year after year, Jim quietly kept tabs on the entirety of this circus, padding methodically from one room to the next, one process to another, tamping down his pipe, tugging at his trim moustache, occasionally arching an eyebrow, mumbling but never becoming visibly overwhelmed or excited when, as frequently occurred, trouble arose with a ruined gel, expensive spill, escaped specimen, or shattered slide. Even when true disaster struck in the form of a tissue-thawing, animal-killing power outage, Jim was sanguine to the max, his fastidiousness an unspoken embrace of the glacial pace of true science—a realm I perhaps was ultimately too impatient for.

Naturally the advent of an eager new graduate student to assist with this toll of tedium was a godsend, and no professor in his right mind would overlook an opportunity to offload some of the myriad daily chores required to keep a lab functioning. I would quickly learn to handle a raft of chemical and bio business, but my first job required the least training: cleaning and feeding the animals housed in the annex.

It seemed straightforward. Tortoises and iguanas ate fruit and other vegetable matter and really only needed the torn, shit-addled newspaper that lined their cages changed; I'd had plenty of both as a kid. Aquatic turtles and frogs had to be fed and have their fouled water siphoned and changed, a procedure I was also familiar with from tanks of baby snappers and Painted Turtles that lined the counter of our basement rec room for years. In a corner stood a wooden, screen-lidded box with adult, juvenile, and baby crickets that went variously into gecko tanks, frog terraria, and a condominium of plastic boxes containing the products of Jim's Frankenstein-like penchant for crossing different chromosomal strains to see what freakish things he could generate. A quiet, black-and-white-banded California Kingsnake (*Lampropeltis getula californiae*) needed only the occasional thawed mouse. Occupying the room's largest cage was a colorful, two-meter Hispaniolan Boa (*Epicrates striatus*). This snake was no one's friend.

I don't recall Jim saying anything special about this animal. In my experience, boids were gentle, somnolent neck wraps found in schools, pet shops, and fine strip bars everywhere, so I was taken aback when, opening the side panel of its large wooden terrarium, this one hissed loudly and coiled rapidly into a corner. I should have shut the panel but instead waited to see what it would do. Which is why I had a clear view as it exploded from the corner like a fat bolt of lightning to clamp its gaping mouth over my forearm.

I'd been bitten by hundreds of harmless snakes, most with teeth too small even to penetrate skin. But those that *could* inflict a wound—largish gartersnakes, watersnakes, and milksnakes—generally offered a swift nip in hopeful warning of being left alone, then quickly retracted. The boa, however, did not let go. In fact, as I stumbled backward with my free hand on its neck, blood gushing from a stylish, U-shaped needlepoint of some eighty wounds, it actually started chewing, walking its moveable jaws across my arm to inflict new and deeper bites. Had there been witnesses, the spectacle would have been found either slapstick or horrific as I thrashed around the room, knocking into cages with fifteen kilos of snake refusing to yield its vise grip and attempting, it seemed, to maneuver into position to swallow my arm.

In a flash of lucidity I staggered to the sink, flipped on the cold water, and stuck the animal's head under the icy stream. It let go. (Comically, after recalling this story to a friend recently, he handed me a news clipping in which another hapless herpetologist documents an identical arm-swallowing problem with a python, complete with cold-water solution.)

I went directly to the campus clinic, had the wounds cleaned and disinfected, dutifully received the required tetanus shot, and had my arm wrapped in thick gauze through which blood continued to seep for hours. When I returned to the lab, I said nothing and went straight to a desk. Prepping chromosomes across the hall, Jim glanced up, looked at his watch, traced the arcs of blood on my clothing and the gauze protruding from my sleeve, and grinned.

"Got you, eh?" he chuckled, squashing a microscopic pile of cells under his thumb. "Have to watch that one."

JIM'S RESEARCH CENTERED on the relationship of various mechanisms of reproductive isolation—those things that ultimately prevent different populations from breeding with each other and lead to the creation of new species. These mechanisms included bioacoustics (frog calls), population genetics (gene distribution), and his ultimate focus, cytogenetics (essentially how DNA is packaged and passed from cell to cell)—examining the role of chromosome variation in amphibian evolution.

Among related species, chromosome numbers can vary through fission and/or fusion of single chromosomes or the occasional addition of extra full sets of chromosomes, a phenomenon known as polyploidy—a term that would find permanent purchase on my lips. Chromosome characteristics tend to be species specific, and their arrangement—the actual physical configuration of a genome, or karyotype—can be seen by squashing actively dividing cells on a slide and staining the (hopefully) spread-out chromosomes.

When, for whatever reason, the karyotype changes significantly within a population, members can no longer breed successfully with individuals from other populations of their species retaining the original karyotype and thus become effectively isolated, a first step on the slippery slope to speciation. This happens because when gametes—the sperm and egg, which each contain half a parental chromosome complement—meet in fertilization, the homologous (corresponding) chromosomes from each parent must pair effectively in order to establish a somatic cell lineage (from the Latin *soma*, for body) that will, through division and differentiation, produce a functioning organism.

If chromosomes cannot pair correctly, the genetic imbalance leads to developmental chaos; depending on the degree of divergence between parental karyotypes, an embryo might be anything from completely inviable to functional with provisos. A classic example of the latter is a mule, the nonbreeding, hybrid offspring of a horse and donkey.

Although horses and donkeys are closely related species, the horse karyotype comprises 64 chromosomes while the donkey equivalent is 62; when the resultant 32-chromsome and 31-chromsome gametes meet up, they result in a 63-chromosome mule. Such progeny are almost always sterile because the odd number of chromosomes makes their even distribution to subsequent gametes impossible.

Changes to DNA sequences comprising structural and regulatory genes, however, have been small since horses and donkeys diverged, so the resulting animals are otherwise viable, with temperament and dietary requirements intermediate between prima donna steed and stubborn ass, adding up to high work capacity and low maintenance. Thus, although mules display desirable physical and physiological hybrid vigor, they're a bust reproductively.

How does such chromosomal chicanery contribute to speciation in amphibians? Mirroring amphibians' great diversity, the rates at which their chromosomes evolve are highly variable—extremely slow in some salamanders, extremely rapid in certain frogs. Jim wanted to know why.

One of his pet interests was how life-history traits—particulars like when an animal mated, how and where it had babies—correlated with chromosomal evolution and speciation in the terrestrial-breeding frog über-genus *Eleutherodactylus*. Ranging throughout tropical America, this group has diverged exceptionally rapidly in the Caribbean, where its members display a broad range of chromosome number. With many hundreds of species, Jim had plenty of karyotyping ahead.

Another type of change that had Jim's attention was the phenomenon of polyploidy. As if they weren't strange enough, amphibians and reptiles dabbled extensively in this phenomenon. Which is where our slow creep back to the blue-spots begins.

BIOLOGY IS PLAGUED by a conflict between the scientific need for reductionist empiricism and the human predilection for sweeping generalism. It's like this: you're looking to understand a Russian doll by studying one component in the set, but the enterprise is subsumed by your desire to relate this to the rest of the frickin' toy store. Everyone is a theorist at heart, notwithstanding exacting, arcane journal article titles like "Sexual Differences in the Vomeronasal Epithelium of the Red-backed Salamander." I would be no different, laboring in the laboratory gulag on intractable genetic problems, constrained by convention to largely report on *what* I was finding, when I really yearned to know what it *meant*. Cosmic significance. But a decade in the academic trenches would serve mostly to dredge more mysteries from the biological Pandora's box containing the frequently co-occurring phenomena of polyploidy, hybridity, and unisexuality—terms that formed the tip of a very large iceberg lurking beneath almost all of Jim's mentoring.

If you are, as a popular television program teases, smarter than a fifth grader, you know humans have 46 chromosomes—

pairing sets of 23 from Mom and 23 from Dad. The basic chromosome number (n), or *haploid* condition of our species, then, is $n=23$. The pairing of two haploid sets—the normal state in somatic cells—is termed the diploid condition. Thus, the human diploid number is $2n=46$. All cells except sperm and eggs have 46 chromosomes. We have sex so that haploid chromosome sets in sperm and eggs have a happy reunion in a diploid embryo. Simple.

When a somatic cell divides in the process known as mitosis, these 46 chromosomes, otherwise lounging around the nucleus in a great, unconcerned tangle, condense, join with their homologues into 23 cute little pairings, and replicate. The duplicated chromosomes (there're now 92, or 46 pairs) crowd to the center of the nucleus like a class lining up for attendance, split apart, and are sequestered equally into two identical daughter cells of $2n=46$. This happens in our bodies about a bazillion times a day, and because lasting errors remain surprisingly rare, mitosis is judged a rather conservative process. Tidy even. Not so meiosis, the specialized division that produces gametes.

In meiosis, after the chromosomes replicate, related chromosomal arms cross over, swapping genetic material, and two divisions (Meiosis I and II) produce four daughter cells, each with a haploid chromosome complement of $n=23$. The subsequent coming together of these somewhat genetically shuffled male and female gametes during fertilization (planned or unplanned) serves to restore the diploid number of $2n=46$ in our offspring and genetic variability in the population.

The same basic scenario occurs in most animals. But once in a while, more often than generally known, meiosis breaks down and one or more divisions fail, resulting in gametes with *unreduced* chromosome complements. If an egg bearing an unreduced diploid ($2n$) chromosome number, for instance, is fertilized by a haploid sperm (n), the result is an embryo with three full sets of chromosomes: a triploid ($3n$).

The outcome of an extra set of chromosomes varies across taxa: some triploid organisms manage fine; others not so much. For instance, special reproductive tricks allow continuing triploid lineages in many insects, and triploid trout are artificially induced in aquaculture—these sterile fish grow faster and larger than normal diploids, which shunt vast energy reserves into sexual maturation and reproduction. Mammals, conversely, are completely intolerant; triploid embryos invariably perish early in development.

One way around the triploid reproductive conundrum is to avoid it, and if you must be a polyploid, be one with an *even* number of chromosomes. Frogs and toads have figured this out and boast several tetraploid ($4n$) and even octoploid ($8n$) species. But the most outrageous chromosome parties are thrown by the African Clawed Frog genus *Xenopus*, in which dodecaploid ($12n$) species are known. Jim Bogart worked with many of these, repeatedly arguing in print that given their widespread occurrences, such "aberrations" likely played an important evolutionary role, especially tetraploidy, a de facto doubling of the genome that opens the door for all sorts of innovation to accrue at redundant gene loci. Unequivocally demonstrated for many genera of plants, such doubling episodes are likely behind the establishment of several higher-order animal groups; it was even recently suggested that vertebrates evolved from an octoploid ancestor.

Jim's heady journey to the center of this microscopic world wasn't always apparent to the wide-eyed herpetology students who accompanied him on field trips to the woods surrounding Guelph. In the bush, Jim moved as methodically as in the lab, wisps of pipe smoke betraying his whereabouts as we fanned out—a trail to follow when, invariably, he found something no one else had. Students would gather as Jim hoisted a large Yellow-spotted Salamander (*Ambystoma maculatum*) from the damp forest floor, its somnolent Devonian smile completely out of time with the '60s-style iridescent spots randomly splattered over a coal-black dorsum, and explained how forests were full of these orna-mental animals that, because of their cryptic, burrowing habits, no one ever saw; they would listen attentively as Jim held out a mosslike tetraploid Gray Treefrog (*Hyla versicolor*)—differenti-ated from its bark background only when he plucked it from the tree like a street illusionist palming a coin from behind a specta-tor's ear—and described how its range abutted that of its diploid counterpart, Cope's Gray Treefrog (*Hyla chrysocelis*), and divulged that these forms sometimes hybridized to produce triploid off-spring whose trilling calls were neatly intermediate in frequency to those of their parents, a phenomenon he carried tape record-ings of to illustrate.

Understandably, students' attention drifted during these verbal voyages into the dark heart of delinquent DNA; to their eyes the aesthetic of these unknown creatures offered marvel enough. But they'd have to snap back to molecular attention when one of them invariably fished a leaden blue-spot from beneath a log and presented it to Jim, who would declare, for no reason they could discern, "It's a hybrid. Probably triploid."

SEVERAL SPECIES OF *Ambystoma* call the vast woodlands of northeastern North America home. The Blue-spotted Salaman-der (*A. laterale*) has a northerly distribution from eastern Mani-toba to southern Labrador, south through the Maritimes and New England, and westward through the southern tier of the Great Lakes. This small, blue-black species is a generalist, occu-pying a wide range of boreal and sub-boreal habitat. A distantly related species, Jefferson's Salamander (*A. jeffersonianum*), larger, lead-colored, with tinier, less-profuse flecking along its lower flank, is restricted to undisturbed Carolinian hardwood forest in the lower Great Lakes and southern New England. DNA differences suggest these two last shared a common ancestor some 20 million years ago, then subsequently evolved in isolation to constitute distinct species. They remain distinct and easy to tell apart; the problem is that these two species—let's represent normal diploid chromosome sets in *laterale* and *jeffersonianum* as LL and JJ, respectively—now form two ends of a very messy hybrid continuum that includes $2n$ LJ, $3n$ LLJ and LJJ, and even the occasional $4n$ LLLJ and LJJJ. Again, Jim wanted to know why.

Researchers had long reasoned that, on some rainy spring night millions of years ago, an overzealous blue-spot or Jefferson's got its wires crossed in some dark forest pool and made whoopee with the wrong salamander. Water-breeding amphibians generally have the same routine: male attracts female, male grabs female, female lays eggs, male fertilizes them. With frogs, females are attracted by the male's call and grasped in a specialized embrace called amplexus, and the sperm is released over the eggs as they're extruded. In salamanders, however, males deposit sperm on the ground or pond bottom in neat packages called spermatophores, then attempt to interest females with romantic nudging, tail waving, and straddling. If the female is receptive to a male's booty-shaking, they amplex and he maneuvers her over top of what he hopes is one of *his* spermatophores. She picks it up internally, where the packaging dissolves and eggs are fertilized before they're laid.

But amphibians in the frenzied hormonal throes of mating are frequently observed to amplex individuals of the wrong species, and ponds are often littered with spermatophores; the water is filled with sperm and eggs—a genetic accident waiting to happen. An accident like hybrid salamanders.

Regardless of the details (and they are perverse), somehow, somewhere in distant time, a diploid hybrid LJ female was generated. By some quirk of hybridity—a glitch in the otherwise viable coexistence of two different genomes, as in the mule example—the second meiotic division failed. Instead of generating the usual haploid eggs, each contained the same *diploid* set of LJ chromosomes as Mom. A further quirk of hybridity allowed these eggs to enter normal embryonic development on their own, establishing a unisexual, more or less clonal lineage of all-female LJ salamanders that then spread into populations of both Blue-spotted and Jefferson's salamanders. There another genetic "mistake" occurred. Although their eggs didn't require fertilization to develop, hybrid females nevertheless mated with available males. Occasional fusion of unreduced LJ eggs with normal haploid sperm (L or J) then yielded triploid embryos, at least some of which were viable: again, somewhere, somehow, continuing unisexual lineages of both LLJ and LJJ triploids were established. How?

As we've seen, eggs sometimes spontaneously develop with no genetic contribution from males, and the resulting offspring are clones of their mother. The same breakdown of Meiosis II responsible for clonal LJ females allows triploid salamanders to produce triploid eggs. These clonal female offspring mature and go on to produce more triploid female clones, and so on. Such continuing unisexual lineages are termed parthenogenetic (*parthen* = virgin; *genesis* = birth), and the animal world contains many forms, all pretty strange.

In 1900 German-born biologist Jacques Loeb induced parthenogenesis when he pricked unfertilized frog eggs with a needle and found that in some cases an embryo formed; physical disruption of the membrane appeared to spur the eggs into development. It turns out that a special form of parthenogenesis employed by hybrid salamanders relies on just this trick: physical mating with males occurs, but the sperm serve only to stimulate eggs into division before being discarded. This process is called gynogenesis (*gyno* = female).

It's an interesting paradox: to reproduce, LLJ and LJJ females *must* mate with males of one of the two parental species even though the sperm is generally rejected. Thus, continuing unisexual hybrid lineages are *embedded within* populations of normal diploid species, threatening to overwhelm them. A genetic Trojan horse.

NOBODY KNOWS FOR sure why parthenogenesis and gynogenesis occur in higher animals; these are seen as primitive tricks, senseless invertebrate atavisms trotted out at the occasional degenerate vertebrate soirée. What *is* known is that unisexuality is highly correlated with hybridization; does the presence of two different genomes in the same nucleus trigger triploid and hence unisexual cascades? More important, if you had a suspected triploid unisexual hybrid in your hands—something that seemed intermediate in nature to A. *laterale* and A. *jeffersonianum*—how the hell would you know what you were looking at unless you could see its karyotype in a squashed cell or remove tissue that held genetic clues to which parental species were involved? Exactly—which explains those damn holes.

My time with Jim Bogart taught me that to truly know anything about these animals meant entering both the molecular and the chthonic domains they inhabited. And taking up residence. For evidence of how such an obsession could ultimately occupy a mind, I needed to look no further than the allusion to his cherished tetraploid Gray Treefrog on the license plate of Jim's beat-up old Toyota: HYLA 4N.

4

BULLETIN FROM THE PACIFIC

*An old woman sees a venomous snake on the road whose tail
has been run over. She takes it home and nurtures it until it's healed, then
treats it like a pet. It likes to coil around her arm, sleep with her for warmth and
seems totally happy. Then one day out of the blue it bites her. As she's
dying she says, "I thought we were friends—why did you bite me?" It responds,
"Because I'm a snake. You knew that when you picked me up."*

AFRICAN FOLK PARABLE

S TUART—I THINK THAT was his name—tightened his left
hand around a cold Fiji Stout and held the bolo out to
dangle between us with his right.

"What did you say it was related to?"

"Sea snakes and kraits—cobras more distantly," he answered.
"It's a frickin' elapid."

"Doesn't look *that* nasty," I said. Elapids are the second great
worldwide group of venomous snakes, whose deadly neurotoxic
cocktail contrasts with the more hemotoxic venoms of viperids.
Stuart spun the dull, decidedly kinked animal between thumb
and forefinger like a mobile turning in the breeze.

"Well . . . tread marks will do that."

I'd picked up the dark-brown, thirty-centimeter snake in the driveway of a backpacker's resort on Fiji's main island of Viti Levu. Actually I'd picked up two, both dead; the second had suffered even more from repeated squashings by staff-driven vans and swerving golf carts. At the time, December 1986, Stuart believed they were something like only the eleventh and twelfth records known to science of the secretive Fijian Bolo (*Ogmodon vitianus*), and scraping up the two carcasses put me in possession of one-sixth of all specimens in existence. Or so he said. Of course I'd had no idea it was that rare. In fact, I'd never heard of it until that morning, and everything I'd found out since suggested why.

Camera in hand, I'd been chasing lizards around the grounds when a gardener—observing through the jade leaves and fuchsia blossoms of a hibiscus while he halfheartedly raked dried sea-grape and broken palm fronds—called out: "Hello! Mister! You want him snake?"

He was a smallish, wiry man whose whole body twitched when he spoke; I suspected that he spent far too much time in the kava circle.

Kava was the ubiquitous, mildly narcotic emulsion made from the root of the Kava Pepper and once consumed by most native Fijian men. The muddy concoction was ritually passed around a circle in coconut-shell bowls—increasingly more slowly as its anxiolytic effects took hold; this could continue for hours each day, resulting in somnolent, red-eyed males who did little beyond complain about how nothing much ever got done. It was easy to see why the industrious East Indian population that arrived as indentured labor with the British-run sugar cane industry came to dominate most of the islands' key institutions—a constant sore point with ethnic Fijians that resulted in the occasional sleepily executed coup.

I also suspected that bloodshot buddy simply wanted to drag me down to the shore to point out yet another Yellow-lipped Sea Krait (*Laticauda colubrina*), the deadly but docile black-and-white–ringed denizen of inshore reefs I'd tripped over a dozen times in my travels through the island kingdoms of the South Pacific. Instead, he'd steered me to the front of the hotel and pointed to the *Ogmodon* hugging the pavement between rapidly drying remnants of last night's epic rains.

"Bad," he said, fist up. "No him like," he waved his finger. "Live under," he thrust his arm forward in a screwing, tunnel-like motion. "Never him see," he covered his eyes, then spread his hands to wiggle his fingers downward. "Come up, rain sometime." He paused, pointing vaguely to the sky. "Then chief say bad thing is happen. Very bad," two fists pounded together. "Me no him take," his hand was on his breast, then pointing at me. "Maybe him come you?"

This interpretive dance made me feel deaf, and truly, buddy appeared to speak no known language. But I thought I understood: he didn't want to have to clean these very bad omens from the driveway, and the fortuitous appearance of someone that might do so was, well, a very good sign.

Good indeed. After finishing up my master's and nine months of traveling, I was heading to Toronto to start a doctorate at the Royal Ontario Museum, where I was certain that bequeathing someone a pair of unusual Fijian snakes would quickly ingratiate me. So I'd peeled the carcasses from the pavement and dropped them into a bottle of cheap gin purchased at the hotel bar.

Forty percent alcohol barely sufficed on the preservative front (specimens are usually fixed in 10 percent formalin and rehydrated in deionized water, then transferred to a solution of 70 percent ethanol with a few drops of glycerin to keep things good 'n' Gumby-like), but I'd be home in a few days and could strengthen the mixture then. Heading toward my tent at the hostel's campground, I stopped by the pool for a cold Fiji Stout. I placed the gin bottle next to a chaise lounge and eased down onto it. Stuart was sitting next to me, leaning back with a book, red-faced from the sun, beer, or both.

"Hey," he said, noting my brew, "stuff's pretty good, huh?"

Before I could answer, he took in the gin bottle and bolted upright, eyes wide. "Holyfuckingshit! *Two* bolo? Where the *fuck* did you get those? You a herpetologist or something?"

Shocked to have my inner geek outed whilst trying to project traveler cool, I had no time to contemplate the infinitesimal odds of such an unlikely encounter or its inevitable consequences. "Yeah . . . I guess . . . "

I felt as if I'd stood up in a circle of repentants in a church basement and said, "My name is Leslie, and I'm a herpetologist." The first step toward recovery is admitting you have a problem, but it doesn't work when you're with someone who is still mid-binge.

Stuart was a biologist from Idaho—well, really, a herpetologist who had to work as a general biologist in his job as a park ranger, though he was always out herping and there were some cool herps in Idaho and he was here to chill out because he just got separated—well, not really separated but divorced 'cause it was never going to work out 'cause she was his boss, but then, not really divorced he guessed, because they weren't really married though it had been eight years but anyway he didn't really give a shit 'cause he was really just happy to be free and besides, she was a fisheries biologist for fuck's sake, and ichthyologists were always trouble and just didn't fucking get it.

"I mean, really—*fish* . . . ," he finished. "Fuck."

Delivering all this with a huge grin, Stuart tugged hard on his bottle. "Hey, what the fuck—let's rent a car and go herping!"

Off the wagon—my beach vacation was done.

IN THE WAY you sussed out points of interest or cool restaurants before a trip, Stuart had studied up on Fijian herps. The bolo, he informed me, was one of the world's least-known snakes. With its pointed snout and small eyes, the rarely encountered burrower appeared on the surface with rain in only certain places at only certain times of the year (likely looking for a mate, making the driveway deaths all the sadder), but little else was known. Did it lay eggs or bear live young? (Eggs.) What did it eat? (Earthworms and beetle grubs—the only elapid to prey purely on invertebrates.) Where did it forage? (Native Fijians insisted it hung out in the soil under decaying logs and rose into the logs at night to feed.) Where did it come from? (Melanesia; its closest relative as ascertained by DNA sequencing was *Toxicocalamus*, a genus of New Guinean forest snake.) Strange as the bolo was, however, it was far from Fiji's only reptilian enigma.

The Fiji Boa (*Candoia bibroni bibroni*), one of a handful of Pacific boids, lurked in remnant lowland forest on several islands and in various parts of Viti Levu. With a trunkload of Fiji Stouts, Stuart and I battled through dense brush near the capital of Suva, taking it on the chin from thorns and bugs, learning from villagers about the mystique of a snake we couldn't find.

The boa was sacred in the old Fiji religion, kept in pits near the spirit house and worshipped by chiefs and priests who ritually consumed them when they weren't eating people. Their pagan reverence could be related to the boa's chromatic shiftiness: it's able to completely alter its ground hue from dusky brown to light pink in a few hours. This ability is highly unusual in snakes, though the ability must be atavistic—snakes arose from lizards (more on this later), in which the trait is widespread. Color change in snakes is so rare as to be newsworthy; when the mildly venomous, rear-fanged Kapuas Mud Snake (*Enhydris gyii*) was discovered in Borneo in 2006, it made the wires not because it was the 360th new species of plant or animal described in the last decade from an area of sky-high biodiversity, but because it was able to morph from red-brown to almost white in only a few minutes.

Doubtless the Fijian chiefs believed consuming boas could confer similar chameleonic power. Humanity has always viewed color shifting as transformative and magical—so much so that anyone outside scientific circles rarely realizes that an animal might possess the ability; an ecotourism website advertising hikes on one of Fiji's least-developed islands naïvely notes, "You might even see a python—there are brown ones, red ones, and even pink ones!"

Beyond changeling abilities, however, how species of the largely New World subfamily Boinae—only distantly related to the pythons of Africa and Asia—became scattered on a few South Pacific islands and Madagascar presents a lingering biogeographic question. Likewise for two gorgeous and highly endangered lizards. Painted in deepest emerald green interrupted by bold white, dwindling populations of the Banded Iguana (*Brachylophus fasciatus*) were found across Fiji as well as the islands of Wallis, Futuna, and Tonga; the even rarer endemic Crested Iguana (*Brachylophus vitiensis*) was found only within the Fijian archipelago. This was even more enigmatic than the boid mystery, as exactly zero iguanids were found in the Old World. A proto-*Brachylophus*, then, must have rafted to Melanesia from South America, in the same manner that the Galapagos

Islands—one thousand kilometers removed from the South American mainland—obtained founding populations of their more famous iguanas, genus *Amblyrhynchus*. Fiji is a much longer, hungrier distance to float (some seven thousand kilometers), and yet it appears that not only did iguanas establish themselves out here but subsequent radiation occurred as well; subfossils sifted by archaeologists from middens and firepits around the South Pacific show that much larger iguanids had been wiped out in historical times by human predation.

Anthropogenic threats are always a problem for larger reptiles, but with captive breeding programs underway for Fiji's iguanas at nature parks and ecological reserves, the bigger problem these days is the nonindigenous Indian Mongoose. The mythical weasel-hero of Kipling-esque cobra battles—which regularly scared the crap out of us as it streaked in front of our car in a last-second, ground-hugging blur—has proven a scourge for native reptiles and amphibians wherever it has been introduced to control rats in cane fields. Then again, the equally ubiquitous Marine Toad (*Bufo marinus*)—another international pest-control journeyman known as Cane Toad outside its South American home—has done as much worldwide damage to native faunas.

Most of Fiji's terrestrial herpetofauna—a mix of native and introduced species comprising three frogs, two iguanas, three snakes, ten geckos, and twelve skinks—had interesting backstories, the subject of discussion whenever Stuart and I encountered them: splayed-arm Cane Toad pancakes adorned roads with great regularity, especially after rain, an oddly pantropical phenomenon I'd witnessed in places as diverse as Australia, the Caribbean, and Bermuda; the sound of skinks scuttling through dry leaf litter raised the question of whether they were native or one of several species that hitchhiked here with Polynesian voyagers and modern Pacific traders; the large Oceanic Gecko (*Gehyra oceanica*), another pop-eyed Polynesian stowaway, growled and yapped like a small dog from forest haunts as we plowed through underbrush in search of the elusive boa; and everywhere was the smaller gecko *Lepidodactylus lugubris*, a parthenogen whose clonal proliferation made it a pest in the many places it had been introduced. Hiking a jungle trail a month earlier on the Tongan island of 'Eua, a halo of butterflies distractedly circling my head, I'd flipped a rock to find one guarding a pair of elliptical eggs, a sight that cast the familiar conundrum of unisexuality in a new context—the species had never been recorded on this South Pacific outpost and yet here it was, merrily multiplying, from here to maternity.

Clonal reproduction made island colonization scenarios more likely for a species—not to mention for scientists trying to figure out how organisms disperse. Only one individual is then required to found a population, and Noah's Ark notwithstanding, the probability of a single female washing up on an unoccupied island was infinitely higher than the probability of a male and female finding their way either together or independently. Although biologists long reasoned that female reptiles could found island populations without the helping hand of parthenogenesis—being gravid on arrival or relying on the widespread capacity for storing sperm for later use—cloning certainly made it easier.

Biologists had observed in several vertebrates the expected capacity of parthenogens to spontaneously revert to sexual reproduction, but they were both shocked and stoked to recently discover the reverse is also true—parthenogenesis is a facultative ability in otherwise sexually reproducing reptiles, coincidentally two large but curiously island-hopping species: the Komodo Dragon (*Varanus komodoensis*) and the Burmese Python (*Python molurus bivittatus*). In two instances, female Komodos raised in European zoos and never exposed to males produced offspring—all genetic clones of Mom. The possibility that Komodos could pull off this trick when conditions dictated might partially explain the odd persistence of this fearsome species—world's largest lizard at over three meters, a hunter-scavenger with a biotoxic bite—in the face of historical human persecution since its discovery in the 1600s (though it has now been protected for some fifty years) and its apparent reoccupation of certain areas through overwater dispersal.

THE LONDON ZOO contains a popular Komodo exhibit. In one large pen lurks a dusty, monstrous female named Sungaï, which, unlike any other known reptile, responds to her name, understands commands, and scarfs chicken carcasses from a wooden facsimile of a hollowed-out deer carcass—a comical scenario. Out of sight in a smaller pen are several of Sungaï's clonal progeny; cock-headed, colorful, half-meter lizards living in trees as young Komodos do for up to four years out of fear of being cannibalized by adults—Mom included. The scene all seems so . . . prehistoric.

A former colleague who has become one of the world's leading authorities on plant parthenogenesis is searching for a genetic control of the ability; if such a mechanism exists, then the rare expression of clonal reproduction in higher animals could rely on an atavistic trait that goes back billions of years to early life on earth, pre-dating the plant-animal kingdom split. The accident of meiotic breakdown associated with hybridity or polyploidy that seems so often to trigger parthenogenesis then

takes on new meaning—and potential. Artificial cloning of plant
and animal stocks is big business, but the discovery of a natural control would rock the world; it could revolutionize every
aspect of agricultural practice; it would mean easier breeding to
diverse environments, yield increases, fewer pesticides, and for
the farmer in Africa, complete autonomy from seed companies.
Discovery of a genetic control would be a significant contribution and a potential Nobel Prize. But as I imagine Sungaï con-
tentedly flicking her long, forked tongue at visitors crowding the
glass, only two things come to mind: a B-grade movie in which
clonal Komodos terrorize London and thundering herds of what
were surely their prehistoric precursors—parthenogenetic dinosaurs as obnoxiously abundant as unisexual salamanders.

One thing people don't want to see breeding at will is the
Burmese Python. But facultative parthenogenesis could explain
why this behemoth, clumsily introduced to the Florida Everglades by a slew of uninformed owners whose pets outgrew
their capacity to deal with them (or, apparently, to reason), has
multiplied out of control there (though this incursion seems fair
reciprocation for transplanted alligators in Los Angeles's flood-
ways and New York's sewer system).

From the mid-1990s through 2003, Everglades National Park
officials removed around fifty Burmese Pythons. Then, in 2004
alone, sixty-one snakes were removed, and the toll has accelerated apace. Biologists logically believed these were discarded
pets; after all, around thirty thousand *Python molurus* enter the
U.S. each year. But when hatchlings were found deep within the
park, authorities had to admit that the adaptable species, dependent only on a permanent source of water, seemed firmly established. The problem is huge, literally and figuratively. Adults can
attain the scary length of eight meters, eating machines that prey

upon mammals, birds, reptiles—even, as it turns out, alligators. Epic tilts between large pythons and alligators worthy of a Japanese horror flick are now the norm. In one well-publicized instance a four-meter python burst open after swallowing a two-meter gator; officials came across the scene shortly afterward, and a graphic picture of the mess hit the wires.

Pythons are prolific: the female lays, incubates, and protects up to one hundred eggs. The forty-five- to sixty-centimeter hatchlings grow quickly when food is abundant. That male and female pythons were apparently meeting up to procreate in the park's gloomy corners was a scary enough scenario. But then a well-isolated female at Amsterdam's Artis Zoo produced eggs containing developing embryos in five consecutive years, and DNA analysis proved clonal reproduction. If female Burmese were capable of a spontaneous switch to parthenogenesis in the absence of males, eradicating them from the vast Everglades was suddenly a much bigger problem. Authorities doubled their efforts and even trained a snake-sniffing beagle—Python Pete—to help out. Whether this move will help remains to be seen.

Global trade and travel has spread the problem of introduced species everywhere, but Florida—with its subtropical climate, mix of terrestrial and aquatic habitats, busy ports, and high human immigration—is particularly vulnerable. Escapees from homes, ship cargo, parks, and attractions (*Visit Reptile World! See mighty pythons and cobras! Buy pecan pies and fireworks!*), as well as from exotic plant and animal farms, have all had an effect.

Fiji had introduced geckos, skinks, and toads, but its two frog species were native. *Platymantis vitiensis,* a tree frog that lays eggs in the water that collects in plant axils, where leaves attach to stems, and its leaf-colored, ground-dwelling sister species *P. vitianus*—rarely seen and vulnerable to both mongooses and toads—were hanging on, unthreatened, as of yet, by another South Pacific invader: the Aussie Brown Tree Frog (*Litoria ewingii*) was now common enough in New Zealand that it could be heard calling from roadsides in every month of the year, its effect on vanishing native *Leiopelma* frogs yet to be quantified.

AFTER ANOTHER GRUELING, unsuccessful day hunting Fijian boas, we were feeling the need for general anesthesia—I in particular. I'd cracked a tooth in half on a pebble concealed in some rice I'd eaten in Suva. Such an occurrence wasn't uncommon in this part of the world, where they dry rice on the road, and it would happen to me again. That particular time, however, was the most painful one, with South Pacific breezes whistling over the exposed root of an upper molar. The resort was holding its weekly kava ceremony for the latest crop of backpackers. Stuart figured it was as good a time as any to see what kava was all about; I figured anything short of cyanide would help.

At the appointed time a dozen of us gathered in a circle on the patio. Fiji Stouts in hand, Stuart and I watched a couple of Fijians grind up the kava root, place the resulting pulp into muslin, then knead it relentlessly in a large, wooden, water-filled bowl. When the water had turned unappetizingly gray, coconut-shell cups were dipped and passed, propelled by requisite mutterings and chants. The drink's nose was a bouquet of dirt and decay with a hint of lawn clippings, the start pure peppery mud-puddle and the finish like the inside of a garbage can. Each sip made your lips tingle; your mouth was eventually numb enough not to taste anything. This ceremony went on for about an hour.

I wasn't sure the kava, as with many drugs whose effects come on gradually, was making me anything but bilious until I tried to stand up. By then it was dusk and a cloudburst had moved in. After several minutes of being pelted by huge drops, I'd resolved to go inside or at least change seats—though I couldn't recall having moved to the one I occupied at the time. A lot of time seemed involved in that thought, even more as I tried to connect it to some kind of action, and in the attempt I suddenly realized that I couldn't move. Or was it *wouldn't*? I tried to will myself up but felt attached to the chair, which was now sliding backward up the wall with me in it. Wait, no—it was the ground moving away. But that was only because I was . . . standing . . . up. Right. Was I wet? Was it still raining? Where were those coconut shells? And where was my beer? A lot of questions when I really didn't care about answers. Much chatter and sliding furniture. Someone, maybe everyone, was laughing.

"Hey," the now-familiar voice of Satan rang out in the dark, "this is what it rained like before you found those bolos. Let's go look for snakes."

"Huh?"

The brief rain had left slinky vapors twisting off still-warm pavement. Stuart and I scoured the roadways around the resort for an hour before giving up and going to the beach to search above the high-tide line for sea kraits that often lurked there (*Laticauda* split their time between land and sea, coming ashore every ten days or so to digest food, have sex, lay eggs, or shed their skins). Again finding nothing, we sat down with newly opened beers on a shelf of fossilized reef raised above the beach. A full moon glowed behind the billowy edge of a towering cloud, spilling onto the beach and pooling at our feet. Everything was black and white and black. Shadow and light and shadow.

Another couple of weeks and I would be back in the thick of academia, something I'd been anxious about over the past weeks. The time. The money. The commitment. I'd jumped in with Stuart's mad dashes around the island largely to avoid stewing about the coming few years. In that moment on the beach, however, I felt more relaxed than I'd ever been. I looked down at Stuart's feet. How did I run into this guy? Who *were* these people? Black and white and black. Like that rope. Which was moving. Over his feet. Shadow and light and shadow. Like that deadly sea krait gliding across his toes. Now he was looking down, too. We were frozen.

"Man, that's a . . ."

"Fucker," he said, flicking it away with a simple, slow-motion kick. Airborne, the snake lashed around with its tiny mouth open, invisible fangs catching nothing but space. It landed on another reef shelf and thrashed off into a crevice. Stuart whistled softly, then held up his beer, and we clicked bottles.

"That could have been worse," he laughed.

HERPETOLOGY'S HIDDEN THREAD, it seemed, was luck. Lucky you didn't get bitten, or, if you did, lucky the bite didn't kill you, because it surely should have. Fortunately, I would come to know this truism mostly through observation. Despite hundreds of nonvenomous snakebites on my ledger, I didn't come too close with the dangerous ones: not when I mistook a venomous Cottonmouth (*Agkistrodon piscivorus*) for a harmless watersnake in an Oklahoma cattle tank; not when a sack of über-scary Banded Kraits (*Bungarus fasciatus*) liberated themselves in the bunkhouse of a Vietnamese logging camp while we slept; not even when the man I was returning to Toronto to work with, a certain Robert W. Murphy—mentor, friend, shit-disturber, and poster boy for the eponymous law in ways too numerous to count—purposely broke the necks of a half-dozen rattlers to keep them alive but immobile in the shower stall of a hotel room in Baja, where I discovered them, not quite as immobile as they should have been, on a late-night trip to the bathroom.

Like the beach scene with Stuart, this was the stuff I would never—*could* never—tell my mother. And she would fortunately never imagine it when I stood in the June sun at my doctoral convocation, grudgingly robed in an ill-fitting gown at the only graduation I would attend in a quarter century of possibly misguided education. Dabbing away tears of pride—and relief—she would forget all the toads and lizards and snakes that I'd collected or surreptitiously purchased and that then escaped in the house, as well as all the bites and tetanus shots, the swamp-rot and decomposing muck that was my clothing, and the yogurt containers filled with live, leaping amphibians jamming her refrigerator. With any luck she would also forget the time she was late for Mass because my gartersnake found its way from a cakebox in the trunk to the dashboard heat vent, where it lodged, head protruding like a prairie dog, while Dad drove warily to a tiny country church, where a scowling priest pronounced it the devil at work.

No, ON THAT day Mom would simply see me as one of a long line of bright young scientists clutching newly minted PhDs. My peers, however—earnest and bespectacled overseers of cutesy studies on salmon fecundity and duckling behavior and lemming distribution, destined for jobs with some dusty government ministry—would know the truth. Standing only as close as they dared, they would see me for the biological pariah I had become: a condemned man clutching a rolled death warrant, the notation beside my graduate-class picture "Most likely to die . . . soon," a neon sign on my back blinking "Warning: Herpetologist."

And Bob Murphy would have the job of shepherding me to this auspicious acme.

EVEN WITHIN THE magnanimous fraternity of zoology, a modern career in Eye of Newt and Toe of Frog still amounted to a circus act that garnered little respect. In ways both cherished and chided by recruits, it was a biological *Exile on Main Street*. Stuart had proved that.

"If you want to study herps, you have to be preadapted to fight," Murphy would tell me, "because you *are* going to engage in controversy."

It didn't matter that herpetology was a historically noble pursuit. It didn't matter that once upon a time the world's pre-eminent paleontologists dwelt among its ranks, before someone decided birds were dinosaurs and opened up the portfolio to ornithologists. It also didn't matter that herpetology was an illogical category (thanks again, Aristotle) or that studying chromosomes made you functionally more of a geneticist. It didn't matter because whether you worked with turtles, lizards, frogs, or salamanders, you were doomed by association with the snake guys; a Faustian bargain with Cobras 'R Us that many her-petologists—nerds, freaks, and misfits that they were—wore as a badge of honor. Or a belt.

Like punk rockers flaunting "individuality" with Mohawks and safety-pin uniforms, many drawn to herpetology feel a need to look the part. Thus, an inordinate number of bikers, strip-pers, and other fringe types count herpetology among their hobbies and aren't shy about it. Then again, neither are some science-minded practitioners: snakeskin boots, poison arrow frog T-shirts, and necklaces of crocodile teeth long flourished at meetings of the good ol' boy Herpetologists' League (HL), more mainstream Society for the Study of Amphibians and Reptiles (SSAR), and even Cope's august American Society of Ichthyolo-gists and Herpetologists (ASIH).

The problem with ASIH was that, other than occasional sea snakes turning up in coral-reef carpet bombings or minnows accidentally snared in a net full of tadpoles, ichthyology and herpetology had no more in common than their practitioners. This incongruity explained the egregious display tactics at modern-day meetings, where dressing like A Guy Who Studies Frogs ensures you won't be mistaken for A Guy Who Studies Fish. In contrast, ornithology meetings do not feature eagle-talon jewelry, no self-respecting mammalogist would be caught dead wearing a coonskin cap, and neither discipline boasts an equivalent to the popular herp bumper sticker, "My Python Is Bigger Than Yours."

Despite identity issues and sideshow potential, herp meetings held a potent cerebral draw. Herpetologists remain at the cutting edge in taxonomy (the naming of animals), systematics (their relationships), and biogeography (their distribution). Meeting presentations frequently combined these into an irresistible tonic of theory, laboratory wizardry, and adventure—often in the world's wildest landscapes. Just such a talk introduced me to the whacked-out world of Bob Murphy.

Before traveling the South Pacific, shopping for a PhD supervisor at an ASIH meeting in Victoria, B.C., I watched Dr. Bob (as most called him) deliver his groundbreaking theory on the biogeography of Baja California lizards and snakes with a trademark mixture of vitriol and laconic wisecracking. Grumbles of skepticism rippled through the mostly old-school audience, erupting into open contempt during question period. Slouching in a black Motörhead T-shirt and silver-rattler belt buckle, the Punk King of Herpetology deftly rebuffed challenges with a blizzard of data-analysis mumbo jumbo. Methodology arguments broke out. When one particularly obstreperous southerner pressed him on interpretations, Murphy responded with a shrug.

"You can believe whatever you want," he'd leveled from the stage, characteristically twisting one side of a Fu Manchu between two fingers, "but you're a complete fool if you do."

Where did I sign up?

DR. BOB, IT turned out, swam so effortlessly through herpetology's ocean of archetypes that he was often, in the same instant, both unbearable cliché and refreshing didact who defied categorization.

Like many herpetologists, Murphy couldn't remember a time when he wasn't interested in animals. As an adolescent in Texas, he collected snakes in a creek and ferried them home primarily because his parents "couldn't stand them." Though briefly sidetracked into marine biology by a high-school mentor and a family move to California, he steered back onto the herpetological track when he discovered that chasing desert lizards was easier, more fun, and—more important—a hell of a lot warmer than donning scuba gear to float around in the frigid Pacific.

He also found he had a soft spot for lizard behavior—the comical head bobbing and push-ups employed in territorial displays and sexual signaling. He liked watching a lizard take off and being able to tell what it was simply by the *way* it ran or what it ran *to*. He enjoyed tracking down animals solely by knowing what they did for a living; if something ate ants, you looked for the supply of food. The desert, he learned, was a more fine-grained environment than most realized, with exceptionally discrete ecological partitioning: here there were bushes, over there rocks, in between dunes, each with its own distinct fauna. The ocean had seemed more homogeneous, perhaps because Bob's brain was numbed by the frigidity of the Humboldt Current that hovered just offshore. Bob didn't like cold.

In the end, Bob's fate was sealed by his own poor

thermoregulation. And so, by association, was mine. Our friendship would be the story of two battling ethers: I, continually luring him toward the cold-hearted north; he, finding endless ways to drag me to the heat of the south. It was a battle with a happy, synergistic outcome.

Meeting up at a sushi bar the evening after his talk in Victoria, Dr. Bob and I drank beer long into the night and ate intertidal creatures we'd only ever seen in museum jars—things the chefs kept under the counter for themselves and even waitresses winced at. The meal quickly degenerated into a pissing contest of gastronomic indiscretion; we unflinchingly sucked back each new organism the staff presented. Neither of us faltered, no matter how foul the offering, resulting in a draw.

Bonding over nausea thresholds, we shared our histories of childhood snake chasing and disdain for both religion and mainstream academia, loudly carrying on this discovery until we realized we were frightening other patrons.

"The problem with these meetings," I lamented drunkenly as we were ushered onto the street, "is that they're *so* fucking boring."

"Exactly. What they need is rock 'n' roll," said Dr. Bob. "I've been thinking about maybe bringing my drum kit to a meeting and presenting some data to music."

I should have just laughed. Instead, not only did I sign on as Murphy's grad student but we shook hands on an absurd plan to produce the world's first scientific rock opera. The trail to that dubious stage would lead through dark forests of philosophy, the searing desert of academia, and the muck of my dissertation. In the end the journey would be another saw-off: I'd give Murphy his rock opera, and he'd gift me the life-threatening experiences of a lifetime.

But first we would wade through a few frigid swamps.

5

SLIME BUCKETS

Knowledge is experience; anything else is just information.

ALBERT EINSTEIN

THE LATE MARCH woods in Haliburton, Ontario, were quiet and sullen. Morning's blue sky had succumbed to gray. Light breezes flowed unimpeded through empty forest; nothing but sap stirred among leafless hardwoods and crusty, leftover snow.

Thick, gray ice crowning a large beaver pond was barely free of the shore, and water glistened darkly in the few places it had pulled back. The trees looked frozen in time. A warm south wind smelled of rain, and I was pretty sure that later all hell would break loose.

At that moment Bob Murphy, now my doctoral adviser, burbled down through the Slurpee-soft spring ice, dip net and all, up to his neck.

Schadenfreude followed Bob everywhere in Haliburton, its acme the sight of him bolting up out of brown, frigid water accompanied by sounds akin to someone fishing through an ice-filled cooler of beer at a Texas barbecue. As a reptile specialist and confirmed desert rat who found even saunas chilly,

Dr. Bob was rocked on occasions too numerous to recall by the bug-infested, rain-soaked, cold-enough-to-freeze-your-balls-off landscapes of his adopted country. To his eternal credit, however, he was willing not only to learn about the sex lives of salamanders but to jump (or fall) in as my field assistant despite the project's regimen of cold, wet misery. Ever generous, Bob's enthusiastic participation and technical savvy were the stuff of great student-teacher relationships. And his boreal gaucherie the stuff of pure comedy.

That night in town, people crowded into McKeck's Place to watch NHL Stanley Cup Playoffs on the big screen. Springtime here, as in most of Canada, meant hockey, maple syrup, and a long-awaited respite from the cold. But whereas humans measured spring's air of renewal in cultural terms, many animals were tied to a more stringent metric—it was the only time of year an individual might see another of its kind. Naturally, such encounters engendered a certain kind of urgency—one that also got biologists excited. Maybe too excited: while most folks cheered another punch-up on *Hockey Night in Canada,* Dr. Bob and I were supervising an orgy on the south shore of Lake Kashagawigamog.

Swept on strong gusts, the predicted rain sifted through the trees, coalescing as large drops that tumbled from naked branches. Muffled noises in the leaf litter melded with rain and a growing cacophony from the pond; in the dark, they were the kind of sounds that made your skin crawl. The night was alive, and the ground around us moved. No Hollywood special-effects tech could have marshaled what we tracked in our headlamps.

Thousands of glistening amphibians had risen from the quiescence of the forest floor. Blind with purpose, they zigzagged toward the pond in drunken clusters, bouncing off each other like billiard balls. This night hosted the Cold Crew, the denizens of earliest spring: burnished Wood Frogs (*Rana sylvatica*), tiny Spring Peepers (*Pseudacris crucifer*), striking Yellow-spotted Salamanders, and, in greatest abundance but most difficult to see, glabrous Blue-spotted Salamanders and their unisexual cronies. What this slippery mélange lacked in diversity it made up in sheer numbers: more of them lurked within a meter of where we crouched than the average person saw in a lifetime.

Given the creatures' cryptic habits, few biologists could even fathom the amount of matter represented by living amphibians in a typical temperate forest: up to 75 percent of the resident vertebrate biomass, according to a study at the University of New Hampshire. And yet, you could stand in one spot in that same forest for a thousand years and never see a single amphibian. The best time to appreciate this secret world was when the animals converged to play out the drama of breeding, a short but prodigious burst of ritual advertisement, frantic courtship, and furtive mating—spring break in Daytona Beach without the alcohol. As time marched on in the Haliburton woods, so would the parade: Chorus Frogs (*Pseudacris triseriata*), American Toads (*Bufo americanus*), Red-spotted Newts (*Notophthalmus viridescens*), Gray Treefrogs, Northern Leopard Frogs, Green Frogs (*Rana clamitans*), Mink Frogs (*Rana septentrionalis*), and Bullfrogs (*Rana catesbeiana*) would aggregate in time-honored sequence through April, May, and June—an exquisite choreography rooted in the deep history of eastern North America's rich amphibian fauna.

It was a dance I had come to love.

WHEN I WAS a kid, snakes wound continually through my hands and dreams, darting at will from the exposed pastures of experience into the tall grass of the subconscious. But working with salamanders had brought a paradigm shift; the creatures I now juggled were clammy, unconcerned, almost sessile beings with none of snakes' nervous, danger-evoking energy. Theirs was a different world, ungoverned by the heat of summer swelter, furtive movement, or vicious striking; instead, it was ruled by droning rain, surprise snowfalls, and the slow, halting proscriptions of ice. I would spend much soggy, hypothermic time in this Kingdom of Spring, piqued both by its capricious hostility and by its startling genetic subterfuge. These forces became my true mentors, delivering an understanding of the world that was tied as much to the muck of a pond bottom as to the molecular muck of a nucleus.

Working in Jim Bogart's lab, I'd spent two hectic springs driving around Maritime Canada at night, aurora borealis hanging over my shoulders and Orion tilted low on the horizon, fishing blue-spots from ponds and ditches, employing forensic genetics in the lab to identify and track postglacial dispersal of the various forms. It should have been enough. But these enigmatic animals didn't easily surrender their secrets, and so there I was again, four springs into our work at the Haliburton beaver pond, sitting in the dark in the rain, still wondering what the hell was going on under the ice, and keeping a protective eye on Dr. Bob.

Ringing the pond was a low fence, black construction plastic stapled to wooden stakes, its bottom buried in the soil and restaurant buckets countersunk to ground level every few meters on the forest side of the barrier. On any moist spring night, these receptacles brimmed with ambitious amphibian immigrants that were counted and then released on the pond side of the fence. Except, of course, for the blue-spots, from which we desired more information than could be gleaned by observation alone.

Each morning during the month-long breeding season, we'd transport bucketfuls of salamanders to a field lab in a nearby cottage. Here, the animals were briefly and harmlessly anesthetized while a single drop of blood was collected from a painless toe-clip and flash-frozen at $-196\,°c$ in liquid nitrogen; the samples were later used to check the ploidy (number of sets of chromosomes) of every individual. We recorded the animals' sex and size, then returned the creatures to the pond at nightfall as if nothing had happened. It was the amphibian equivalent of partying at the lake with a few hundred friends, being abducted and probed by aliens, then being dropped back at the party before anyone noticed you were gone. Hey—where'd I leave my beer?

The work was tedious and time-consuming, and the more it rained, the more animals showed up: some days we processed over five hundred. It was also sticky business; like many salamanders, blue-spots have a viscous, milky tail secretion—resembling white glue—which they wield for defensive purposes. Predators like shrews encountering this noisome epoxy can have their eyes, nose, or mouth glued shut and die of asphyxiation. The substance is exuded under even mild stress, and accidentally touching a tail could result in fingertips that wanted to stick together in unnatural ways and hours—sometimes days—of unwelcome, unwashable residue. Dr. Bob coined the term "slimers" after his first attempt to wipe a small but tenacious dose onto his pants. He succeeded only in repeatedly sticking his thumb to the fabric.

The bounty in our buckets, however, always seemed like the migration's aftermath. And so this night, the first good rain of our fourth breeding season, we'd wanted to see firsthand what the invasion looked like. Dr. Bob and I watched mesmerized as animals converged from every direction, swarming indifferently over snow, ice, rock, and timber. Internal switches and hormones governing such behavior were firmly locked onto phase one: *Must Get to Water*. Put something in front of them, they went over it; put them in something, they climbed out. Water, if they reached it, was both sanctuary and medium for phase two: *Must Mate*. In our lights, startled frogs leapt into the darkness, while at the pond's edge salamanders appeared to sense the weight of impending biological destiny; pausing briefly, they took one last look around before plunging under the ice. Unlike Bob's accidental dunkings, these plunges purposefully closed the loop in an ancient prescription.

Amphibians—the group that had ultimately vaulted us onto land—indeed offered a strange and fascinating story. One well worth listening to.

BECAUSE SOME REPTILES are amphibious, no amphibians are reptilian, and many amphibians aren't amphibious at all, one might rightly be confused as to the scientific meaning of "amphibian." The word's Greek roots refer to a doubtful nature or duality of existence—organisms that seemed to both (*amphi*) live (*bios*) in water and live on land, appearing, disappearing, and reappearing in one realm or the other. Coined in the mid-seventeenth century and later formalized by our friend Linnaeus, the term has since been applied to a range of our own mimetic inventions—from seaplanes to airboats to tanks.

Despite its widespread usage, "amphibian" recalls for most of us the classic connotation of animals that migrate to ancestral ponds to mate, lay eggs, and take their leave while the young hatch, battle through an aquatic larval stage, then miraculously metamorphose to wander into the same hostile landscape whence their parents came. We're naturally compelled by this narrative arc of struggle, survival, and transformation. Crack open Robert Hofrichter's *The Encyclopedia of Amphibians*, however, and you'll quickly see that only a fraction of them follow this clichéd pattern: "Many species have developed astonishing survival strategies and have grown independent from large bodies of water. They colonize subterranean cave systems, alpine regions, rapidly flowing mountain streams, human settlements, tundra and desert areas. They can withstand aridity and frost; they carry their young in their mouths, on their backs and in their stomachs; some even lay their eggs in foam nests on trees. Amphibians [in fact] surpass all other vertebrate groups in the diversity of their survival and reproductive strategies."[11]

A ringing endorsement for amphibian multiculturalism—but what, then, if not amphibiousness itself, defines such a group? There's a bit of *amphi* in that answer, too.

Together with the primitive jawless fishes (lampreys and their ilk), cartilaginous sharks and rays, and bony fishes, amphibians make up the Anamnia. More descriptor than taxon, Anamnia includes those vertebrates whose eggs lack an innermost membrane, or amnion. Reptiles, birds, and mammals, in contrast, belong to Amniota, a group whose embryos feature this extra protection. But there's more: in conjunction with those three classes, amphibians *also* compose Tetrapoda—the four-limbed vertebrates. These overlapping designations suggest that the main transition from fish to amphibian involved the evolution of limbs to allow for part-time padding around on land, while the watershed from amphibian to reptile, and thus adaptation to a *fully* terrestrial existence, involved acquisition of the amniotic membrane. Thus, amphibians are most readily defined by an essential schizophrenia: they are tetrapods with anamniotic eggs.

The whole mess got started back in the Devonian, when amphibian ancestors arose within Rhipidistia, a freshwater group of the lobe-finned fish order Crossopterygii. One-time fossil symbol of this critical period in the evolution of vertebrates is the gill-and-lung-equipped *Eusthenopteron foordi*. Because the move to land is often seen as the most important watershed in our own evolution (overlooking, as did Aristotle, the acquisition of a backbone), we find such creatures particularly riveting. On a hot summer day in southern Alberta some years ago, I'd gained insight into the power of this past from a journeyman fossil hunter.

Rene Trudel was a slight, energetic man with a penchant for cigarettes. After spending the day on a fossil tenure he supervised near the St. Mary's River, we'd retreated to Trudel's place to cool down in the shade with a cold beer. Passionate and talkative, he spun tales of collecting in the world's hinterlands until the beer was exhausted and dusk had sucked up the heat like a door ajar in winter. He fondly rendered each anecdote, but Trudel positively ignited when talk turned to his work on the Devonian deposits of Miguasha on Québec's Gaspé Peninsula. His recollection of his first encounter with *Eusthenopteron* was compelling: after weeks of fruitless, backbreaking work, he'd been on his hands and knees wrestling a nodule from the deposit's face when the rock suddenly cracked open and put him eye-to-eye with the three-dimensional, open-mouthed head of the fabled fish. "Dat was *reeelly* sometin'," he'd chuckled, shaking his head and stabbing the dark with a cigarette, its ember throwing just enough light to catch the sparkle in his eye. In that instant I saw that whatever else Trudel might have been—fossil merchant, miner, mercenary—he was mostly a guy who'd glimpsed his own soul staring back at him from the gaping jaws of a 370-million-year-old fish.

For all its cachet, however, *Eusthenopteron* was still just a fish. At the time, the earliest known "amphibian" was believed to be

363-million-year-old *Icthyostega*, from the rich deposits of eastern Greenland. Long referenced as a textbook transitional form,
it has lately been construed as more of a limbed fish, ancestral to
the true amphibians that dominated the subsequent Carboniferous. Distinctions remain fluid as new fossils put our knowledge
in flux; for instance, *Tiktaalik roseae,* a limbed rhipidistian—or
"fishapod" as discoverers whimsically labeled it—found in Arctic
Canada in 2004, rolls back the appearance of tetrapod accesso-
ries in lobe-fins to 375 million years ago.

Icthyostega nevertheless displayed at least an eye for terrestrial
real estate: clear reliance on lung breathing, dorsoventrally flattened and reinforced skull, mobile neck, posterior elements of
the gill arch pitching in to support the pectoral girdle and front
limbs, and hind limbs with seven toes on each foot (the penta-
dactyl, or five-toed, condition shared by all modern terrestrial
vertebrates, came later).

The discovery of a transitional form like *Icthyostega* that so perfectly fit expectations had been cause among paleontologists for
celebration, back slapping, and, sadly, overspeculation. *Icthyostega*
was contemporary with another transitional form, eight-toed
Acanthostega, whose skeletal insufficiencies showed that it was
even less able to exploit the land niche, tipping paleontologists off
to what these beasts were really doing: desperately gasping for air
in warm, oxygen-poor swamps. Where lobe-finned fishes used
their tails for locomotion and pectoral and pelvic gear for balance, *Icthyostega* and *Acanthostega* did the reverse, relying on lobes
or limbs for locomotion and tails for balance, pulling themselves
through shallow, anoxic waters and occasionally using their
stronger front limbs to haul out much like seals. In any event,
certain members of this evolutionary grade apparently excelled
at gasping and found land more to their liking. With plant and

insect groups exploding in the Devonian tropics, opportunity knocked in the form of a burgeoning terrestrial environment, and proto-amphibians answered.

As with many nascent animal groups, early amphibians were positively beastly compared with today's generally pocket-sized offerings: *Mastodonsaurus giganteus* from the Late Triassic reached four meters and had pointy, nasty teeth worthy of a crocodile; huge lower fangs poked up through openings ahead of the nostrils. It was freakish but typical of the dabbling evolution engages in when a lineage tests new morphological, physiological, or ecological ground. This experimentation is adaptive radiation—wherein a number of forms cobbled from a basic *bauplan* try out as many ways to live as are possible in as many places as are available.

Amphibians underwent an adaptive radiation in the Carboniferous that enabled them to reign as dominant terrestrial vertebrates for over 200 million years. Eventually, the familiar three modern orders of amphibians emerged: the limbless, eel-like, burrowing caecilian; the tailless, leap-adapted frog; and the sleek, classic-tetrapod lines of the salamander.

Appearing in the Early Jurassic, caecilians remain the least understood group from every conceivable standpoint. Limbless burrowers resembling giant earthworms with mouths, they feature reduced, skin-covered eyes, poisonous skin secretions, a pair of freakish sensory tentacles that spring from their heads, and penislike structures for internal fertilization. They include a mix of egg-laying and live-bearing species, with newborns ranging from larvae that grovel in moist soil to metamorphs with giant external gills to juveniles that feed on their mother's skin. Little known and rarely seen, close to two hundred species circumscribe a worldwide tropical distribution. A sparse number of herpetologists working on these highly specialized beasts are viewed as even more esoteric than their peers, if that is possible.

In contrast, the foreshortened, bug-eyed morphology of the frog is one of evolution's true genius strokes. From inauspicious origins in the Early Jurassic, frogs have survived 185 million years and several mass extinctions as the most successful order of terrestrial vertebrates. And they have the stats to prove it: with some 5,400 species, close to 90 percent of modern amphibians are frogs. Until it was recently fragmented by taxonomists, the tropical American superfamily Leptodactylidae alone contained fifty genera and eleven hundred species—some seven hundred in Bogart's beloved *Eleutherodactylus*, the largest vertebrate genus and the only one to have a member wholly preserved in amber—a nifty piece of 37-million-year-old jewelry.

As poster child for a successful, global, adaptive radiation, frogs occur everywhere but extreme polar regions (though they aren't shy about subpolar latitudes, reaching well above the Arctic Circle in North America and Eurasia) and make a living in every conceivable way. Leptodactylids again offer a microcosm of frogs' staggering diversity: adult body sizes range from one to twenty-five centimeters; some are stocky and toadlike, others resemble sleek bullfrogs, and many have adopted a treefrog morphology. Ecologically, they range from purely aquatic to purely terrestrial in a spectrum of habitats—even subterranean. Some lay eggs in water, others on plants, some in foam nests, and some in soil. Some larvae develop in water, others on land, and some directly in modified oviducts, emerging fully metamorphosed.

The name frog comes from the Old English *frocga*, which (no surprise here) derives from Old Norse *frauki*. Humans have always had the deepest fascination with frogs. Representations in art, symbolism, superstition, mythology, fairy tales, magic, religion, and commercial logos flog everything from intelligence to fertility to resurrection. Aside from warty, dry-skinned toads—linked to evil, witchcraft, and the netherworld—the remainder of frogdom typically symbolizes good. Positive vibes, man, as Kermit might say.

Despite our affinity for frogs, however, we still see salamanders as the quintessential amphibian. Logic tells us that their piscine movements, tails, and four more-or-less equal limbs most closely resemble whatever first crawled out of that Devonian swamp. And indeed salamanders have found many imaginative ways to recall those halcyon days of straddling the land-water interface.

Among five hundred or so species are, of course, terrestrial adults that migrate to ponds to breed, but some species, depending on conditions, either metamorphose to terrestrial adults or remain permanent water-dwellers, retaining a larval morphology through sexual maturity (picture a race of humans as giant babies). The water-born larvae of some newts transform, live briefly on land as brightly colored juveniles, then undergo a second metamorphosis, returning to water as an aquatic adult. Some salamanders live permanently in water and surface to breathe; some respire without having to surface, having jettisoned lungs and co-opted the outer skin as a giant respiratory surface. Others have given up similarly hard-won morphological ground: blind, unpigmented species adapted to life in subterranean waterways; degenerate, eel-like beasts with reduced digits or no rear limbs; a cornucopia of forms that retain external gills ranging from inconspicuous buds to feathery fronds of fuchsia flesh. Salamanders can be among nature's most colorful creations, with phantasmagorical patterns and adornments that seem painted in a ceramic studio. They can also be drab as dish-water. Of course, you should never judge a book by its cover.

Even seeing a lot of salamanders won't tell you much about their way of life. The late Mike Rankin, assistant curator of her-petology at the Canadian Museum of Nature in Ottawa and a man who had hundreds of salamanders pass through his hands each year (albeit in jars), summed up the position of most biolo-gists when I'd told him I worked on salamanders: "Good for you. I don't know much about 'em except they're slimy and hard as hell to find in August."

True that. Most terrestrial salamanders spend their time in underground retreats, moving deeper during drier months and below frostline in winter. In spring, chock-full of hormones that accumulate over winter, water-breeding species await cues to begin a pilgrimage to ancestral ponds; when the ground thaws and a rainy night provides for optimal travel, it's goin' home time.

I felt privileged to witness these nocturnal scrambles. Not simply because they were deeply fascinating or because so few people ever saw such things but because so few will ever have a *chance* to: disease, shrinking habitat, and road mortality in many migratory species have made such spectacles increasingly rare. Habitat destruction tops the list of threats and includes the effects of clear-cutting, stream channeling, pond filling, wet-land drainage, agriculture, and pollutants. Because their semi-permeable skins, moisture requirements, and typically biphasic life cycles make amphibians indicators of local environmen-tal health and climatic trends, their current worldwide decline (Chapter 12 covers this phenomenon) bodes poorly for a global environment on which we also depend.

Because amphibians are adapted to certain temperature and moisture regimens for breeding, larval development, and adulthood, climatic flux at any juncture can affect both populations and overall distribution. Global warming will favor a few species but be detrimental to most. In northeastern North America, for instance, increasingly frequent midwinter mild spells have prompted premature breeding by some species, whose efforts are then destroyed by freezing when weather returns to seasonal norms. At the other extreme, exceptionally hot spring days cause water temperatures in breeding habitats to skyrocket, accelerating fungal, algal, and bacterial growth with accompanying rapid depletion of dissolved oxygen, an effect that can kill eggs or cause developmental abnormalities. Problems are exacerbated when shade vegetation that moderates water temperature is cut from the margins of aquatic habitat.

Human activities and fragmented habitats can drive local amphibian extinctions, but what happens during naturally occurring climatic shifts? Results are ultimately the same—changing distributions of species adapted to particular ecological or climatic associations. The difference is that these occur gradually over vast periods of time as part of a larger integrated system of changes in continuous habitat—like those following retreat of the last continental ice sheet.

I'VE OFTEN WISHED I had been alive during the Pleistocene. A childish whim, I know, but merely viewing the aftermath of glaciation doesn't do justice to its powerful imagery. For instance, the car-sized boulder Bob and I leaned against in the Haliburton woods once floated a kilometer high on a frozen sea and was stranded here when the ice melted back. As the ice front retreated northward, this area became the spillway for a giant river hundreds of meters deep. Kashagawigamog ("long and flowing water" in the Ojibway tongue) is all that's left of this Goliath waterway, but thick, rocky soils and sandy outwashes bear witness to deposition that occurred as the meltwater subsided. (Most of the sediment ended up farther south, where it's underappreciated. Chicagoans and Torontonians laboring in city gardens are blithely unaware that the fertility underfoot owes its existence to vast amounts of rock, dirt, and vegetative mass trundled southward by Pleistocene glaciers, sorted and settled in fluvial vanguards, then raked like so much expensive topsoil by the ebb and flow of Super Lakes that make today's "Great" ones seem like wading pools.)

After the ice, tundra changed rapidly over to boreal forest and then, at the height of postglacial warming, around five thousand years ago, a hardwood version more typical of the central United States; a cooling trend since has maintained the area's familiar mixed forests. The march of climates and ecosystems was mirrored by a succession of animal species. Present distributions of amphibians in Ontario say a lot about these past changes, perhaps none so much as the Blue-spotted Salamander complex, a case study in the potentially bizarre interactions of genetics, evolution, glaciation, climate, environment, and human interference. As we were slowly finding out, the group comprised many forms, traded genomes like hockey cards, raised and lowered ploidy at will, and generally gave sex a bad name. The kind of thing that made you go *Hmmm . . .*

TO AN UNTRAINED observer, the salamanders crowding our buckets at the Haliburton beaver pond all looked similar: ten to twenty centimeters long, dark bluish-brown with conspicuous, lichenlike, baby-blue spotting that resembled the flecked enamelware of your grandmother's roasting pan. The reality, of course, was far more complex. The buckets actually contained several distinct forms: male and female *A. laterale* as well as triploid LLJ and tetraploid LLLJ females.

Currently the ranges of *Ambystoma laterale*, *A. jeffersonianum*, and other hybridizing species of *Ambystoma* overlap here and there, but this overlap was more extensive once. As cooling and warming trends square-danced over the millennia, Carolinian forests and their fauna repeatedly came into contact with their boreal and prairie equivalents. Because each ecosystem contained unisexual salamander swarms dependent on at least one diploid species of *Ambystoma*, the result was unisexual tides washing back and forth across eastern North America to pool in various geographic nooks and crannies. So strange(r) things were bound to happen; remember—it's an orgy out there.

Sure enough, the squirming masses Dr. Bob and I dredged up in Haliburton led to questions aplenty. Although some of my master's work had looked at whether L and J genomes occasionally swapped genetic material in a shared hybrid nucleus, and Bogart and I had demonstrated at least one such instance, I'd put such cytogenetic musing aside for my doctoral project to focus on population composition—an ecological snapshot of the unisexual hybrid phenomenon. And that picture consistently showed some 75 percent of salamanders at the Haliburton beaver pond to be unisexual females. I did the math: if the remaining 25 percent comprised equal numbers of male and female *A. laterale*, then almost 90 *percent* of the overall population was female, all relying on a tiny, overworked contingent of male *A. laterale*. A dream dating scenario for salamander studs or disaster in the making?

Perhaps unsurprisingly, hybrid salamander complexes were first identified because of these wildly unbalanced sex ratios, and early observers logically theorized that exponential reproduction by unisexuals should eventually put co-occurring species out of business. But because triploid hybrids *require* males in order to reproduce via the peculiar process of gynogenesis (recall the paradox of sperm serving simply to stimulate an egg into division before being callously discarded), they are de facto sexual parasites on any species with which they co-exist, and parasitism's most stringent tenet is to exploit but not exhaust the supply of hosts. Thus, the widespread mutual existence of regular diploid species of *Ambystoma* and their unisexual parasites—occupying an area the size of Australia—required built-in control.

Some checks and balances were apparent: herpetologists long knew, for instance, that triploid eggs were less viable than those of diploids, experiencing high mortality; either the eggs were genetic disasters or Mom wasn't all that adept at attracting sperm donors. Bob and I found other glitches, too. Tetraploids (some 15 percent of Haliburton hybrids) had even more problems than triploids: they produced fewer eggs; these suffered yet higher mortality; larval development lagged significantly; metamorphosis was a crapshoot; sexual maturation was delayed.

The existence of tetraploids also meant that not all was going to the clones' conquering plan; clearly in some matings, the usually discarded L sperm was uniting with an LLJ egg to form an LLLJ female. Why, we wondered? Fortuitously and quite unexpectedly, ever-diligent Jim Bogart and colleagues answered by demonstrating how this process was largely determined by water temperature in breeding ponds: all offspring of triploids were triploid clones at 6°C, but at 15°C most offspring of triploids were tetraploid. Thus, fluctuating temperatures caused by everything from habitat alteration to variable spring weather could affect fertilization rates from year to year; more tetraploids over time would mean things were getting warmer—an interesting consideration in light of global warming, and one of uncertain consequence.

Although prehuman events had kicked off a cascade of bizarre genetic processes in these animals, these broad effects of shifting Pleistocene climates would have found equilibrium over time. Now, however, they were crammed into only a few decades by human transgressions. I would come away from my study with this haunting question: how many unisexual hybrid complexes were *we* creating?

THE HOCKEY GAMES were long since done and the bars closed when we finally turned off our lights at the beaver pond. Steering Dr. Bob away from any icebound danger, I listened in the dark to the hundreds of frogs clucking and whistling through a falling aqueous filter. I sensed that even superficial understanding of such little-known netherworlds granted awkward membership; if I were a frog or salamander I felt I'd know just what to do. Billions of raindrops fell in any instant, but I could differentiate between the tattoo drumming over the clutter of the forest floor and the atmospheric circle closing over the pond's surface.

Sounds were always clearer in the dark. Ever since the Devonian bent a nascent terrestrial ear.

6

ROMMY, CAN YOU HEAR ME?

"Even now, just being here, I still get that collector feeling. You know

what I mean. I'll see something and then suddenly get that feeling.

It's like I can't just have something—I have to have it and learn about it

and grow it and sell it and master it and have a million of it."

SUSAN ORLEAN, *The Orchid Thief*

ALTHOUGH THE FIELDWORK I conducted during my time at the Royal Ontario Museum under Dr. Bob now seems part of a vanishingly distant past, the membership I enjoyed in a group of wisecracking doctoral students in the Department of Ichthyology and Herpetology seems as though it were only yesterday. Comedy is like that.

The crowded office I shared with three others featured a couple of computers, reams of paper, books galore, and walls papered with humorous paeans to pop culture and academic absurdity. Jars marshaled on each student's desk identified his or her lot for the three to five years completing a degree would take. Mine had dozens of gray, rubbery 'manders, packed nose-down like pickles in a handful of large vessels; Hugh Griffith's station featured skinks (lizards of the family Scincidae) in myriad shapes and sizes, largely borrowed from other institutions for a phylogenetic analysis of the group; Paul Chippindale, a night owl rarely seen before 4 PM, displayed a smattering of the tiny Spring Peepers whose population genetics he was studying; and most intriguing were the cleared-and-stained Gobiid fishes floating in crucibles of glycerin above Randy Mooi's dissecting scope, eerily pellucid save for wine-red bone and aqua-blue cartilage.

Across the hall cloistered the directors of this zoological theater troupe: Rick Winterbottom, curator of ichthyology and a specialist in marine fishes too small to see; Ed Crossman, another ichthyology curator focused on the polar opposite— giant freshwater fishes like Muskellunge and Northern Pike; and, of course, Dr. Bob, curator of herpetology and black sheep of the triad in every conceivable way. Salamanders, lizards, frogs, fish; unisexuality, systematics, genetics, morphology; world-leading researchers as supervisors—as good an intellectual mill as one could hope for while apprenticing to take the scientific stage. Yet what stuck with me from this heady time was neither the grind of research nor eureka moments of discovery; instead, I mostly remember the endless fun and peals of gut-wrenching laughter emanating from our cell.

As befits mentor-apprentice relationships, traffic flowed constantly between the student office and those of our I&H supervisors. When we'd collected the questions we wished to ask about the data we'd collected from the animals we'd collected, we'd collect our sheaves of computer paper up like a swaddling child and enter Murphy's long, narrow office, navigating a gauntlet of personal collections to reach his desk at the far end. Questions were often jumbled during this distracting passage, evaporating altogether when Dr. Bob inevitably started in about his latest tug-o'-war with the ass of administration.

To begin, Murphy's book collection was the largest outside the ROM's own library, and you could spend hours scanning

out-of-print titles, turn-of-the-century illustrated works, and
a glut of undecipherable material from China and the Soviet
Bloc. His reprint collection—a mountain range of filing cabinets topped by the snows of yet-to-be-filed reports—made Bogart's apartment blocks seem like low-income housing. There
were objects collected on trips to Mexico, China, Fiji, Philip-
pines, Australia, and the Caucasus. A music collection. Camera
gear and photographs. Plastic models of colorful poison arrow
frogs. And everywhere were specimen jars, a trail of taxonomic
crumbs that could be followed back to the outer office, through
the classroom and labs, then across the hall to the collections
room—a vast warehouse of bottled discovery and suspended
secrets. In case we'd somehow forgotten, Bob's office was a neon
reminder that museums, institutions dedicated to the gestalt of
collecting, were, in fact, populated by collectors.

Working in a museum meant dwelling in the very belly of
humanity's gathering instinct, a place where collections were
celebrated and the best contributors to these venerated. Though
often viewed as a malevolent and haphazard practice—god
knows biologists do little to dispel Gary Larson's comical *Far
Side* portrayals—collecting didn't always involve *possessing* an
organism.

"For me it's mostly about gathering *knowledge* of hidden life,"
Hugh Griffith once told me as we sifted leaf litter in search of salamanders. "Being aware of all the stuff you don't see—though it
surrounds you—is enriching."

Like any form of maturity, such hands-off reverence is
grown into. As a kid I was a zealous collector—hockey cards,
motel soaps, Hot Wheels, minerals, fossils, shells, birds' nests,
butterflies. I'd even started a neighborhood museum to press
others into service to "grow the collections" (later learning this
was *the* budgetary catchphrase of real-life museums). Collecting

was in my blood, and I met few in science who didn't share this often pathogenic bug.

In *The Orchid Thief*, Susan Orlean asks an Everglades Park ranger burdened by relentless poaching of animals and plants what it is about collecting living things that so seduces humans: "'Oh, the mystery, beauty, unknowability, I suppose,' he said, shrugging. 'Besides, I think the real reason is that life has no meaning. I mean, no obvious meaning. You wake up, you go to work, you do stuff. I think everybody's always looking for something a little unusual that can preoccupy them and help pass the time.'"[12]

But although these words speak to the existential lure of biology—a practice that obviates the soul-sucking surety that life has no cosmic purpose by investigating its purposelessness—whence the clearly inherited urge to collect?

Acquiring and hanging on to objects not necessary for survival has been a universal of human behavior since our earliest societies. Although many nineteenth-century explorer-collectors hid behind claims of altruism—an urge to contribute to the greater good—a recent study suggests their motivation was more personal.

Collecting and hoarding in rodents is driven by structures within subcortical regions of the brain. Studying human patients who developed abnormal hoarding behavior following injury to these same regions, University of Iowa researchers concluded that a primitive collecting urge was released from normal restraints. Unlike collectors of art or stamps, patients displayed personally disruptive collecting behavior, filling their homes with useless junk and broken appliances. Despite no ongoing interest in the items, they fought all attempts to get rid of them. Remind you of anyone?

One *could* make the conceptual leap that the most rabid

collectors among us are brain damaged, but that would seem more of an uncharitable attempt to redefine "eccentric."

BOB'S MOST OMINOUS collection had nothing to do with science. It was, instead, his hoard of percussion instruments: stacks of bongos, tambourines, maracas, drumsticks, and electric drums; the stacked bass, snares, and tom of a regular kit; and, in the corner, a giant gong that would forever reverberate through our souls—twenty kilos of hammered brass that came to symbolize the delusion of grandeur that was ROMMY.

ROMMY was another of life's strange watersheds that traced its roots to the rubric of the Blue-spotted Salamander. During our few idle hours at the Haliburton cabin, Bob insisted we make good on the rock-opera deal we'd shaken hands on in Victoria. Scheduled to perform this yet-to-be-conceived production at a summer meeting in Ann Arbor, Michigan (committing to fill a three thousand–seat auditorium was Bob's idea of motivation), we'd set about penning the script. Incorporating a real set of data, it told the story of a bumbling graduate student named ROMMY (played by Chippindale, Bob's youngest, most naïve charge) caught between two conflicting theories: phylogenetics as promulgated by his "good" professor (Randy Mooi) and phenetics as advocated by an "evil" rival (Bob would step from behind his drums to don a rubber mask as the sinister Dr. Phenetico). In phylogenetics, species relationships are based on shared derived characters (for instance, all five species of living rhinoceros have horns and thus logically diverged from a common ancestor that had horns), whereas phenetics relies on measures of overall similarity (the three species of two-horned rhinos might be classed together in this scheme, though one is only distantly related to the other two); so entrenched among biological factions were

these differing methodologies that if the two schools were countries they would have been at war.

Caught up daily in the conflict as we were, the storyline was
a supreme act of art imitating life. When we sang the chorus to
"ROMMY, Can You Hear Me?" it was a frustrated real-life Murphy
yelling at a real-life Chippindale, who was asking the hopelessly
redundant questions of any insecure student.

No one could take any of this too seriously, and so it soon
morphed into a ribald comedy laced with inside biological
jokes. I strapped on a guitar as ROMMY's best friend, Cliff; we
recruited other musical, acting, and technical talent from the
ROM and Canada's academic herp community—Hugh Griffith adeptly picked up the bass, my frequent collaborator Larry
Licht from York University played tenor sax, University of
Victoria's Pat Gregory volunteered as narrator, and Jim Bogart
even had a cameo. I&H Curatorial Assistant and guitarist Ross
MacCulloch wrote original lyrics and several scores for the
almost twenty songs, though we ripped off the majority from
Tommy, The Who's landmark rock opera about a deaf, dumb, and
blind boy: "ROMMY" was a concatenation of ROM and our meta-
phorically senseless student.

Somehow we pulled it off, helped by vast amounts of beer
consumed during the performance and a boozed-to-the-hilt
crowd that clapped, laughed, and guffawed from the opening
bar. Self-deprecation was a way of life for herpetologists, but
none had had the absurdity of their existence reflected back to
them from a stage. Nor had anything like this occurred at meetings where novelty generally ran to holding a plate of barbecued
alligator while jawing about a new species of arboreal salamander from the jungles of Honduras. Bob's successful attempt to
rock the conservative foundations of science elevated him to

minor deity in herpetological circles; you could bank a lot of transgressions against that kind of capital.

After the biggest gamble of our academic careers, we were, to a person, triumphant. Like the animals I studied, I was supremely comfortable in my skin, with no sense that a day might come when I'd wish to shed it. Finding an artistic outlet in those staid corridors may have delayed the ultimate realization that I couldn't spend the rest of my life in a lab, but at the time it merely galvanized our department at the ROM, in the minds of most, as a place of creative critical mass, unbridled fun, and abiding strangeness. It also offered de facto proof that when it came to herpetologists, you could always expect the unexpected.

A COMFORT WITH organs and organisms and a reverence for strange life-forms paradoxically engender an even deeper irreverence.

The '70s British television show *Doctor in the House* featured madcap medical students railing against the stern environs of a university, where they found comfort and comedy in the intersection of booze and cadavers, drunkenly smuggling preserved body parts into dorms and social situations. Museums were rife with such activity; virtually everything was bathed in some form of formaldehyde, alcohol, glycerin, or combinations thereof. Thus, frog heads in your coffee, fish skulls in your lunch bag, salamanders spelling out M-U-R-D-E-R in the freezer, and an assortment of cryo-crap that found its way into pockets and drawers tended to reek of a chemical past. Not that there was any shortage of tricks with unpreserved animals.

Hardly a week passed without a "crispy critter"—the dried, twisted body of some poor escaped animal that looked and smelled like it was straight out of a Chinese apothecary—appearing on my desk. A tiny Red-eared Slider (*Trachemys scripta elegans*) the receptionist kept behind her desk was once replaced with a preserved specimen, and days went by before she noticed her new pet turtle was dead. People opened briefcases to find harmless Fox Snakes (*Elaphe vulpina*) shooting out at them—the same snakes that were frequently pressed into service at parties as live neckties. Plenty of amusement began at the reception desk, where our preternaturally perky receptionist answered the phone with a chirpy *Good morning! Ichthyology and Herpetology!*, a syllable-laden sing-song that set just about every nonscientific caller into peals of What-the-fuck? laughter and kept us snickering at our desks. Another endless fount of absurdity bubbled on the other end of the phone.

One day a guy called about a lizard preserved in amber he'd bought for a boatload of cash in the Caribbean and wanted authenticated. Bob invited him down, took one look, and declared it a fake—a lizard embedded in amber-colored acrylic. The man, however, was insistent.

"OK," said Bob, "I'll put it in acetone; if it's real amber it won't be affected, but if it's plastic it will turn white and be destroyed. All right?"

"All right," the man said confidently.

He left with a white lump in his pocket and tears in his eyes.

All manner of crackpots believed the ROM was a confessional where their latest imprudence would be forgiven. People brought in snakes they'd hacked to death with hoes, shovels, and axes or run over with cars, boats, and lawnmowers. They wanted to be told that these were dangerous, deadly creatures and that they hadn't acted in haste by turning them into compost. Invariably—at least when enough animal remained to figure out what it had been—we'd break the news that they'd killed a perfectly harmless creature, taking care to explain its beneficial nature (particularly if a Greek chorus of judgmental children was present), leaving the guilt-ridden party with the impression that his or her murderous indiscretion had left a nest of parentless baby snakes somewhere, hissing and teary-eyed, to fend for themselves. Which, given that most snakes exhibited zero parental investment, was patently untrue, but it made a point.

Every once in a while some bozo would get his identification right, however, so I wasn't surprised to open the freezer one morning and find a Massasauga Rattlesnake (*Sistrurus catenatus*), bagged and tagged "Parry Sound District, Killed by Tourists." It was the kind of thing that steamed you for a boatload of reasons, not the least of which were that the species wasn't aggressive, was easily avoided, and, for the simple crime of having a rattle, endangered as hell. Between fielding phone calls from moronic cottagers convinced that snapping turtles had collapsed their dock or *positive* that they'd seen a rattlesnake where rattlers simply didn't exist, sometimes a scenario of truly inspired insanity arose. We were lounging around one day when our lab assistant, Marj, buzzed in over the intercom.

"There's a man upstairs who says a snake is attacking the furniture in his apartment," she said. "He wants to talk to an *ex-pert.*"

Randy and Hugh snorted contemptuously. Finger on the intercom, I was ready to suggest Marj politely dismiss the guy when she impishly added, "I told him you'd all be right up." Suddenly, we were all experts on reptile-furniture interactions.

With Marj in tow we headed to the entrance dressed in our most blood- and chemical-stained whites like a train of interns marching into the wards to inspect a rarely seen illness. Which, in retrospect, was precisely what we were doing.

"I am having the problem of snakes biting on my furniture,"

insisted a small, dark man with a heavy East Indian accent and large, purpled nose.

"*Reeeally,*" said Randy, stroking his chin.

"I am waking every day, and they are making with more teeth and scratches onto the chair," he insisted, delivering a litany of other evidence.

"How do you know it's *snakes* doing this?" I said, asking the obvious.

"Ah! . . . I am bringing a sample," he said, sliding an embroidered pillow with gold tassels on each corner from a plastic bag and pointing to a spot along an edge.

"This is Dr. Griffith," I offered solemnly, nodding toward Hugh, who was already desperately trying to maintain a straight face. "His specialty is big items. Sofas mostly. This is Marj the . . . uh, assistant. And this is Dr. Mooi, our fabric expert. Dr. Mooi, your thoughts?"

Randy scrutinized the pillow then passed it to Hugh and me. Two microscopic punctures about a centimeter apart looked as though they'd been delivered by a stapler but could, in a fit of wild, hallucinogenic imagination—or complete pathological paranoia—be construed as fang marks.

"I . . . I've never seen anything like this," mumbled Randy with great concern, his double entendre of understatement a clear ploy to encourage Hugh and me to lose it.

To stay in character we went on the offense with rapid-fire questions:

"What kind of snake do you think did this?"

"Cobra." Of course.

"Have you seen one?"

"No." Of course.

"Where would they have come from?

"India." Of course.

"Where would they be hiding?"

"In the furniture. Please—you are saying you are experts?" Had us there.

"Sir, are you aware that snakes only bite when feeding or in self-defense?"

"But they are so attacking every day!"

I bit the inside of my cheeks to keep from laughing. Tears beaded in the corner of Hugh's eyes, his face reddening with the effort to hold back. Marj turned her head to compose herself. Only Randy, his titanic ability to contain derisive laughter honed by months of ROMMY rehearsals, was immune.

"Normally we hang on to things like this for analysis," he intoned gravely, shaking the pillow, "but right now we're too busy with other cases."

It was a clear signal to wrap.

"We have to, um . . . well . . . attend to a Louis XIV table that was ravaged by iguanas," said someone. "Messy business. Sorry. Uh . . . good luck."

The absurdity went over the top so fast that we practically ran back to the stairwell where we all collapsed in teary, gut-wrenching laughter.

Outside, a poor, deluded man clutching a pillow descended into a subway, where he might have received a further shock. As part of a broad campaign to reinvigorate visitations, the ROM's ad agency had installed an inspired piece of creative art in many subway cars: a life-sized Reticulated Python (*Python reticulatus*)—clearly capable of destroying any furniture item in the IKEA catalogue—stretched for meters, across subway-car ceilings, accompanied by what, for ophidiophobes, was an unsettling slogan: "Haven't seen you in a long, long, long time."

LIFE AT THE ROM was a comforting combination of academic excellence and a constantly evolving joke. But the regimen of informative fun was also a collective cry for help, black humor used to dispel the threat we were all too aware of—a lament not only for the institution that housed us but all such facilities. Like many creatures languishing in the ROM's collections, the world's museums were a threatened species.

Not long ago I caught up with my former officemate Randy Mooi at the Manitoba Museum, where he'd recently been installed as curator of zoology. His lab was littered with the usual scientific kitsch—maps, cabinets, computers, machines that went "beep," and plenty of jars full of wispy marine reef fishes. To reveal unique structural characteristics, he clears and stains the animals, a fascinating process in which the stomach enzyme trypsin digests all but skeletal elements, a soak in potassium hydroxide and ethanol renders what remains translucent, and the dyes alizarin and alcian respectively render the cartilaginous and bony bits a graphic red and blue. He spends hours scanning these delicate and beautiful preparations looking for minute differences between species.

That he was engaged in much the same routine as when we were students naturally led us to reminisce about the glory days in Toronto. We laughed over the ROMMY paraphernalia gracing the back of his door before segueing to his current projects, some of which involved toads and snakes; I kept my smug pleasure at seeing an ichthyologist forced by circumstances into research on herps—a reversal of the norm—to myself.

To Randy's side sat a metal cart bearing an eclectic mix of vertebrate junk—vertebits, if you will. An amusing potpourri of stuffed caiman and iguana, dried armadillo and Australian skinks, turtle shells, the skull of some African ungulate, and a leopard skin. There was also a half-meter sawfish blade, Porcupine Puffer Fish, and the rolled-up hide of a Reticulated Python, which a bouquet of tags revealed to be twice misidentified as boa constrictor and anaconda.

Randy explained that his predecessor had earmarked the cartload for deaccessioning, a fancy museum term for taking out the trash. The exotic material didn't fit a new Manitoba-centric mandate, and since all museums were these days pressed for space, it was toast. The purge made a certain amount of sense save for one detail: the material was *precisely* the kind of big-outside-world stuff kids went to museums to see. You could have all the interactive button-pushing, fact-projecting, disembodied dioramas you wanted, but when a kid wanted to know how scutes—the familiar, geometric, interlocking plates of a turtle's shell—related to the bones beneath, they'd want and need to hold a shell to gain any real understanding. With funding, and therefore space, being cut right, left, and center, the grist of much tactile learning would soon have no home.

Like most curators, Randy saw funding cuts to museums more as political showmanship than legitimate fat-trimming. Museum budgets are generally small in the grand scheme of things, and to subsidize them in full doesn't particularly burden the public purse (Britain's museums all have free admission). However, politicians look fiscally responsible when they say, "We're only going to give you half your budget, and you need to fund-raise the rest."

After our initial joking, the conversation led in a dozen disheartening directions; looking to break the spell, Randy nodded at the cart. "At least one man's garbage will always be another man's treasure," he chuckled, and I knew what he meant: museums needed to operate on the notion that the same went for generations, countries, and cultures. Museums were the spokes of a global wagon wheel of knowledge for which virtual versions wouldn't suffice; without real spokes, there was no real wheel.

SOON AFTER MY visit with Randy, Hugh Griffith and I—having not seen each other in a decade—set out to channel more of those good ol' days at the ROM with a critter quest in the Fraser Valley of British Columbia. We went searching for the Pacific Giant Salamander (*Dicamptodon tenebrosus*), rare at this extreme northern edge of a coastal distribution beginning in northern California. Still, the area was perfect for *Dicamptodon*, a denizen of cool, montane forest laced by streams that ratcheted from pool to idyllic pool up steep hillsides, and finding one was an unspoken challenge to our herpetological treasure-hunting skills. There was no map to *Dicamptodon*, but a jar in a museum somewhere put a giant X here.

As we turned off the highway, dense forest evoked a visage of Middle Earth, mystic and mythical. If Bigfoot existed, then this creeping, moss-encrusted understory was just the place you'd expect to find the skulking creature; but we'd settle for a giant salamander. The first stream we ascended seemed perfect for *Dicamptodon*, whose predatory larvae spend several years in water and whose adults aren't shy about the occasional dip. But despite diligent searching, we found nothing. Moving onto the banks, we raked through forest floor debris coated in microscopic plants— a riot of opportunity germinating in a quiet of decomposition— finding nothing but wriggling, wormlike Western Red-backed Salamanders (*Plethodon vehiculum*).

For the next hour red-backs materialized with remarkable but annoying regularity from handfuls of rotted wood and leaf litter. This population seemed unusually polymorphic (the term used when individuals of the same species come in different sizes, shapes, or patterns): some displayed solid, middorsal stripes ranging from blood-red through orange to a bright, rarely seen yellow; there was also an admixture of broken stripes, tail mottling, and unstriped all-black forms. Polymorphism like this can allow a species to live in or adapt to a broader range of microhabitats; conversely, when particular morphs become exclusive to certain locales, a species is poised to fission into two or more taxa under the right conditions.

Ironically, for all the multifarious variation within our own species, *Homo sapiens,* polymorphism is a strangely difficult concept for us to grasp. As collectors and classifiers, we like things simple: if it's long and brown it's this; if it's short and green it's that. The natural world does not always conform to this simplistic model, however, and Hugh and I had well learned that the seemingly superfluous collections of museums were one way to keep tabs on this often confounding range of variation. Much as they also keep tabs on the distributional limits of species like *Dicamptodon.*

These lessons of yore were on our minds as we made our way into another streambed. Wading through a choke of waist-high vegetation, Hugh pointed out various ferns, Devil's Club, Vanilla Leaf, and Stinging Nettles, which announced themselves to my right leg, already bleeding from impact with a streamside rock.

"How do you know so friggin' much about plants?" I asked.

"I never used to," said Hugh, "but I had to learn it to be an overqualified interpretive naturalist."

I think he also learned in order to shore up the scenery in the two novels he'd written. The first was about a disgruntled graduate student who spends a summer on Bermuda studying an indigenous skink (as he did), while the latest, *The Jesus of the West,* traced the adventures of a bitter and (naturally) overqualified naturalist sought out by a famous wildlife artist and old camp mate he hasn't seen in decades. In that story, almost improbably, long-lost buddy accompanies the protagonist on a search for *Dicamptodon.* When I finally read the book, I realized that in a complete reversal of the ROMMY scenario, our lives were now eerily imitating art, especially when the naturalist's friend unearths a *Dicamptodon.*

After laboring in and around another steep, V-shaped streambed, I reached into a hollow under the peeling bark of a crumbling stump, and my hand emerged with living compost; from a black mixture of soil and goo an eye blinked back at me, then another, and soon the gold- and copper-flecked mottling of a stout, fifteen-centimeter Pacific Giant Salamander materialized from the detritus. I shouted, holding it aloft so that Hugh could see. Another hard-won find. More hidden life.

Flush with success, we chattered like schoolchildren on the drive back to Vancouver. We'd done due digital diligence and photographed the creature, quickly turning it back into its domain, satisfied with only this brief encounter. On the way to a pub debriefing, we passed the Richmond Nature Park, where Hugh used to work. Yellow tape and a squadron of police blocked the entrance, and we simultaneously heard on the radio that they'd found human remains.

"Damn," sighed Hugh, with unconcealed sincerity. "Why couldn't that have happened when *I* worked there?"

Hugh's droll sense of humor has seen him through a lot. When Dr. Bob was installed as a curator at the ROM, Hugh, a master's student at the adjacent University of Toronto, quickly struck up a working relationship. He would ultimately sign on as Murphy's first PhD student, but not before, according to Hugh, "Bob took me to Baja and broke my arm."

If you knew anything about Dr. Bob's expeditions, filling in the blanks was frighteningly easy.

7

A DAY IN HELL

The ocean is a desert with its life underground.

America, "A Horse with No Name"

WHEN HE FOUND himself slipping through rotten ice on the Haliburton beaver pond like a hot Texan through butter, Dr. Bob was wont to wax poetic about the desert's more familiar hazards: sunstroke, dehydration, and the host of life lining up to stick things into your flesh. He also enjoyed transporting graduate students with little experience outside the not-so-perilous forests of eastern Canada directly to his favorite laboratory: the bleak, heavily scarified blast furnace of Baja California.

When my number came up in May 1988, amid tidying up my own spring field season, moving in with my fiancée, and daily ROMMY rehearsals, Bob's invitation seemed like a welcome respite from a stressful schedule. Something different. A bona fide vacation.

BAJA WAS INDEED a whole new ball game but not the kind I'd expected. From the moment we touched down in Los Angeles, everything became a hanging question.

"What are we bringing?"

"Not sure yet."

"What are we driving down in?"

"Not sure yet."

"Who else is coming?"

"Not sure yet."

"When are we leaving?"

"Maybe tomorrow, maybe not."

"Where, exactly, are we going?

"Now *that's* a good question . . . "

That "we" included expedition co-chaotician Dr. David Morafka of California State University at Dominguez Hills, a respected herpetologist, Desert Tortoise (*Gopherus agassizii*) expert, and longtime buddy of Murphy's who had a similar get-things-done-in-spite-of-yourself approach. For instance, when the pair finally declared themselves "organized" for this two-week expedition, our provisions consisted of a box of cookies, a couple cans of beans, a speargun, an amateur herper from Arizona who claimed to know how to use it, and a map to all the taco stands on the peninsula. The cookies were gone before we reached the border.

In Baja we followed the Pacific coast south, pulling off in Ensenada for street-side fish tacos, a famously delicious introduction to local cuisine and a surefire way to inoculate yourself with *Salmonella, E. coli,* and three flavors of dysentery. A crumpled map was spread over the hood of Morafka's aging Toyota 4x4. We would continue south to El Rosario, cross the peninsula overnight, then hit the Sea of Cortés at Bahia de Los Angeles. We would work our way south to the resort area of Loreto and beyond to Bahia Agua Verde. We would collect in important mainland sites along the way, but our main objective was to hit key offshore islands to collect rattlesnakes, or *cascabeles* (bells), as locals called them.

Although he'd worked in Baja for both his graduate degrees, Dr. Bob continued to entertain questions about the peninsula's biogeographic jigsaw and staggering reptile diversity (some 160 species). He was particularly interested in how lizard and snake species reached the myriad islands dotting the Sea of Cortés. Since the islands comprised both continental (isolated by rising sea levels) and oceanic (of volcanic, or sea-floor origin) examples, some species had clearly rafted or swum from the peninsula or the Mexican mainland, while others were simply trapped on elevated chunks of land by marine incursions after the Pleistocene glaciers melted. Which of these scenarios applied to which species? And, since many of these castaways were found *only* on one island, which mainland forms were their closest relatives?

Molecular data would suggest answers in the degree of genetic divergence between mainland and island populations, but mostly these questions were the business of biogeography—the where, what, and why of animal and plant distribution. I'd dabbled in it with my master's, trying to figure how unisexual salamanders got where they got. But using these creatures as a biogeographic model was like learning to swim by crossing the English Channel.

As much as it can, biogeography seeks to untangle the threads of contemporary and historical distribution—both the taxonomic and geographic origins of species. Its roots lie in morphology, ecology, and, to some extent, paleontology, making it a favored sideline among systematists (those studying species relationships); if, for example, your computer spits out an analysis showing the closest relative of a California species to bizarrely reside in Sicily (as in the salamander genus

Hydromantes), it requires either fast-footed storytelling or rigorous explanation. Systematists would thus find it difficult *not* to draw biogeographic inferences about the connection of California and Sicily from such data, harking back to even Darwin's and Wallace's struggles to understand the origins and relationships of species in island archipelagos.

Led by a large herpetological contingent, molecular systematists recently coined the term phylogeography (a conflation of phylogenetics and biogeography) to describe their efforts and to prove that their love of jargon knows no bounds. As practiced today, biogeography takes the same rigorous approach as any other science, replacing storytelling with hypothesis testing and modeling. Optimal places in which to test biogeographic theories include areas with well-understood geological histories, restricted distributional corridors, and island archipelagos. Baja had all three.

To make complete sense of relationships gleaned from laboratory analysis, molecular data are considered in the context of an area's geological history. When it comes to Baja, however, what looks like a simple continental appendix on maps is actually an incredibly complicated series of geological grafts. Even a superficial overview of its assembly is enough to make biogeographers run for the simplicity of the Himalaya.

Baja's presently lithe form was established in the last 5 to 10 million years. Yielding to relentless stretching, the North American plate had finally split, tilting a block westward and opening the Gulf of California (Sea of Cortés). The resulting peninsula comprised chunks of land derived from several sources and was surrounded by islands that had either cleaved from these same sources or popped up from the gulf's spreading floor. Fluctuating sea levels during successive Pleistocene glaciations then had the net effect of washing lizard and snake species on and off of these islands, significantly blurring their histories of occupation.

Biogeography's development and context is excellently chronicled in David Quammen's *The Song of the Dodo: Island Biogeography in an Age of Extinction*. Island biogeography is easily studied, and its precepts readily extended to islandlike fragmentation of continental species and ecosystems (for example, one can construe mountaintops or forest remnants as de facto islands). Quammen traveled the globe in pursuit of island colonization and extinction scenarios, spending significant time in the hands of herpetologists, even ending up in a lizard study on Baja's Isla Ángel de la Guarda.

Early in the volume he charts a litany of the world's most outlandish island inhabitants—the Dodo, giant tortoises, pygmy rhino, Marine Iguana, Tasmanian Devil, Giant Earwig, and one species on our current itinerary, the rattleless rattlesnake of Isla Santa Catalina. As Quammen says: "The list could go on with no diminution of weirdness . . . islands are havens and breeding grounds for the unique and anomalous . . . natural laboratories of extravagant evolutionary experimentation . . . That's why island biogeography is a catalogue of quirks and superlatives. And that's why islands . . . have played a central role in the study of evolution. Charles Darwin himself was an island biogeographer before he was a Darwinist."[13]

Baja's island clusters didn't offer quite the same spectacle as the Galapagos, but plumbing their evolutionary idiosyncrasies clearly put us in esteemed company.

SOME HELD THAT most of the species-relationship questions Baja's geography posed could readily be answered using morphological criteria, but not Dr. Bob. After all, it was the Golden

Age of the Tissue Cowboys—an enigmatic cadre of systematists that crawled the globe not so much to collect specimens (though this practice was still necessary) as to obtain tissues that could be used to discern relationships. The rarer and more mythic an animal, the more valuable a chunk of its liver. This *Raiders of the Lost Ark*-meets-*Monty Python's The Meaning of Life* saw platoons of Indiana Joneses raking earth's wildest corners as well as back-yards, markets, and restaurant kitchens, even scraping up fresh eviscerate from interesting roadkills (tissue samples from those Fijian bolos would have been nice . . .).

To avoid having to transport live animals, we generally pro-cessed them in the field—before specimens were preserved in jar-worthy museum poses, tissue samples were messily removed to small plastic tubes, flash-frozen in liquid nitrogen, and trans-ported to the lab. There they were thawed, ground up by hand, and centrifuged; the resulting suspension contained invis-ible protein products of specific structural genes, including a sought-after legion of metabolic enzymes. We then separated the enzymes by protein electrophoresis, which uses high-voltage electricity passed through starch gels buffered to various pHs. The distance an enzyme migrates through a gel is based on its charge and molecular weight, and differences in these charac-ters between specimens reflect the genetic variation in popula-tions. When we stain the enzymes, the gel becomes a neat way for meat-headed herpetologists to visualize the proteins and tell populations and species apart.

I became intimately familiar with the process under Jim Bogart and employed it in my biogeographic analysis of unisex-ual *Ambystoma*. Although the results are often definitive, elec-trophoresis isn't easy to execute: working out correct buffer/enzyme/tissue combinations is fraught with time- and chemical-wasting trial and error. One reason I'd signed on with Dr. Bob was his adeptness at this procedure; he was, as we'd labeled his Dr. Phenetico character in ROMMY, a virtual Starch Gel Wizard.

Methods that showed protein *products* of specific genes— therefore only hinting at differences in the DNA coding for them—would soon be supplanted by the breakthrough of DNA sequencing, a more direct elucidation of genetic variation. But long before the CSI generation, Tissue Cowboys were still happily riding herd on the protein range.

IF CONTINENTS ARE the earth's skin, then deserts are a patch of eczema on its butt. Why does *anything* live there? Because, to paraphrase J.B.S. Haldane, life is not only more tenacious than we suppose, but more tenacious than we *can* suppose.

Rolling over Baja's sere, boulder-strewn interior, I realized that appreciating desert biology required patience, imagination, and the ability to look beyond. The environment, to mine a tired but unassailably accurate cliché, was harsh and unforgiving to both man and beast. In that lay its appeal: this very harshness had led to much invention among organisms that dwelt here, engendering special challenges for those who studied them.

In daytime, when high temperatures turn lizards into a blur of scales streaking across rock or sand, you normally collected them by sneaking up from behind, wielding a fishing rod hung with a small noose. Monofilament fishing line is virtually invisible, and as long as the rod doesn't cast a shadow across a field of vision primed to detect swooping birds, you can slip the weightless noose over a lizard's neck and yank it shut before the creature reacts; if the noose is placed properly, any attempt to escape invariably draws it tighter. In this way—but only with vast patience—you can obtain *muchos pequeños lagartos encantadores* as unblemished specimens for museums.

The Tissue Cowboys had a different approach. For my initiation into the ways of science's Wild West, I was horrified to be handed a 22-caliber rifle and told to shoot any lizard I saw in the head. Hitting the skull was key: you didn't want to mess up precious tissues. Generally speaking, I couldn't hit a carnival duck with a bean bag, but the hazard of ricocheting bullets inculcated swift ascension on the accuracy curve; by the end of the trip I could put a pellet through the noggin of a ten-centimeter lizard from ten meters away, leaving it stone dead on the rock without its having known it was even in danger. This approach, Morafka explained, conformed to the tenets of humane euthanasia as dictated by official animal care protocols. Well, alrighty then.

The perceived austerity of Baja's landscape is put to the lie by the stunning richness of its lizard fauna. Some ninety species populate every microhabitat on offer, found on, in, and under rocks, crevices, live cacti, dead cacti, bushes, detritus, sand dunes, ant and termite nests, abandoned rodent burrows, and several places I haven't seen or even thought of. As Bob observed when he first became interested in desert lizards, there seemed no end to the ways they could shake out an existence, which usually corresponded to the endless ways their mostly insect prey shook out an existence; consequently, different species could be found on different bushes, in different parts of the same plant, or even on the same plant at different times of day or night.

We only scratched the surface, chasing Brush Lizards (*Urosaurus* spp.), Rock Lizards (*Petrosaurus* spp.), Spiny Lizards (*Sceloporus* spp.), and Side-blotched Lizards (*Uta* spp.). Several nocturnal species of gecko (*Coleonyx* and *Phyllodactylus*) could also be plucked from rocks with a steady hand if they were properly mesmerized by a headlamp. Rocks, however, remained warm into the night, rendering the already-speedy little bastards difficult to grab and often leaving you with nothing but a twitching piece of tail. (Autotomy, or tail loss, is common in both lizards and some salamanders; as with death feigning, its biological function is to confuse a predator, creating a brief window of opportunity in which to effect an escape. Regrowing a tail is energetically costly and is thus a last-ditch tactic; many a thesis has been expended on a cost-benefit analysis of this behavior.) To the biologist of old, a chunk o' tail was a useless piece of cellular junk, but to a Tissue Cowboy it was as good as the lizard it came from; tail bits were happily crammed into tubes and dropped into liquid nitrogen before they'd even stopped twitching.

I knew relatively little about lizards. When I was a kid, my exposure was restricted to pet-shop offerings of invariably emaciated iguanas and the nervous, color-shifting anoles we mislabeled "chameleons" shipped en masse from the tropical Americas (true chameleons came from the Old World). Still, in the short windows of observation afforded, I was piqued by several aspects of lizard biology, including parallels they displayed to birds. As in birds, male and female lizards could look quite different, and males made territorial and mating signals with their decorations. The nervous twitching and head cocking in lizards was also very birdlike. Years later, before paleontologists made their revolutionary declaration on the bird-reptile association, I chummed around an ASIH meeting in Oklahoma with a guy from Chicago's Field Museum who indiscriminately attended every presentation on lizards. At a social function, I discovered he was actually a respected ornithologist. Why on earth, I choked, passing a mouthful of warm Budweiser through my nose, had he forsaken the charmed, erudite company of his big-city peers to hang with the pig farmers in biology's barnyard?

"I'm interested in behavioral ecology, sexual selection, and social systems," he said. "It's what drives most of bird evolution.

I want to see how lizard biologists study interactions like signaling and communication in territoriality and courtship."

"But *why?*" I persisted, bluntly missing his point.

"Because it's the *same* system," he retorted. "The behaviors are ultimately derived from the same reptilian source . . . "

"What?"

" . . . so it's really like looking back in time to see what has changed and what has maybe remained similar in these two lineages since their divergence."

"What?"

"Birds . . . ," he leveled, affecting a lizardlike head tilt that clearly said *Surely you know this, dipshit,* "are flying dinosaurs. They're reptiles, dude."

Well touché; after all, there *are* flying lizards. Except that Southeast Asia's genus *Draco* doesn't fly so much as glide on patagia (skin flaps) formed from extended ribs. It's more of a neat trick, but then lizards are full of neat tricks: the lightweight, fleet-footed basilisk (*Basiliscus* spp.) or Jesus Christ lizard can streak upright across several meters of water without sinking; Frilled Lizards (*Chlamydosaurus kingii*) unfurl skin neck-rings so large their heads look like cupcakes; geckos hang improbably from smooth ceilings; fringed-toed lizards (*Uma* spp.) float over sand as if on snowshoes. A dozen forms have independently reduced or lost digits and limbs to take up burrowing through sand, soil, or leaf litter. Some lizards are strict carnivores, some strict herbivores, and many extreme specialists—like the infamous Galapagos Marine Iguana (*Amblyrhynchus cristatus*), the only lizard to feed in the ocean, diving in search of seaweed and extruding the extra salt it takes on through eyes and nose. Some lizards mate for life and others mate with anything that moves. Lizards usually lay eggs, though as with their snake scions, some rule breakers bear live young—a few with placentalike structures that echo, in part, those of the imagined reptile-mammal transition. And, of course, several lineages contain unisexual parthenogens.

Lizards can be stunningly decorated or drably camouflaged. Adults range from coin-sized, insect-scarfing sprites to monstrous beasts that chase down deer. Scientists have recently discovered that many more of them are venomous than the two previously known, the Gila Monster and Beaded Lizard (genus *Heloderma*); some possess snakelike toxins and others deadly chemicals that have never before been found. (This toxic heritage makes sense, since modern taxonomic convention holds that snakes and lizards are *not* sister groups. Because the suborder Serpentes arose deep within the monophyletic clade of what we call lizards—the way birds arose deep within the clade of what we call reptiles—snakes are more properly construed as highly specialized lizards.)

Eric Pianka and Laurie J. Vitt plumb the staggering range of lizard morphology and ecology in *Lizards: Windows to the Evolution of Diversity*: "Lizards are spectacular products of natural selection and have diversified to fill an amazing variety of ecological niches . . . What we have learned about lizards is applicable to nearly every conceptual area in modern biology; indeed in many cases development of entire fields of biology had their origins in the study of lizards."[14]

What's most apparent leafing through the volume's eye-opening photographs, however, is how impressively strange, otherworldy, and far from our standard view these animals can be. Before color photography could do them justice, the twentieth-century doyen of reptile gestalt, Raymond L. Ditmars, had recognized their phantasmagorical nature. He suggested that if you lined up fifty or so different lizard types they would look like a bunch of toy-shop models with so many bizarre knobs and spikes that you couldn't imagine they were real living beings.

But then, so much of what we see in the natural world seems impossible to many without invocation of an external artist. The herpetologist, however, finds this frame of reference flawed, a failure of society to more rigorously pursue the kind of knowledge that supports belief in the possible. Evolution's 300-million-year experiment with lizards is simply another example of what's possible given enough time and the right materials. To both the informed and the naïve, Baja is an open-air gallery of natural organic art holding a permanent special exhibition on lizards.

BAJA'S DECONSTRUCTIONIST LANDSCAPE seemed foreign even to desert aficionados but was especially alien to entrenched boreal senses. Anytime I closed my eyes in the truck, I was invariably greeted with something new and fantastic when I opened them again: Tolkien-esque mounds of rounded, exfoliating granite like stone eggs on a plate; cartoon oases flagged by tilted palms and tangled green sprouting in the middle of brown nowhere; aquamarine ocean lapping monochromatic mountains like old, hand-painted film; and the Boojum Tree—a bizarre, Dr. Seuss–like sprig of a plant towering up to twenty meters over the desert's empty pate, spaced like the last hairs on a balding head.

It was a dreamscape, but there was also the occasional nightmare. As my head bobbed in the backseat one afternoon, curses from the front awakened me to the surreal sight of a motley cluster of *campesinos* brandishing guns in the center of the empty highway, their faces covered with kerchiefs, bandoliers crossed over their chests. Militia? Banditos? Somebody shooting a spaghetti western? We'd been stopped on several occasions by local *policia*, but they usually sported at least one piece of official-dom—be it badge, cap, or shirt—that encouraged us to pull over. These guys bore nothing remotely official, but the M16s were far more convincing. Like rattlesnakes poised patiently beside a kangaroo-rat runway, they'd chosen their ambush well—a depression between two low rises with no opportunity for evasive maneuvers. We had no choice but to stop on the centerline or risk being shot.

Rifle leveled, the leader approached while Morafka resignedly rolled down the driver's window as though he'd been pulled over for speeding. I was trapped in the back of the two-door with my heart pounding; Morafka and Murphy remained cool as cucumbers up front. The exchange was in bad (the Mexicans) and worse (M&M) Spanish, but I followed the thread: were we smuggling money or drugs? *Ciertamente no.* Did we have any guns? *¡No!*

This exclamation sent another stab of fear through me, since my feet were resting on the lizard rifle. The Mexicans were clustering menacingly around when it dawned on me that the boys had been through this scenario before and knew exactly how to defuse the situation: i.e., play to the audience's weakness.

The interrogation continued. What are you doing out here? *Estamos solamente biologistas,* answered Morafka with practiced casualness, brandishing government-stamped collecting permits for the snakes, *Nosotros tenemos como . . . cuarenta o cinquenta. Queres ver?*

At the news our truck was packed with rattlesnakes, the Mexicans took several steps back, gesturing with alarm. After much excited shouting, the leader turned back. OK, he said, let's see. Murphy bounced out, swung down the tailgate, and whipped out a bag that clearly held a weighty, writhing mass. He untied the knot and held the sack open. Comically, the man tried to peer into it from a meter away, leaning in so far he eventually had to place his rifle barrel on the road to support himself. He still couldn't reach. He took a reluctant step closer. *Puta madre! Santa Maria!* he erupted, crossing himself.

Thirty seconds later we were belting down the highway, leaving the *campesinos* scratching their heads over a Close Encounter of the Worst Kind. A bag of venomous snakes could be a powerful carnet.

THE HEAT WORSENED as we forged south. You could only look for animals early in the morning and at night, so we drove when we had to and slept when we could, often pulling off the road toward dawn in the middle of nowhere to bed down. Food was a problem; no one seemed interested in stocking up on anything longer lasting than another box of cookies. Things improved when we reached the coast. We camped on beaches, and speargun buddy proved adept at flopping edible treats like Yellowfin Tuna and Slipper Lobster onto shore with startling regularity.

The only problem was that for reasons unknown, we had no tents. Sleeping in the open was fine from a meteorological standpoint: it was hot as shit and unlikely to rain anytime this decade. The problem was the million other creatures bunking there—mostly pointy, piercing, poisonous ones. If you added in the thorns, spikes, needles, hairs, and noxious secretions of surrounding plants, the decor was definitely on the dodgy side of dangerous. Not exactly feng shui.

The biting and stinging and scratching would start pretty much the second you stepped out of the truck. Myriad invisible sand fleas made themselves known everywhere, and harvester ants—or "pogos," offering the insect world's most toxic venom and a six-hour roller-coaster of blistering pain—were legion in open areas around low, leaf-bearing plants. These plants also held buck moth caterpillars, bristling with toxic hairs that broke off in your skin to cause severe pain and inflammatory dermatitis. Scorpions and a host of nasty-assed arachnids patrolled the ground at night, and we were constantly diving for the trucks to avoid Tarantula Hawks, giant gun-blue wasps with a considerable dangling barb that delivered a sting that rated four out of four on the insect-sting pain scale and left grown men crying and writhing in agony.

I thought I had it all beat by propping the corners of my ground sheet off the sand with sticks to discourage anything from crawling onto it. But around four o'clock one morning I was shocked awake by a red-hot needle being inserted into my knee. Fumbling on my headlamp, in the folds of my sleeping bag I found a nondescript, fingernail-sized brown bug. It was a Western Conenose or Kissing Bug, blood-sucking member of the three thousand–strong assassin bug clan possibly responsible for donating debilitating Chagas' disease to Charles Darwin in South America, and it had drilled its considerable proboscis into my knee, which swelled and throbbed in searing pain. Stiff with fluid, the knee took days to return to normal.

It was war out here. Assassin bugs immobilized insects with their bites, and female Tarantula Hawks used the desert's largest arthropods as nests, paralyzing them before they could wield their own considerable venom in defense. It only took a dozen pogo stings to kill a rat, but horned lizards (*Phrynosoma* sp.), immune to their venom, could feed on the ants all day, while kingsnakes happily fed on rattlers, to whose venom they were immune. These cage matches all took place in and around plants that would just as soon be hung with the carcasses of these animals as play host to any of them.

Why all this deadly dueling? In a surprising word: water.

Water is the life essential at greatest premium in deserts, so organisms go to extraordinary lengths to protect what little they have. Plant or animal, micro or macro, municipality or ecosystem, desert ecology is a politic of trading and hoarding water credits. No entity wants to needlessly expend precious energy, and therefore water, in a prolonged struggle—the cost of replacement is simply too high. Plants are tough-skinned, waxy, and prickly to protect moisture stores from the sun and the marauding insects that would suck it from them; likewise, invertebrates must protect themselves both from desiccation and from being drilled into by other fluid-seeking arthropods. Most desert denizens adhere to the credo that the best defense is a strong offense—all prey is a source of water, and if you need a moist, nurturing environment in which to deposit a few eggs, well, a recently immobilized body is as good as it gets. Plus, when those eggs hatch, the offspring will have something fresh to eat. *Mmmm.*

Still, no matter how noxious, none could hold a mesquite torch to the desert's most efficient and sophisticated venom-delivery system: the rattlesnake. This animal's lightning-fast strike leaves its rodent prey mortally wounded with a major dose of hemotoxic (blood- and tissue-destroying) venom coursing through its body. The little buggers stagger a few meters and keel over from cardiac arrest; the snake then tracks down its meal via pheromones in the venom, avoiding struggle or injury. Ditmars, again waxing poetic, often opined that no greater perfection in weapons designed to kill could be found than in the fangs of rattlesnakes.

On a trip where you were expected to collect as many of these as possible, you had to love such brio.

EACH OF BAJA'S hundreds of islands generally boasted one or two rattlesnake species. Fully 20 percent of thirty species of *Crotalus* distributed throughout the Americas were Baja island endemics (i.e., found only there). Bob wanted to know whether these evolved from founder populations of Red Diamond Rattlesnakes (*Crotalus ruber*), Baja California Rattlesnakes (*C. enyo*), Western Diamondbacks (*C. atrox*), Mojave Rattlesnakes (*C. scutulatus*), Speckled Rattlesnakes (*C. mitchellii*), or a long-extinct ancestor. To do so, he would perform a genetic *Who's Your Daddy?*, comparing mainland species with island endemics. Our first destination was Isla Santa Catalina.

Rattlesnakes evolved on the prairies of North America. Their heat-sensing facial organs, legacies of a pit-viper ancestry, were perfectly preadapted for locating the myriad rodents whose runways bisect grasslands. So the evolution of rattles from tail-vibrating behavior made sense: a reliable audible warning to protect these generally sit-and-wait snakes from shortsighted herds of co-evolving, heavy-footed mammals like bison.

A rattlesnake's rattle is one of nature's slickest inventions. In this complex structure, loosely interlocking segments (modified, keratinized scales) click against each other to produce sound. "Rattling" involves muscle contractions and vertebral oscillations that are among the fastest recorded in vertebrates—and sounds more like a buzz. This process places substantial demand on the respiratory and circulatory systems and has an energetic cost, so rattlers won't rattle if they don't have to. If a species found itself occupying a habitat devoid of large animals, would it still require a costly apparatus designed to deter them? The rattle-less rattlesnake of Isla Santa Catalina is thought to have lost its characteristic structure under just these circumstances, and it further benefits from keeping down the racket while climbing bushes to hunt birds—a very unrattlerlike activity.

We hired a boat, threw in our meager supplies, and roared off. Dolphins followed as we flashed across a sparkling Sea of Cortés; whales spouted in the distance, and a giant Manta Ray erupted from the surface behind the boat, turning like an airplane before flopping back into the ocean. That night several specimens of *C. catalinensis* turned up in our headlamps, prowling through low thorn scrub. If you didn't know better, you would think it more of a lithe jungle viper than a rattlesnake, more gracile than the typical heavy-bodied specimens we caught the following night on Isla Santa Cruz, plump and reddish diamondbacks that Dr. Bob was convinced were *C. ruber*. (Years later, DNA data would change this interpretation, aligning the Santa Cruz animals with *C. atrox*, and the nascent tree rattlesnake, *C. catalinensis*, with chubby *C. ruber*.) On parched Isla San Marcos we were dropped off by a drunken boat driver terrified of our buzzing cargo; when he failed to return at the appointed time, we spent a hungry and thirsty night on the island. The drunk's brother had the presence to rescue us next day when his sibling confessed to the abandonment. We had only one more stop.

Named for its resemblance to a giant turtle breaking the water, Isla Tortuga is a tiny black dome of lava that appears on few maps. We were repeatedly told that Tortuga was the devil's home and that no one *ever* set foot on it. After convincing a reluctant pilot to ferry us out the eight kilometers—he wouldn't even let his boat touch the rocks, and we had to jump out—we quickly discovered why: the island was raw, black lava radiating hellish heat. The air was 45°C, the ground outside of shade a sizzling 70°C. The only water was in the pathetically small bottles we carried.

Taking our first step away from where we'd debarked, we immediately clocked the telltale buzz of an endemic *C. tortugensis* emanating from a shady hole in the lava. Then another. And another. *Jeezuz!* The island was only one hundred meters across and several hundred long, yet every footfall elicited warning from a nearby serpent—a veritable minefield of menace. We'd quickly realized that we had to get out of the freakin' sun and that the only shade consisted of emaciated shadows thrown by a handful of Saguaro Cacti wilting to our right. Tiptoeing over, we saw to our horror that each shadow harbored several massive rattlers. Hundreds of deadly snakes thrived on tiny Tortuga, most clustered in the one place a human could survive more than a few hours. A nightmare with nowhere to hide. *Indiana Jones and the Temple of Doom.* Business as usual for Bob.

What followed was a snake-bagging frenzy. While one of us held open a nylon bag, the other swiftly picked up two or three with a pair of tongs and dropped them in before tying off the bag and switching duties. With snakes on the move everywhere, you had to maintain a constant 360-degree vigil. Within fifteen minutes we'd cleared a patch of its ophidian hazard and tied off several fat bagfuls of *C. tortugensis.* Did we need that many specimens? No. Did we need a safe place to sit down? Definitely. We would be there for several more hot and horrid hours before the boat returned—if it ever did—so we'd let most of the snakes go later.

M&M were lying on the ground in the saguaro shadows, hats pulled down over their faces. Without looking up or moving his hat, Bob pointed mutely toward the mound of writhing sacks stacked in the shade of a boulder.

"Yeah, that was *too* easy," said Morafka.

LOOKING FOR HERPS, given their cryptic habits and propensity for camouflage, is a scavenger hunt at the best of times. But that's part of the appeal: for every frog that hops into a pond there's a handful you don't see; for every lizard you spot there's a dozen you won't. And snakes? You don't even want to know. Sure, you develop a search image that raises the probability of finding something, but the hunt still requires work: turning over rocks, tearing apart logs, digging in muck, poking in holes. But somewhere between Cope and Ditmars and Henry Ford, collectors discovered the La-Z-Boy of herpetological activities—one to which no other branch of zoology can lay claim: road driving at night.

Given the right conditions and a cooperative stretch of pavement, you can reap a king's harvest of scampering, slithering, or slimy critters. A road at night is a herper's best friend; a kind of one-stop shopping in the Foul and Loathsome aisle at Nature-Mart. If it's warm, reptiles adorn the asphalt, soaking up heat; cloudy and humid, amphibians start to mobilize; raining, everything's on the move.

Road driving requires its own set of skills. In eastern Canada, where I logged the majority of my night routes, you had to be able to distinguish, at up to one hundred kilometers per hour, in pouring rain on jet-black pavement, at least three species of salamanders and five species of frogs. We also used road driving to locate ponds: if you clocked an earsplitting chorus of Spring Peepers, you stopped the vehicle (ostensibly safely; in reality not so much), grabbed nets, containers, earplugs (really), and boots, and sloshed off into the blackness. The scene was often creepy— you alone with your light playing on the surface of unfamiliar waters that harbored god knew what. I'd had pike and lampreys take a run at me in the dark but was only truly unnerved when a beaver swam up behind me and slapped its tail on the water so loudly that I stumbled and filled my waders with ice water.

Like everything else about Baja, however, road collecting there was a whole new ball game. No rain, no breeding ponds, no water. One night, when fog enticed a catalogue of creatures onto the road, we drove half the length of the peninsula, Morafka's brake foot grotesquely twisted onto his lap in a half-lotus while he pulled at the left side of his scraggly moustache (he'd already pulled out the right side). While Bob finger-drummed ROMMY tunes on the dashboard, we talked politics and listened to mariachi music between screeching halts to collect creatures that would empty their bowels, bladders, and musk glands on us. Once I clambered out excitedly to pick up a dead rattlesnake that wasn't; while I was making this unwelcome observation, a scorpion scurried up my leg.

Years later I encountered a similar scene in California's Death Valley. When a freak fog descended it was like a switch had been thrown, and the once-empty road sprang to life. There were millipedes, centipedes, spiders, and solifugids—strange, ghostlike arachnids that sported enormous fangs and appeared to blow across the pavement like wisps of dried grass. A baby Desert Horned Lizard (*Phrynosoma platyrhinos*), button-cute and the size of a quarter. And plenty of snakes. Juvenile Great Basin Gopher Snakes (*Pituophis catenifer deserticola*) sadly squashed in record numbers. A tiny Desert Night Snake (*Hypsiglena torquata deserticola*), with its mild manners but paralyzing dose (if you were its lizard prey) of rear fang–delivered venom. The usual assortment of determined Sidewinders (*Crotalus cerastes*) throwing measured coils ahead and to the side in what seemed an awkward, legless limp over pavement but was, in sand, one of nature's most exquisitely efficient forms of locomotion—so much so that desert-dwelling vipers on other continents had convergently arrived at it. There was even a gorgeous, gray-white Desert Rosy Boa (*Lichanura trivirgata gracia*), subtly striped in pastel pink, reminiscent of Marty's nature hut pet all those years ago. Handling

the harmless animal reminded me again how tactile a constrictor is—it can flow innocently through your hands like water or
resist with the muscled grip of a menacing handshake. Like a
greeting from your subconscious.

ON THE LAST morning of the trip, a rising sun flaming over
the landscape found me tearing through the creosote as I had
so often, only this time I was neither chasing a madly scurrying
lizard nor bearing a proudly packaged specimen in hand. Rather,
I was running for help with a thrashing, aggressive, two-meter
Desert Coachwhip (*Masticophis flagellum*) fastened to my forearm.
I'd spotted it crossing the road in the first sideways throw of light,
and although M&M were largely uninterested in this common
rat-scarfer, they'd encouraged me to rush into the desert in pursuit. The snake flashed into a bush at lightning speed, and all I'd
managed to grab was its retreating tail; true to form, like a snapping whip, its head shot back over its body to strike me on the
hand. Then, like Bogart's boa, it hung on, rapidly chewing its
way up my arm like a dog mawing a tennis ball, refusing to stop
even when offered escape.

With my blood-spattered shorts flapping against gouged
and infected legs, I was like the classic Canadian rube in over his
head in the Great Unknown south of the forty-ninth parallel. I
longed for the less hazardous environs of home. Still, I'd gotten
off lighter than Hugh; Dr. Bob hadn't broken my arm, but he'd
definitely snapped my boreal myopia. Both drawn and repulsed
by the desert's catalogue of dangerous critters, I'd passed the
requisite indoctrination and survived the hazing. Sensing the
import of his helpful mentoring as he pried the snake from my
arm, Bob made one of his patented attempts at cold-blooded
comfort.

"This is nothing . . . ," he drawled. "Wait until you get to the jungle."

I reckoned I could wait a bit.

· · (8) · ·

ANOTHER MESSY FREAK SHOW

The answers only rattle the questions harder.

MICHAEL CALDWELL, barroom napkin note

IF YOU WERE a North American news junkie in the late
summer of 1996, you might recall that the daily screed of war,
famine, murder, and O.J. was interrupted by frightening pictures of freakish frogs with missing, incomplete, or even extra
legs and digits.

Yes, the continent's fear impresarios were remounting The
Strange Case of the Deformed Frogs, a mystery that had played
to packed houses and rave reviews the previous summer after
a group of Minnesota schoolchildren encountered a virtual
plague's worth of misshapen anurans exiting a farm pond. With
fans of media theater on high alert, deformities now seemed
to be turning up everywhere. Critics convulsed, the public
kvetched, and a gallery of scientific Sherlocks issued dire warnings that the slippery canaries in our environmental coal mines
were finally croaking "Auld Lang Syne."

In reality, herpetologists had known that frogs had been in
worldwide decline for a while. Populations were vanishing and
species undergoing complete extinction at alarming rates—

even in pristine, protected areas. Celebrated mid-'80s disap-
pearances included the jewel-like Golden Toad (*Bufo periglenes*)
of Costa Rica's Monteverde cloud forest and the bizarre Australian Gastric-brooding Frogs (genus *Rheobatrachus*), whose young
developed in the mother's stomach.

But there were plenty of less esoteric examples. And plenty
of potential causes you didn't need to be a scientist to cite—
habitat destruction, pollution, disease, global warming, ozone
depletion, Thatcherism, Reaganomics, perestroika, Madonna.
However, this apparently sudden rash of deformities seemed to
hold out an example in the making—one we could ignore only
at our peril.

I watched this alarmism unfold on television in southern California, where I now worked as a magazine editor, with
certain bemusement. First, the story wasn't really news to me.
Deformed amphibians had been dropped off at Bogart's lab in
Guelph on many occasions: a Northern Leopard Frog with a
bone-white, underdeveloped limb sprouting stiffly from the
center of its chest; a one-eyed Green Frog; and a handful of
newly metamorphosed Blue-spotted Salamanders sporting
extra digits, split limbs, and hermaphroditic gonads. All had
been fetched from farm ponds, making the current anguished
clucking over potential reasons for the deformities by a host of
solemn news anchors seem moot.

Of the known potential causes of such monstrosities—
chemical contaminants, parasite infection, UVB radiation—only
the first could account for such a broad range of defects either
directly or in synergy with other causes. And since the deformities came from farm ponds, the culprit was almost certainly a
pesticide, herbicide, or fertilizer. The question wasn't whether
chemicals were involved, but which ones and how they might
act or interact to effect the changes.

This assessment wasn't just the hubris of a cynical former scientist. My academic swan song, in fact, had been to hum a few bars in an extensive investigation of this very phenomenon in Québec's St. Lawrence River Valley. At the time of the Minnesota reports, colleagues and I had a paper in press that would be the first to link pesticide use to deformities, acute and chronic toxic effects, and abnormal DNA profiles in frogs. Although our findings would rightly be debated, they were, to quote the study's initiator, Martin Ouellet, who'd tracked Frankenfrogs in Québec since 1992, "clear-cut." But as blithe American news anchors showed, who cared what a bunch of hoser herpetologists thought?

MONTREAL'S REDPATH MUSEUM is the oldest building in North America built specifically to be a museum. Donated to McGill University in 1880 by sugar baron Peter Redpath, it was intended to house and display the significant collections of über-geologist Sir John William Dawson. The smallish building of neoclassical design opened its doors in 1882 and looks sternly over McGill's central campus, buffered from hectic Sherbrooke Street by a grassy, manicured sweep and divot-pocked playing fields. Today it curates collections in ethnology, biology, paleontology, and geology, hoardings largely begun by the same starched dudes responsible for the Smithsonian and Royal Ontario Museum. In North America's pantheon of museums, few hold the same historical continuity as the tiny Redpath.

For those of us lodged in it, however, it merely meant another revered institution, another clutch of irreverent colleagues. Montrealer Tim Sharbel obtained a college degree in wildlife management before taking a lab-tech job at the Redpath and gaining a maestro's command of the key techniques of cytogenetic and systematic research—chromosome banding, electrophoresis, and the early throes of DNA sequencing. Despite an exotic Lebanese–French Canadian background and a gift for languages, Tim was a down-to-earth guy with the usual suite of Montreal vices—hockey, hash, beer, and women. His roommate, Hinrich Kaiser, was a cheery but reserved German with seemingly unlimited funds to trash through the eastern Caribbean in search of frogs, usually accompanied by Tim. The pair gained intimate knowledge of Caribbean natural history, geography, culture, and rum, and had several new species and biogeographic revelations to show for a spate of nasty sun scaldings, infections, poisonous plant burns, intestinal parasites, and skin fungus. Clifford Zeyl arrived at the Redpath from Guelph. As an undergrad he'd worked in Bogart's lab, collaborating with us in a study of the unisexual salamanders on Kelleys Island in Lake Erie, where some individuals combined genomes from three separate species. He now looked at the relationships of sex and parasitic DNA to evolution in rapidly multiplying microorganisms; the shift to unicellular subjects aside, he remained a herpetologist at heart.

In the spring of 1992 we'd all gathered at the laboratory of the Redpath's curator of herpetology, Dr. David M. Green, a knowledgeable A-type who'd conducted both his MSc and PhD under Jim Bogart, finishing up just as I'd begun my tenure in Guelph, and whose focus was frogs.

In addition to a dozen other titles, Green sat as national coordinator for the Canadian Working Group of the international Declining Amphibian Populations Task Force. Yes, there was an international task force. No, it knew neither what it was dealing with nor how dire things would actually become. Yes, it would garner much press and not a small amount of government monies. And sadly, no, when the writing was on the wall it would not be able to do a single thing to stem the tide of extinction.

Green's various involvements turned much of our thinking

toward conservation biology, recasting many of the evolutionary questions we pursued in the context of the immediate climatic and anthropogenic factors affecting them. I started to see fluctuating population composition in unisexual salamander communities as an ecological phenomenon caused by small-scale habitat alteration and large-scale climatic shifts.

One of Green's specialties was Fowler's Toad (*Bufo fowleri*). Those living at the northern edge of their range were under threat from climatic factors that affected breeding success and hybridization with the more widespread American Toad. Sharbel was similarly concerned about hybridization between two small stream salamanders—the Northern Dusky Salamander (*Desmognathus fuscus*) and Mountain Dusky Salamander (*Desmognathus ochrophaeus*)—in the Chateauguay River basin in extreme southern Québec. This, he'd enthused over a plate of *shish taouk* at a favored Lebanese lunch haunt, was a classic wildlife management issue: could we get a handle on how extensive this hybridization might be and whether it threatened the integrity of either species, both of which were near their distributional limit here?

The conservation angle was a fresh call to arms. You couldn't spend a decade mired neck-deep in the muck of something as arcane as unisexuality without wondering how you might apply at least one thing you'd learned to something people actually gave a shit about. The global decline in amphibians was such a cause, and small-scale issues like hybridization were perfect testing grounds for methods that might be more broadly applied. Sharbel thought a method I'd used to quantify ploidy in salamanders might be the perfect tool.

Flow cytometry (FCM) employs an argon laser beam to precisely measure DNA in cells fired past it one at a time in a high-speed stream. Used for years to detect human cancers and genetic abnormalities, it had acquired many nonmedical applications during the previous decade. When Dr. Robert M. Dawley of Cornell University successfully used FCM to examine a complex of diploid-triploid hybrid minnows, I'd readily adopted it to determine ploidy in the thousands of salamanders we were handling in Haliburton. We now no longer needed to count laboriously obtained chromosomes under a microscope—a single drop of blood run through a flow cytometer could tell you plenty in seconds.

THE RALLYING CRY "Field trip!" in a herpetology lab is akin to "Road trip!" in a college fraternity. Think *Animal House* with real animals—plus frogs and snakes. So strong are the combined urges of collecting and escaping the lab that anybody's field trip instantly becomes *everybody's* field trip. Add the fact that any car crammed with herpetologists is a de facto expedition even when it's only headed to the mall (every passing ditch and vacant lot being a harbinger of potential treasure), and you had a formula for the halting, Murphy's Law (strangely, no relation) scramble that was a field trip.

Zeyl and I had made several jaunts together back in our Guelph days. One memorable Labour Day while Bogart was away, we'd waded into the Eramosa River Valley to round up local species to show students attending that fall's herpetology class. The excursion turned into a snake-catching bonanza that included what seemed to us a world-record Eastern Gartersnake—a spear-headed, bratwurst-thick, meter-long monster—a half-dozen supercharged, aggressively snapping milksnakes, and the never-to-be-repeated thrill of flipping a large limestone flake to reveal four snakes of three species: two large Northern Water Snakes (*Nerodia sipedon*), an Eastern Milksnake, an Eastern Gartersnake. Without time to corral each safely, we'd been bitten savagely and repeatedly. I have visions of Zeyl swaggering along the grassy banks of the Eramosa in his standard tie-dyed T-shirt and threadbare cut-offs, a clutch of madly striking snakes in each hand and blood running down his arms as if he'd just finished shift at the Dickens-esque abattoir that hovered over the valley like a Pink Floyd album cover.

Sharbel, Kaiser, and I had also journeyed into the field together, usually with Michael Caldwell—a PhD candidate under Redpath director and paleontologist emeritus Bob Carroll—in tow. We logged the first record of a Red-bellied Snake (*Storeria occipitomaculata*), kissing cousin to the familiar DeKay's Snake, from l'Île d'Orleans just east of Québec City, plus a new voucher—the archetype on which any new description is based—of an LLJ unisexual from the original type locality of l'Île Perrot west of Montreal (an LLJ specimen collected here back in the day was inappropriately described as the unisexual "species" *Ambystoma tremblayi*, but the voucher had been lost in a fire). Each minor achievement, however, seemed to be offset by major comic disaster: flat tires, poison ivy, broken equipment, lost items, and "soakers" always found their way into the mix.

On this particular outing we headed south and west of Montreal along the south shore of the St. Lawrence River. As we flew along the highway, volcanic domes rose abruptly from the flat former floor of the Champlain Sea, a post-Pleistocene inundation by the Atlantic Ocean. These were the fragmented northern edge of the ancient Adirondack Range, part of the greater Appalachian mountain chain. Many supported unique flora and fauna, some relicts of more widespread distribution in warmer times, others simply following this physiographic axis to reach their northern limits.

Few would guess that the Appalachians' most impressive

faunal asset was an ungodly diversity of salamanders. Repeated displacement, isolation, fragmentation, and divergence caused by 30 million years of advancing and retreating ice sheets have led to an array of highly speciose groups. As such, the southern Appalachians are regarded as a classic area of endemism—a biogeographical region in which species are constantly being generated—home to the richest salamander fauna in the world (seven families, nineteen genera, and some seventy-five species). Feeding on small life-forms, these salamanders make a huge contribution to nutrient cycling in both terrestrial and aquatic habitats. Thus, the relict domes boiling up from the St. Lawrence valley could become ecologically vulnerable if, among other things, their salamander faunas were threatened.

Such was the case on the northern slope of the Adirondacks in southern Québec, where *Desmognathus* inhabited streams that began as subterranean springs, seeped down mountainsides over exposed bedrock in cool, deciduous forest, and dissipated at the slopes' base. In addition to ubiquitous Northern Dusky Salamanders, a handful of streams also contained the mountain dusky. A few strange-looking specimens further suggested that the two species engaged in limited hydridization.

Geographically overlapping species usually maintain ecological distance by occupying different microhabitats, but repeated land clearing for farming followed by natural succession and reclamation had blurred these microhabitats. To get a handle on the level of hybridization, we would need a large sample size. Because these species were vulnerable, tissues for genetic determinations had to be collected via nondestructive means, something biologists were often hard-pressed to do but that was now imperative.

We piled out of the car and into the woods, meticulously searching rocky debris in and around two adjacent streams.

Unlike amateur herpetologists and enthusiastic youngsters playing the land for hidden animals, however, we were careful to
replace each of our divots, leaving ecosystems as undisturbed as
possible. We turned up over one hundred individuals from one
stream and seventy from the other. Although it was hard to tell
what was what with these very plain, very similar, very brownish sibling species, northern duskys were generally darker and
plainer (*fuscus*, in fact, is Latin for dusky, dark, or somber). When
it came to identifying mountain duskys whose dorsal patterns
are notoriously variable, however, it was a toss-up whether you
were palming *la vraie chose* or a hybrid.

We held each wriggling finger-length salamander still with
a wet sponge against a clear plastic box lid and measured it;
we inspected translucent bellies for the presence of eggs; we
snipped off tail tips for electrophoresis and gene-flow analysis;
and we collected a drop of blood from each for FCM. We carefully replaced each salamander where we had found it.

When we completed our lab work we found that hybridization had occurred at low levels in only one stream, where *D.
fuscus* genes had then introgressed into the *D. ochrophaeus* population. Such unidirectional hybridization suggested only par-
tial genetic compatibility between the species, and a wildlife
management perspective held that as long as the area's streams
and forest buffers remained further undisturbed by agricultural
activity, salamander populations would likely stabilize to maintain species integrities and traditional levels of biodiversity in
these ecosystems. What concerned me at the end of our day in
the field, however, wasn't how we could save salamanders from
the farmer's plow but who would pay for surreptitiously filling the pack of lab equipment I was carrying with kilos of wet,
slime-covered stream rocks.

WHERE PRACTICAL JOKING at the ROM had been benign, at the Redpath it was often monstrously mean. I'd discovered a reeking, fabric-destroying lizard head in my jacket pocket on a train ride back to Toronto, and in turn—long after the fact so that he didn't see it coming—Sharbel found his desk-chair cushion filled with pond water. Caldwell, who seemed adept at fathering children, found a home vasectomy kit complete with alcohol swabs, surgical scissors, suturing material, and a Band-Aid in his desk drawer. Another student, who stepped into a roadside port-a-potty to relieve himself as we stumbled home from the pub on a −20°C night, found himself rocketing down the steep, ice-covered street atop which it had perched, the contents of this plastic tomb sloshing around his sputtering head. But our most creative pranks were reserved for Der Kaiser, whose budgetary largesse, frequent absences, easygoing nature, and lack of retaliatory game made him the perfect victim.

During one of his frequent trips to Germany, when we'd all noticed once too often that his orderly, dust-free desk was out of synch with the surrounding tumult, we removed his computer monitor and keyboard, obtained a similar setup from the museum's waste stores, smashed the components to pieces, spread them on his desk, and laboriously placed a massive, 150-kilo fossil atop the mess, creating the all-too-realistic effect of the rock's having been dropped from a height to obliterate his computer. When Hinrich returned from the fatherland, his priceless reaction was greeted with howls of pant-pissing laughter. But that prank was nothing compared with our jackass acme, the ultimate herpetological indignity.

In a small jar behind Der Kaiser's desk floated a tiny frog. Brownish, like pretty much any frog bobbing in alcohol for more than an hour, it was the voucher for a new species of *Colostethus*.

Describing it would be the crowning achievement of Hinrich's nascent career, a first significant step on the road to making a scientific name for himself; as such, the animal was precious beyond scope. On another shelf sat one of those cheesy souvenir snow globes you shook to watch plastic flakes tumble through the shrunken facsimile of a city. The two items seemed made for each other.

The switch was complicated: the fluid in the snow globe contained glycerin, which made a mess when we cracked it open; we pried the cityscape from its base and dropped it into the jar of alcohol from which we'd removed the voucher; we retrieved an identical-looking but less-important frog from the collections and tied the voucher specimen's telltale numbered tag to the faux frog's leg and placed it in the snow globe; someone then had the idea to further piss off Kaiser—literally—by refilling the snow globe with urine. Both the "clue" jar with its junk plastic city and the snow globe containing the ersatz voucher were positioned where they had originally sat, while the real, undamaged voucher was hidden safely away.

The joke was spectacular. Despite our history of high-handed gags, Kaiser ranted, raved, and turned red—a cartoon character passing steam through his ears. He was convinced we'd finally crossed the line by wantonly floating his sacred, undescribed species in a globe full of piss. He took it as symbolic of what we thought of him, which, crass as our adolescent reasoning had been, was clearly unintended. Maybe we *had* crossed the line.

IN HERPETOLOGY, CROSSING the line was as easy as crossing the street. Perhaps because *the line*, as perceived by greater society, was laughingly ad hoc, and *the line*, as perceived by science, didn't exist by design. For those caught between the worlds of fallible humanity, pursuit of pure, cold fact, and animals that drew their own dangerous boundaries, *the line* was simply a blur sweeping back and forth between provocation and death.

This callousness extended to intellectual ambit. Graduate students frequently found themselves galled by an institution that on one hand preached individuality and the need to challenge scientific dictum but on the other practiced conformity to entrenched methodologies and thinking. You could escape mainstream confines to a certain extent in seminar groups where rules were secondary to topical discussion, but they were few and far between. As a result, herpetologists tended to find their way directly to whatever free-think tanks existed on campus.

Over my postsecondary career I'd benefited from a host of brilliantly subversive mentors and happily found our Redpath group always subsumed with something thought-provoking that wasn't taught, discussed, or mentioned in regular biological curricula. We all seemed to crave a piece of this anarchic action (Green himself was working on a species-definition theory based on the mathematical concept of fuzzy sets), and Caldwell and I, in constant discourse over virtually every sacred biological cow, set out to formalize it. Thus was born a student discussion group to consider topics that hovered just outside the conventional structure of evolutionary thought or ran as unseen threads through its intellectual basement: ideas like the roles of senescence (aging) in biological organization; entropy (evolution as an emergent process driven by the Second Law of Thermodynamics); nongenetic considerations like self-organization principles and chaos theory, with its attractors and fractal patterns reflected so frequently in the natural world; the vast, unknown-to-the-West Soviet literature built on the Marxist tenet of dialectical materialism, in which nature progressed through constant dialogue with itself—like

the feedback loops found at every level of biological organization. A countercultural group required a countercultural name,
and we chose Sid Vicious's Sewing Circle (svss), capturing the
notion of an irreverent punk collective.

We met weekly at the venerable McGill Grad Club, pints of
beer in hand and photocopied readings on a polished, board-
room-style table in front of us. There was no professorial presence or designated leader, but meetings always started politely
with question-begging salvos and roundtable trade-offs. Finding
our way around topics that we knew nothing about and that no
prof wanted to touch was intoxicating. Also intoxicating were
the many pints and hash joints we consumed, surreptitiously
blowing smoke out an upstairs window as discussion heated up.
As empty glasses climbed in dangerous, shatter-prone pyramids,
voices rose and opinions on the *thème du jour* hardened around
two predictable poles: Why? and Why not? This, of course, was
largely the point. We often seemed to have reached an impasse
when the gathering inevitably adjourned to the pool tables, but
what had really happened was that we'd each come away with
something to think about; staking a position was just a way to
buy time to reel silently under the weight of new information.

I came away from the svss and my time at McGill with the
conviction that everything I thought I knew amounted to not
much, that we really had little idea about the metaprocesses
driving evolution or the real reasons and biological meaning
behind many of the things I'd observed among reptiles and
amphibians. Natural selection acts on variability to cull the useless and maladapted from the ranks of organismal diversity, but
as such it is a secondary process. Something else is pushing up
from beneath to drive the generation of variation—a constant
potential or differential waiting to explode into chaotic change

when the gatekeepers of self-organization momentarily turn their backs. There is a disorderly force behind all the order we see in the universe. We live in a biological house of cards. Everything we do is an experiment, and each might be the one to dislodge the card that brings it all down. Like deformed frogs and disappearing amphibians.

FROGS WITH EXTRA legs weren't new to science. Polymelia, as the condition is known, had been observed and published on from time to time. Comment, however, had more to do with zeitgeist than empirical investigation. During the mid-twentieth century, when the so-called New Synthesis marrying paleontology, evolution, and genetics drove most of biological thinking, and the notion of punctuated equilibrium (long periods of stasis broken by big evolutionary jumps) was in vogue, researchers alluded to a potential evolutionary role for such perturbations. A well-cited 1974 paper by Leigh Van Valen of the University of Chicago went so far as to argue that frog populations with high instances of polymelia might be natural models for the origin of higher taxa. We now see this viewpoint as embarrassing codswallop, but scientists of the time were actively searching for ecological and genetic models for macroevolutionary events, and the force of repetition of even an errant idea could upload it to the received view. As a young graduate student I repeatedly encountered reference to a "Van Valen effect" in evolutionary literature and was prone to treat it as gospel in lieu of any reason not to. Perhaps this was one reason scientific skepticism seemed so deeply entrenched when the deformity tsunami broke in the mid-'90s, an age of environmental battlefields between private and public funding sources.

In his 2000 book, *A Plague of Frogs: The Horrifying True Story*, author William Souder follows the search for reasons behind these apparently sudden occurrences and identifies the frequent collision course between the lumbering scientific method and what seems obvious:

> Clearly, something had gone terribly wrong at [the Minnesota] farm pond in that brief hot summer of 1995. It happened again the next year... The same thing, or something like it, seemed to be going on in Canada. Somehow an annual cycle repeated over countless millennia had suddenly misfired. In the narrow band of time from spring to fall, whole populations of animals were taking a wrong step somewhere between genotype and phenotype. Intuitively, [the schoolchildren] had reached certain conclusions in the space of a single afternoon that it would take many scientists many more months to begin to believe.
>
> The students assumed, for starters, that deformed frogs are not a normal occurrence. This was to be fiercely debated. The students also guessed that something in the water had caused the deformities. This, too, was to become a subject of the most intense inquiry. Finally, the kids speculated that if something in the local water could do this to frogs, it could very likely have harmful effects on other kinds of animals, including people.[15]

Where were the skeptics when Van Valen was proposing that severe physical deformities were proof of Darwin's incredible foresight? Perhaps we did not know enough about the genetic basis of development at the time or of effects of UVB, parasites, or chemicals with mutagenic properties—despite what we knew of drugs like thalidomide. Martin Ouellet, a young veterinarian from Québec City, was under no such illusion.

In 1990 Stanley K. Sessions and Stephen B. Ruth published a

paper describing a connection between parasitic infection and amphibian limb deformities. In a population of Pacific Treefrogs (*Pseudacris regilla*), they observed numerous limb abnormalities associated with the presence of a trematode (flatworm or fluke) parasite, *Ribeiroia ondatrae,* embedded more or less where limb buds would appear in developing frogs.

When The Strange Case of the Deformed Frogs hit the wires, several scientists vigorously pursued this observation as certain explanation. The *Blame Trematodes!* bandwagon was appealing; after all, these villains were responsible for plenty of human misery—some 200 million people in tropical regions worldwide were afflicted with the debilitating fluke-transmitted illness schistosomiasis. But in southern Québec's agricultural reaches, where Martin Ouellet was finding populations of scarily deformed frogs, there did not seem to be an increase in parasitic infection or in the snail vectors that released the parasite's swimming stage into the water to bury itself in the tissues of unsuspecting tadpoles. Ouellet was convinced that something else was behind the outbreaks; discarded chemical containers littering many of the frogs' habitats suggested what that was.

Ouellet began a broad-based study with colleagues at the Canadian Wildlife Service. He collected data on every imaginable physiological and physical parameter and assessed the genotoxicity of any water involved. He also wondered how he might quickly assess potential DNA damage in frogs, and, apprised of the power of FCM by our *Desmognathus* study, he approached our lab. Could FCM shed some light on the alarming occurrences of acutely sick and deformed frogs, as well as the potential risk for apparently healthy animals?

The ability to identify toxically stressed animal populations before they either manifested symptoms or were wiped out

completely would be an important advance in wildlife management and conservation biology, and FCM had succeeded in the
past at evaluating other so-called invisible hazards. In one study,
increased variability in the amounts of cellular DNA—characteristic of replication error and chromosome fragmentation—was
shown in radiation-exposed turtles dwelling in the effluent of
a nuclear power plant. We hypothesized that both normal and
deformed frogs from Ouellet's populations would show similar
hidden DNA damage.

Ouellet spent the summer of 1993 collecting frogs—and
drops of blood—from ponds and ditches adjacent to corn- and
potato fields subject to heavy rotation of pesticides and herbi-
cides. Cornfields were treated with atrazine, glyphosate, buty-
late, and carbofuran—a notorious mutagen whose toxic effects
had sparked a World Wildlife Fund call for a total ban. Potato
crops required treatment with linuron, metribuzin, phorate,
azinphos-methyl, cypermethrin, deltamethrin, oxamyl, man-
cozeb, metalaxyl, chlorothalinol, and diquat. I list these not for
the poetry of the names or to imply that each is a deadly toxin
(some are likely relatively safe). Rather, I do so to show the magnitude of a chemistry whose breakdown products might interact
alone or in concert with other stressors. The joint application
of so many substances, each with at least some unpredictable
consequence, is a giant, scary, uncontrolled experiment. For an
amphibian whose tissues and semipermeable skin are bathed in
this chemical soup from the watery womb of development to
adulthood, the experiment is a double whammy.

Not surprisingly, FCM showed widespread DNA damage
in animals associated with agricultural chemicals. The results
were clear-cut, as Ouellet might put it, or suggestive, at least, to
the world at large.

Science moves at a pace between slow and glacial, so three years passed before the data were gathered, analyzed, and published. Because we had initiated the study years before the Minnesota discoveries, our paper uncovering the connection was timely when it hit the wires—basically as I sat in California watching TV. Our findings were a significant contribution to understanding a growing problem: The Strange Case of the Deformed Frogs was part of a broader global phenomenon of disappearing amphibians.

The often rancorous debate about frog deformities continues. Strengthened by experimental and field observations, the *Ribeiroia* connection appears strong, though it cannot explain the full range of deformities. UVB radiation has largely been discredited as a singular causative factor; rather, both UVB and chemicals are seen to lower immune response and other defenses in developing frogs, making them more susceptible to both disease and parasitic infection, particularly in farm ponds where the influx of fertilizer and manure increases the number of snail vectors for *Ribeiroia*.

At the same time, agricultural chemicals have posed a significant threat on their own: pesticide runoff from potato fields killed some fifteen thousand trout on Prince Edward Island in 2002; a landmark study at UC Berkeley released the same year demonstrated that even tiny concentrations of atrazine, a particularly long-lasting herbicide linked to cancer risk in humans, severely interfered with sexual development in African Clawed Frogs (*Xenopus laevis*), the amphibian equivalent of a lab rat—male frogs had ovaries embedded in their (often multiple) testes, smaller vocal organs, and levels of testosterone a factor of ten lower than normal—less, even, than female frogs. Atrazine is one of a growing class of synthetic substances known as gender blenders, which mimic, convert, or interfere with hormones that regulate a wide variety of developmental processes. And it was everywhere.

Contributing to our understanding of this hazard was a fitting end to a storied chapter in my career. I turned my back on academics soon after my stint at McGill. The orderly matron of journalism ultimately claimed my attention, but herpetology's lascivious vixen, with her dangerous embrace and many whispered secrets, was never more than a wink away. I could change careers, but deep down I would always be a character in *The Far Side*. Fans of the wildly popular comic understand.

In the 1980s and '90s cartoonist Gary Larson, a self-proclaimed closet herpetologist, gave us daily doses of nerdy kids in horn-rimmed glasses, net-wielding scientists, and critter-crammed jars between python, crocodile, and dinosaur zingers. His lasting impact was in reminding us that the image of A Boy and His Frog is every bit as iconic as the Rockwell-esque notion of A Boy and His Dog.

Whereas most simply laugh at Larson's twisted portrayals of talking bugs and bug-eyed kids, biologists find these averring of deep personal truths and emotional connection. Around the planet, university biology departments are papered with fave *Far Side* vignettes. At the ROM, a *Far Side* adorned the door of Murphy's office. In it, a Tarzan character swung dramatically through the jungle—not holding onto a vine but penduluming with head gripped in the mouth of a very large snake. Someone had scratched out the original caption and written "Dr. Bob goes to China."

He thought it was funny. We thought it was possible.

9

BONEHEADS

Scales to feathers / You and I

JONI MITCHELL, "Don Juan's Reckless Daughter"

T HE WAY DAVID GREEN answers my question about how he got started down toad trail, you'd think he'd synchronized responses with every herpetologist that ever lived. When Green says he can't remember a time when he wasn't interested in animals in general and herps in particular, he's reading from the shared cosmic script of a den of ubiquity—likewise, I reckon, when he recalls the plastic cereal-box dinosaurs he hoarded, played with, and guarded with his life at age three. Hey—we *all* played with frickin' dinosaurs, Dave.

Why?

Here's my theory: Kids are fascinated with large, rumbling machinery, and dinosaurs are animate evocations of childhood's pantheon of mechanical icons—*Tyrannosaurus* towers like a steam shovel, its head a swooping, toothed bucket; armored *Ankylosaurus* is a tank bristling with weaponry; giant *Apatosaurus* (né *Brontosaurus*) is an elephantine land ship; sail-backed *Dimetrodon* evokes a schooner, ichthyosaur a toothy submarine, and pterosaur a fighter jet.

To a child's mind, dinosaurs are impressive simply for being supersized and cool looking. At some point, however, they morph from caricatures of the nature we know to vanguards of the nature we will never know, touchstones to an unfathomable dimension of earth history. For the biologically minded, fascination with this ancient machinery turns to consideration of the physiology required to run it, the ecology that supported it, and its legacy of design. Lost in the sleepy folds of deep time, dinosaurs remain the monsters under evolution's bed, forever loveable in the mind's eye—albeit owing mostly to the immunity that 65 million years brings.

I'd spent plenty of time in the ROM's dinosaur gallery, but my real paleontological education began with my McGill buddy, Michael Caldwell, along the fractured shore of northwest Nova Scotia, where two revered sites near the towns of Joggins and Parrsboro straddle a spur of land washed by the Bay of Fundy. Here, Nova Scotia's blood-red sandstone caps the only place on earth where fossils of the earliest known reptiles occur alongside those of related amphibian forebears. The form of preservation is also unique: critters were often encased in the hollow, sediment-filled stumps of lycopods (scale trees), trapped during cyclic flooding of swamp-forest that flourished near the center of the supercontinent Pangaea in the Late Carboniferous.

Three hundred million years after the fact, monstrous Bay of Fundy tides are eroding these stumps out of strata exposed in towering sea cliffs. About one in ten contains something of value, the scientific importance of which is incalculable. To wrest a stump from the rock requires many man-hours and careful, painstaking work; it also requires boatloads of paperwork and bulletproof permits, since the area is a provincial heritage site. In the summer of 1993 a posse including Caldwell, Tim

Sharbel, and me struck out for Nova Scotia with Caldwell's then supervisor—McGill professor, Redpath director, and eminent paleontologist Dr. Robert Lynn Carroll. Carroll's earlier work on material collected near Joggins ensured the town a gold pin on the global scientific map and put the site firmly in the public mind as a natural treasure. But that same public would soon give Carroll a black eye.

We bunked down under towering pine and fluttering maple in a cluster of old-style cottages near Parrsboro, where Carroll immediately took amusing and endearing charge—as if we were elementary schoolchildren on a first-ever outing.

"Well . . . breakfast is at seven," he sounded in his extra-loud, extra-tinny, vaguely midwestern voice. "And you should probably be in bed early because we'll have a long day tomorrow."

Next morning we clustered hungrily around a Formica table to eat cold, sugar-shock cereal, barely warmed Wonder-toast, and Tang—the powdered excuse for orange juice "enjoyed" by astronauts in space, soldiers in battle, and Kool-Aid–weaned kids. It clearly had no place in an earthling's diet, but then neither did most of the garbage on offer. The coffee was instant, the only additive an edible oil product that Tom Sawyer could have used to whitewash Aunt Polly's fence. While we picked through this homage to processed food, aching for bacon, eggs, or anything else with a farm pedigree, Carroll carefully assembled lunches on the counter as if he were sorting socks from the laundry— a single white-bread sandwich of either peanut butter and jam or lonely slice of baloney and mustard, plus a small apple and kindergarten-style juice box. When someone had the temerity to ask after a second sandwich, Carroll was flummoxed, as if the request threw off the entire mission.

"Well . . . do you *really* need another one?" he twanged. "There's only so many slices of bread, you know."

He handed each of us a popcorn-light paper bag with our name on it and herded us into a van for the short drive to the day's dig. As we grinned and feigned mock disbelief, it took everything we had to keep from bursting when, in protest, someone stuffed his entire sandwich into his mouth at once while the rest of us choked on suppressed laughter. When we found ourselves famished and dehydrated after a long morning on Carroll's chain gang, however, the miserly rations lost any humorous overtone. As did the six beers he bought for seven people.

FOR A CANADIAN herpetologist, standing on the beach below Wasson's Bluff—the main confection in Parrsboro's extensive bakeshop—was like salivating before a layer cake of the known universe.

On top are the familiar mixed-boreal decorations that largely circumscribe the country's current herp distributions; this pelage droops from crumbling-soil icing smeared on a boulder cobbler left by the final Pleistocene ice sheet. Other Cenozoic deposits have mostly been scraped off by repeated glaciations, so a lowering gaze takes in Mesozoic strata, largely Jurassic modulating into Triassic layers that mark the breakup of Pangaea and location of the oldest dinosaurs known in Canada. Then, buffered by indefinite Permian horizons, the so-called Coal Measures (coal layers), which for generations have fueled both industrious mines and inquisitive minds.

In front of you now are Upper Carboniferous rocks bearing a diversity of amphibians, the first recognizable reptiles, and reptilomorphs—reptilelike transitional forms. Just as the plant explosion of the Devonian set the stage for terrestrial arthropod radiation and a protein source that lured proto-amphibians from the water, an insect explosion in the Carboniferous encouraged the evolution of fully land-dwelling vertebrates; in addition to the amniotic egg that could develop on land, reptile ancestors exploited the burgeoning arthropod energy source with a new jaw mechanism that exerted more static pressure to hold struggling prey and crunch them up.

You visualize this ancient progression standing atop plant-riddled rocks and the crisscrossing trackways of strange creatures that speak to the otherworldly industry of the times. Soaring lycopod forests, dense thickets of bamboolike horsetail ancestors, and giant seed ferns proliferated. As the vast coal deposits suggest, the carbon bound in this organic mass was buried instead of being respired; as a result, atmospheric oxygen levels reached almost 30 percent by the Permian (they dove to 13 percent by the close of the Triassic before climbing back to today's level of 21 percent around 20 million years ago). Air so oxygen-rich that it could burst into flame from lightning strikes also encouraged the emergence of gigantic arthropods; two-meter *Arthropleura*, resembling a heavily armored millipede, and dragonfly ancestor *Meganeura*, the largest insect ever with a seventy-five-centimeter wingspan, provided good reason for small tetrapods to hunker down in hollow stumps.

As you contemplate all this, water pulling away behind you on a fifteen-meter tide recalls the ocean that formed as Pangaea came apart in the Triassic. Fluctuating sea levels in the Carboniferous meant that rivers in this location, like the Amazon, oscillated between freshwater swamps reminiscent of those in which Devonian crossopterygians gave rise to amphibians, and brackish waters supporting a familiar sea fauna: beds of primitive clams, eocarid shrimp, tube worms, and even timeless horseshoe crabs, unchanged to this day. Also like the Amazon, the murky waters were patrolled by many predators—huge rays, large bony fish, two-meter crossopterygians, and plenty of doe-eyed coelacanths.

In addition, the site offers a human history to consider—one particularly relevant to our party. Although Carroll had accomplished much here under his Redpath association, the institution's founding director, Sir John William Dawson, had first established the site's importance.

Of Scottish descent, Dawson was proudly but briefly shipped from his Pictou, Nova Scotia, birthplace to the University of Edinburgh in 1840, where he studied geology and natural history. Returning to Acadia in 1842, he was introduced to none other than Charles Darwin table guest and chief uniformitarian (bet you thought you'd never see that word again) Sir Charles Lyell, on his first visit to the Canadian Dominion and much interested, I do say, in comparing our Coal Measures with similar strata in Britain.

The two struck up a working relationship, and Lyell was duly influenced by what he saw at Joggins. On Lyell's second visit, in 1852, the pair uncovered the first remains of a stem-tetrapod (we'll call it an amphibian) from Upper Carboniferous strata near Joggins, *Dendrerpeton acadianum*. Dawson then moved west to Montreal as professor of geology and principal of McGill University from 1855 to 1893, where his influence and collections helped lead the institution to world renown, drawing faculty like Carroll and students like Caldwell, who, a century later, were closing the circle in Nova Scotia.

INVESTIGATING FOSSIL STUMPS was an indelicate process. To start, they had to be removed intact; any bones they contained might be tiny disarticulated fragments anywhere within the stump, depending on where the sediment-filled bottom had lain before final inundation. Extracting a stump involved chiseling around its edges, then prying it out with a crowbar. Lithographs from the 1800s show men swinging pickaxes at the surrounding matrix, and far into the twentieth century more drastic means, like dynamite, were often used to liberate stumps from cliffs and reefs.

Under Carroll's careful coaching, by afternoon the first day we'd removed several small stumps and cracked them into manageable pieces, then carefully broke (this sounds contradictory, but it's actually a paleontological skill) them apart with rock hammers to comb for fossiliferous material. Finding nothing, we proceeded to the finale: smashing the remains to smithereens like the tool-wielding monkeys in 2001: A Space Odyssey.

A local man who operated a small museum atop the bluff was leading an interpretive "stump tour" down the beach and was caught unawares by the sight of our party—we were the first scientists in years who had shown up to work the sacred cliffs. Hectoring a pod of paying tourists past ponytailed dirtbags merrily pulverizing what he was describing as priceless fossils, he was at a loss to explain why we would do this or who might have sanctioned it. The tourists looked quizzical, the man disgusted; thinking little of it, we waved innocent hellos from our dusty quarry, backed by a gallery of partially excavated stumps slated for destruction.

Next day Caldwell, Sharbel, and I found ourselves far down the beach during lunch (there was plenty of time to kill after the five seconds we took to down the meal), wandering and wondering over other discoveries along this impressive strand. We knew that in 1985, North America's arguably most impressive fossil find had been unearthed at Parrsboro—over a hundred thousand pieces of various tetrapods that had dwelt in and around a lava-rock talus 200 million years ago. The fossil find was the world's single largest and the first involving fauna of this period. The site also included the world's smallest dinosaur footprints, each the size of a penny. Unsure of its location—or much else—and with the incoming tide about to cut off retreat, we returned to our own excavation.

Carroll and a student were laboring over yet another promising stump. Hefting our tools, we'd just joined in when a high-pitched voice broke over our shoulders.

"*There, see?*" it urged frantically. We wheeled to find a bespectacled woman pointing a shaking, accusing finger our way, flanked by a guy with a video camera. They stood a few meters off beside a large log, as if they'd snuck up on all fours to pop from behind it.

"Where's your permit?" she yelled, as if we were deaf. Clearly she had no idea whom she was dealing with.

"Uh, here," said Caldwell, moving to diffuse the situation, reaching for the official paper in his back pocket, and simultaneously stepping toward the log.

"*Don't touch me!*" screamed the woman hysterically. Then, to the cameraman, "Did you get that?"

We were stumped.

That evening, shaky footage of pulverized fossils ringed by our startled faces made the TV news, clear evidence of a criminal element stealing Nova Scotia's precious natural heritage while the government turned an oblivious eye. None of it was true, of course, but the story hit the papers, setting off a storm to rival anything that blew in off the Atlantic. The self-appointed caretaker-entrepreneurs had reacted with undue zeal in harassing Carroll, interfering with his legitimate work, accusing him of vandalism, and calling in media—but their efforts worked. For

Caldwell, used to fieldwork in remote areas of the Arctic, it was a rude awakening; for me, an eye-opening introduction to the supercharged world of fossil hunting. I'd never look at a hollow stump the same way. And yet the debacle raised a reasonable question.

Who *should* own the rights to the world's first reptiles—animals important enough to be commemorated on a Canadian postage stamp? Although the stamp's forty-cent price identifies it as having been issued sometime in the Pleistocene, you can't help admiring the artist's attempt to capture both the look and the perspective of a pioneer lineage—an alien in an alien world. Figured in iguanid green with whiplike orange tail, the animal strikes a bent, uncertain posture on widely splayed limbs, the smooth, domelike head (faithfully lacking ear openings like its amphibian ancestors) tilted awkwardly toward the viewer. And yet few who read the stamp's fine print would understand its true import:

> *Hylonomus lyelli*
> Land reptile/Reptile terrestre
> Carboniferous Period/Période carbonifère

Hylonomus was like a lone Viking staring out to sea on the northern tip of Newfoundland some four hundred years before Columbus, the Spaniards, the French, and the English swept in and took over every corner of the Americas. A true vanguard.

With memories of barely imaginable histrionics and almost reptilian territoriality on that Nova Scotia beach, we loaded the single, plaster-encased one-hundred-kilo stump we'd been allowed to remove in the end into the van and, like Dawson before us, hightailed it west to Montreal and the sanctity of McGill's Redpath Museum.

Because the Redpath was erected to house Dawson's extensive geologic collections, it was thus his building. Wherever we moved in the tiny, creaking edifice, we trod in his footsteps and, by association, those of the beginnings of terrestrial life on earth. Babysitting the amphibian-reptile transition lodged in the Redpath's bowels was unique comeuppance, an association with human and beastly spirits that might occur to you while you were drinking in the lab as various late-night experiments ran their course, or while touring impressionable women through shadowy corridors after a night at the pub. The sort of behavior that was itself deemed vaguely reptilian.

AS IT TURNS out, "reptilian" is bandied about as freely in taxonomic circles as social ones. Reptiles, birds, and mammals conjointly possess extra-embryonic membranes for their developing young, and thus comprise the monophyletic, i.e., of a single common ancestor—Amniota. Yet birds and mammals are recognized as monophyletic groupings of their own, each with singular origins amid the taxonomic bricolage known as reptiles. As presently construed, Class Reptilia comprises a diversity of forms largely united because of the *absence* of characters that define their descendant groups of birds and mammals. In other words, any amniote without fur or feathers is shuttled into Reptilia.

You don't really need a systematist to tell you that modern "reptiles"—turtles, crocodiles, snakes, lizards, tuataras—are a rogue's gallery of likely long-separated forms and that if birds and mammals cropped up in the middle of that mess, something is seriously wrong with the way we currently classify animals. The kind of false or default relationship that classes such as Reptilia imply is termed paraphyly (from the Greek *para*, "near to"). We can solve the problem of paraphyly by either expanding a taxon to include those clades that arose from it (for example, including birds and, possibly, mammals *within* Reptilia) or splitting it to give all monophyletic components equal status (meaning that mammals; turtles; crocodiles + birds; and snakes + lizards + tuataras would all be separate classes). However this taxonomic shuffle eventually plays out, one thing is clear: reptiles have always been, well . . . reptilian enough that they were recognized as such by their discoverer, Sir William Dawson, when they were first described in 1860.

From humble origins as tiny, agile insectivores that cowered in stumps, reptiles rapidly diversified into a multiplicity of forms that variously specialized in eating arthropods, molluscs, plants, and other vertebrates—including each other. They would, as we know, go on to rule the earth both literally and figuratively, their evolutionary achievements immortalized in a hundred ways by a global culture of self-appointed caretakers, including the cereal-box models that landed in David Green's hands. Like the fall of the Roman Empire, the sudden end to so glorious a reign at the very height of its majesty perplexes and haunts humanity; the dinosaurs' mysterious disappearance offers sharp testament to the essential fragility of even the most exalted products of evolution, which puts our own species in jeopardy of similar cosmic mortality. But that's a notion for another book; here, we seek to understand only the basic origins of the familiar living reptiles.

The fossil record suggests that the ancestors of mammals were first to peel from the trunk of the amniote tree. Turtles were the likely next, although a lack of fossils demonstrating intermediate stages in their high degree of skeletal modification means that no one is sure—complete skeletons of primitive turtles appear "suddenly" in Upper Triassic strata.

The next and largest branch contains the major groups of Mesozoic amniotes, which split early into two distinct lin-

eages (and a gymnastic of syllables): the Archosauromorpha—
crocodilians, pterosaurs (flying reptiles), and dinosaurs—and
the Lepidosauromorpha, represented in modern fauna by the
Lepidosauria, comprising Squamata (lizards and snakes, the
most successful living reptiles, with seven thousand species)
plus Sphenodontida (the sole survivors of this once proud Triassic lineage are the endangered Tuataras, *Sphenodon punctatus* and
S. guntheri, which persist on a few tiny islands off New Zealand,
where they bark doglike warnings and crush giant crickets in
beaked jaws capable of tearing the head off a chicken).

Primitive lizards appeared in the Late Permian, about 250
million years ago. Several lineages radiated rapidly into the
vacant niches left by each tectonic, climatic, and extinction episode, scaling up and down in size and mode of locomotion with
startling results. Lizards that glided through the air on skin folds
stretched over modified ribs evolved at least three times; limbless burrowers arose on dozens of occasions; toes were variously
adapted to scamper over sand, water, rock, and even overhanging surfaces; arboreal forms developed specialized characters
like protrusible tongues, prehensile tails, grasping digits, and
independent eye movement. Sorting occurred early; some
modern genera were already apparent by the Early Tertiary.

Even Varanoids—the most advanced lizard lineage by dint
of size, swagger, and predaceous lifestyle—took things to
extremes: you wouldn't want to encounter a deer-munching,
three-meter Komodo Dragon on Komodo Island's forest trails
today, but a relative roaming Australia during the last Ice Age
made the Komodo look like a puppy. At six meters and over
three hundred kilos, *Varanus prisca* ("ancient giant butcher") was
the nastiest lizard ever, ambushing animals ten times its weight
and dispatching them with immense claws and curved, shark-
like choppers.

The most impressive creatures to stem from Varanoids, however, were the spectacular mosasaurs—large, predaceous aquatic forms with saw-blade tooth arrays and paddlelike limbs. Known from some fifty species of up to fifteen meters distributed worldwide, mosasaurs ruled Mesozoic seas from 92 million years ago as contemporaries of the largest predatory dinosaurs and disappeared in the same mysterious mass extinction at the end of the Cretaceous, 65 million years ago. Basically they came, they ruled, they went; a short, 27-million-year pool party in geologic terms but an important one biologically—a fact that makes Caldwell, who has written and lectured extensively on them, wonder how herpetologists can talk snake and lizard evolution but ignore mosasaurs, the third most diverse group of squamates.

"Unlocking the mystery of the mosasaurs," he tells me, "may well solve the mystery of the origin of snakes. The herp guys need to pay more attention to the fossil record."

Known for his controversial views on snake origins, Caldwell is an enthusiastic advocate of the theory—first advanced by none other than E.D. Cope—that snakes originated in water from mosasauroid stock. He is aided by several discoveries in Cretaceous marine deposits of "snakes" with pelvic-girdle and rear-limb remnants. Another school, however, believes that the lizard–snake transition occurred on land, mirroring the many burrowing/limb-reduction scenarios observed in both fossil and contemporary lizards; indeed, the most primitive assemblage of living snakes consists of blind, fossorial forms. Both sides of the debate also claim recent new ammunition.

Ecological forces can clearly lead to elongation of the body, reduction of the trunk, and loss of limbs, but they might also explain the dramatically different eye structures and focusing capabilities of lizards and snakes. The comparatively degenerate eyes of snakes could be evidence that fossorial or nocturnal ancestors operated in low-light conditions; yet other eye and orbital characters suggest similarities to aquatic vertebrates. In one analysis of ophthalmic data from a wide range of vertebrates, taxa clustered more along lines of ecological adaptation than phylogeny: burrowing lizards and burrowing mammals were grouped together, and snakes shook out a long way off with primitively water-dwelling vertebrates, a finding that strongly supports their aquatic origin. Conversely, a rival group's analysis of DNA sequence data shows no close relationship between snakes and modern varanids, to which the former should logically be most similar if the mosasauroid connection were true, offering default support for a land origin. Does either study suggest to which lizard group snakes *are* related? No. The latest on the origin of snakes? No one is sure.

At best, we know that snakes diverged from a basal lizard stock before the close of the Jurassic and were already fossilizing by the Early Cretaceous, 130 million years ago. The most complete of these skeletons is two-meter *Dinilysia patagonica* from Argentina. It shares characters with modern boas and pythons, which are considered somewhat primitive among living snakes. Another fossil boid from Egypt, *Gigantophis*, at fifteen meters is the largest snake known and was capable of swallowing a water buffalo. Specimens of the boid *Paleryx* from Germany, described in 1850 by our buddy Richard Owen, feature scaly skin impressions.

The first "modern" snakes to appear in the fossil record are also boids. Like their descendants, these were largish, heavy-bodied serpents with primitive skull structure and vestigial limbs—external spurs attached to a remnant pelvic girdle and used in fighting and copulation. When the dinosaurs packed up shop, they left myriad ecological vacuums; as their mammalian meal tickets became widespread and diverse in repopulating these, boids followed suit, until they were the earth's dominant snakes. About 36 million years ago, however, their monopoly was broken by a group of faster, more gracile snakes, the colubroids. As mammals had with dinosaurs, colubroids had hung out in the shadows awaiting their day in the sun. It came with some help from plate tectonics.

The continents had been gradually shuffling away from the equator, their climates cooling dramatically; as plates reached their present positions in the Miocene, about 20 million years ago, lowering temperatures confined boids largely to the tropics. Colubroids swept into vacated and emerging niches, and three families spread like wildfire to eventually make up over three-quarters of all living snakes, thus giving the epithet Age of Snakes to the Cenozoic Era. These were the Viperidae (true and pit vipers with erectable fangs); the Elapidae (fixed-fang relatives of cobras and kraits); and the Colubridae (a polyphyletic catchall of mostly harmless forms).

This rapid radiation of advanced snakes was again closely tied to that of their largely mammalian prey. Today's snakes show much more diversity, however. Several lineages became secondarily aquatic in either fresh or salt water (the latter was invaded on at least three separate occasions), and representatives of nonburrowing lineages have taken on true burrowing lifestyles (remember the Fijian bolo?). There are snakes that hang underwater like algae-covered sticks to ambush fish; snakes that hunt frog eggs laid in arboreal nests; bird eaters, bat eaters, slug eaters, egg eaters, lizard eaters, and eaters of other snakes; even flying snakes that flatten their bodies and use exaggerated S-patterns to glide from tree to tree like Frisbees. How are advanced forms related to basal groups? No one is sure.

As for relationships *within* the Lepidosauromorpha, no one seems sure of much. There is more certainty about which archosauromorphs gave rise to the preternaturally persistent crocodilians, the doomed flying pterosaurs, and the equally doomed dinosaurs—plus that gang's successful winged descendants, birds. As my Chicago buddy noted all those years ago, birds actually *are* modified dinosaurs. And if birds are really reptiles in the phylogenetic sense, then paleontologists have lost a deeply embedded groove first etched by Cuvier, Owen, Agassiz, and Cope—but got themselves a whole new game.

AT HARVARD, ROBERT Carroll studied under celebrated paleontologist Alfred Sherwood Romer. Romer's death just shy of his eightieth birthday in November 1973 marked the end of an era in classical vertebrate paleontology. Those like me who hadn't yet begun university would nevertheless come under the sway of his considerable legacy.

Another who'd studied under Romer was one Thomas S. Parsons. At Romer's instructions—issued two years before his death—Parsons undertook a revision and update of the great man's landmark in comparative anatomy, *The Vertebrate Body*. Labeled "Romer and Parsons" in student argot, the prescribed textbook in my first vertebrate zoology course was the only one I ever read cover to cover—perhaps because it provided crucial context to an evolving worldview. Romer himself captured this sentiment in the fourth edition of his *Man and the Vertebrates* (since retitled *The Vertebrate Story*): "To understand the meaning of any . . . natural phenomenon we try to place it in its proper setting, its relation to other phenomena in time and space. There is no reason to treat ourselves otherwise. Man does not live in a vacuum, has not come out of a void. A fact of prime importance for an understanding of man is his position in the world of life, his relationships to other living things."[16]

During my doctoral days, I was a teaching assistant at the

University of Toronto in several vertebrate anatomy labs cleaved from a large class of biology and pre-med students. The course instructor was Tom Parsons.

Parsons carried himself chin forward in the style of a nineteenth-century lecturer but was more approachable and lacked the haughty diction. He did, however, have a deep and abiding love of the arcane, an attachment to anatomical minutiae that fit his nerdy look: pen- and probe-studded pocket, gray crew cut, Buddy Holly horn-rims, oily, exfoliating brow, and a red, crenulated nose that appeared soaked in the same preservatives as the animals we dissected. He had an encyclopedic recall of skeletal details for a staggering array of extinct and extant fauna and an enjoyable, anecdote-filled teaching style. Wearing his horribly stained lab coat, reeking of formaldehyde, latex, and rotting animal fat, he kicked off each lab section with a rapid-fire talk about what students would encounter in the day's dissections, then made his rounds of the benches, poking and prodding at greasy shark or cat carcasses with bare fingers that he wiped on his lab coat while the rest of us used tools and gloves and masks as if we were in biohazard lockdown.

I also experienced Parsons from a student's perspective. Years before I met Bob Carroll, he had come together with Parsons to present life on earth to me as a series of repetitive anatomical experiments, some fleeting and randomized, others cycling familiar themes through misty eons in an almost hopeful manner, the way a baby repeats promising movements in its search for a way to stand. This happened when I audited a Parsons course in advanced vertebrate paleontology, where Carroll's recently published magnum opus, *Vertebrate Paleontology and Evolution*, was the required text. Chapter after chapter had tracked repeated trends to dwarfism, gigantism, rib expansion, elongation, limb reduction, bipedalism, armoring, ornamentation, carnivory, herbivory, flying, swimming—each offering lessons in how one adaptive idea might hold a winning ticket to the evolutionary lottery of a subsequent epoch.

Among those groups that most piqued Parsons was the Archosauria—possessed of more upright posture and efficient fore-aft leg movement than the scampering, splayed-foot early reptiles—which included crocodiles as well as the primitive thecodonts that gave rise to both dinosaurs and pterosaurs. Parsons liked to point out that given a different roll of the evolutionary dice, we may well have ended up with a planet ruled by crocodilians: over a span of a hundred million years, crocs tried out running, standing upright, getting small (to scamper up trees), getting big (one land species, *Parasaurus brasiliensis,* was the largest carnivore to ever roam the earth), and, when nothing better seemed to stick, diving back into water, literally and figuratively. It was to be their last stand. Today's pantropical crocodilian species parrot the lineage's earliest armor-plated examples in both structure and amphibious way of life—conservative to the potentially bitter end. Almost all of them are endangered, and it's sad to think that we—soft, pink, bipedal mammals—might wipe out a group that withstood the lengthy onslaught of the dinosaurs and survived several global extinction events. Then again, the crocs blew their chance.

Appearing in the Middle Triassic, dinosaurs quickly (in geologic relativity) came to dominate the land from 150 million years ago to the catastrophic end of the Cretaceous. Early paleontologists split dinosaurs into two main groups based on pelvic-bone orientations—Ornithiscia and Saurischia. The latter was subdivided into the herbivorous sauropodomorphs (the really big guys, like thirty-meter, eighty-thousand-kilo *Diplodocus*) and the carnivorous theropods (*Tyrannosaurus* et al.). Ironically, "birdlike" ornithiscians did not give rise to birds; instead, our fine feathered friends derived from highly active theropod saurischians—the "lizardlike" dinos. It's not the only miscue Owen and company wish they could take back.

FROM THE START paleontologists assumed that dinosaurs were ectothermic like the reptiles they resembled. Contrary rumblings occasionally bubbled up but never in the popular press. Then came Adrian Desmond's 1975 book, *The Hot-Blooded Dinosaurs*, suggesting that maybe dinosaurs weren't clumsy, slow-moving battleships, as they'd been portrayed. This *idée du jour* found favor in an era where flighty theories of all kinds were capturing imaginations (remember Erich von Däniken's *Chariots of the Gods?*). The hot-blooded dinosaur theory, however, had serious teeth to it, popularizing a 1940s concept that had recently gained momentum behind the efforts of cowboy paleontologist Dr. Robert Bakker. According to Bakker and a ballooning rank and file, all dinosaurs were endotherms—like us.

His surety ignited a decades-long controversy about everything from the cellular structure of bone to foraging physiology to predator-prey ratios in fossil dinosaur communities. In the end, arguments against the idea that the largest dinos were endothermic were the very ones supporting the notion that smaller, fast-running, and flying dinosaurs had to be so. Buoyed by recent discoveries of feathered, birdlike theropods that preceded the evolution of flight, scientists are now in almost universal agreement that birds are the closest living relatives of dinosaurs and thus other archosaurs. This paraphyletic interpretation places crocodilians closer to birds than to other living "reptiles" and pushes the certainty of endothermy in at least some dinosaurs farther back in time.

With our view of pelicans skimming the ocean, buzzards on a carcass, or rheas thundering across the pampas now fundamentally swayed by archosaurian overtones, it seems a fault of collective human logic that this link was denied for so long. That is, until you contrast marauding theropods like *Tyrannosaurus* with the hummingbird sucking nectar at your backyard feeder and consider the conundrum that flight threw into the equation.

The problem began in 1862 with *Archaeopteryx lithographica,* the winged, feathered, stunningly preserved Upper Jurassic fossil from Germany's Solnhofen limestones. Largely saurian skeletal elements made it the perfect intermediary between birds and reptiles—the most famous "missing link" of all times. Although recent fossil evidence largely confirms that feathers evolved for warmth in fast-running, vision-oriented theropods and flight was secondarily achieved, like other watersheds this idea was a hard sell. Unwilling to accept that Tweetie might be related to those loud, obnoxious theropods that lived down Fossil Road, for years ornithologists attempted to scuttle the bird–dinosaur theory.

But whether flight was a ground-up or top-down phenomenon is moot. Birds are dinosaurs are reptiles. And if scientists weren't such territorial boneheads, we would have figured that out long ago. Although most prefer to ignore the implication, herpetologists are de facto ornithologists, while ornithologists are simply herpetologists in denial. So if you *really* want to teach children about evolution, you'll need to stuff a few plastic birds into those cereal boxes with the dinosaurs.

10

SAVING THE WORLD A JUNGLE AT A TIME

Curiosity was a form of lust,

a wandering cupidity of the eye and mind.

JOHN CROWLEY, "Of Marvels and Monsters," *Washington Post*

I REMEMBER THE moment I realized just how dangerous the company I kept actually was.

It was in a walk-up chophouse overlooking Hoan Kiem Lake in the musty core of old Hanoi. Five Royal Fish featured a rather catholic menu by local standards (meaning it didn't specialize in dog, monkey, or snake) and was thus frequented by a growing tide of foreign flotsam littering the shores of the new Vietnam, a Communist enclave of former austerity now rifting with some 75 million nascent consumers. Convoys of businessmen and their diplomat proxies were increasingly looking to dock in Hanoi, and Five Royal Fish was a de facto wharf.

Famished from a long day in a fetid hotel room pickling specimens collected by our joint Canadian-Russian expedition, I'd been plowing head-down through heaping plates of steamed mustard greens, garlic chicken, and deep-fried pork rolls, chasing it with quarts of Tiger Beer and fastidiously ignoring the swirling tales of drunken frog conquest in distant rice paddies.

But when talk turned to the irresistible macabre of snakebite, I'd tuned in.

Nikolai "Kolya" Orlov, burly curatorial technician at the Zoological Institute of the Russian Academy of Sciences, stared at the noticeably notched end of a middle finger and explained through mouthfuls of carp how he'd once been bitten by a viper of genus *Calloselasma* in Vietnam's Central Highlands, a million miles from anywhere. The snake had struck through a bag he was holding.

Professor Emeritus Ilya Darevsky, esteemed doyen of Russian herpetology and Nikolai's boss, held up the attenuated and permanently hooked digit where he'd once found a deadly Levantine Viper (*Macrovipera lebetina*) dangling by a fang as it pumped venom deep into the tissue. He wasn't able to recall precise details, but then Darevsky, whose encyclopedic knowledge was offset by absentmindedness, could be missing half a hand and not remember, or care, how he'd lost it.

Beside me, Dr. Bob, the man responsible for this messy synod, nodded smirking assent while clutching chopsticks with his own misshapen index finger, courtesy of some carelessness with a Black-tailed Rattlesnake (*Crotalus molossus*). That bite had led to a frantic drive-for-life to the nearest hospital, an arm that turned black and swelled to the size of a watermelon, and, so he claimed, lifelong allergies to everything except beer. In the practiced, acidic manner he employed for emphasis, Bob recited the litany of people he knew who'd lost life and limb to snakebite.

It might have been the critical mass of gathered tales that hastened my epiphany. It might have been toxic levels of MSG. Or maybe I'd just wised up. But at Five Royal Fish I'd finally understood, with no little horror, that if I continued playing *Wheel of Misfortune* with these maniacs, I could be next. Also clear was that my death would *not* be a paving stone on the road to saving the world's biological resources but simply another demonstration of human fallibility; an exercise in head-shaking stupidity destined for inclusion in *The Darwin Awards,* offering endless amusement to those straddling the toilets on which such books were inevitably thumbed.

I'd been a Johnny-come-lately when it came to jungle work—which isn't to say that when Dr. Bob asked me to join this 1994 expedition to the lost forests of Vietnam I wasn't ready. I was. Ready to observe former colleagues in my new guise as a journalist. But expeditions, like wars, have a way of pressing experienced bodies into service. All too soon on that tour of duty I was back in the thick of it, catching, identifying, and preserving animals. Home on the range. Despite pathological levels of stress, I looked for all the world as though I'd been doing it forever. But inside I was less certain. Was I a writer? Was I a scientist? Or just a nervous wreck doomed to pen stories about what happens when a bag of cobras lands in your lap?

I JOLTED AWAKE when my head was pile-driven into the roof of the van. Moans and curses erupted from the churning darkness: luggage was everywhere, and a laundry duffel had hemorrhaged its fetid contents over my shoulders; empty beer cans, jars, nets, and snake sticks rattled under the seats.

Grinding through the remote mountains of North Vietnam, we were midway through a five-week trip on one of the worst roads yet. Though only recently accessible, the area was already a media sensation after a new species of living bovid (the group of ungulates that includes cattle and buffalo) had been discovered there. Scientists called it *Pseudoryx nghetinhensis,* but the denizen of steep, thickly forested mountains was simply *Sao la* to the indigenous Thai minority who shared its home. Given that it sounded like a menu item and was most frequently found in jungle cookpots, I fancied the name had to do with how it tasted.

Pulling this dream expedition together had been tough, but like many of his pie-in-the-sky ideas, Dr. Bob had prevailed, and so here we were, slinging along in the belly of the beast with jungle veterans Darevsky and Orlov, plus ROM entomologist Doug Currie, a slight, wisecracking Albertan with a penchant for dry understatement and blackflies—a natural pairing. At this juncture, however, the dream felt more like a nightmare. I peeled someone's snakeshit-soaked T-shirt off my face and glanced around: Bob was festooned with a Japanese tour bus's worth of camera gear while Doug warily plucked a bag of agitated cobras from his lap where they'd landed and handed them to Kolya.

"I believe these are yours," he said, shutting his eyes to resume slack-armed emulation of a bobble-head Buddha.

Kolya reached over, rolled his eyes, and exhaled through puffed-out cheeks, his permanently placed toothpick resembling a pin puncturing a balloon. He knotted the bag tighter and dropped it at his feet.

Eyeglasses askew and hands clamped firmly on the seat ahead, Ilya continued humming along to the cheesy Russian version of "Those Were the Days" making its tenth round on the tape deck. Up front, ever-clueless guide Xiang rubbed the swelling egg on his windshield-weary forehead while driver Hai, cigarette glued to his lower lip, stared intently into the blackness, occasionally swerving to avoid random villagers strolling the hard-packed road in the dark.

Slapstick as it seemed, our modern voyage paid no small tribute to those who'd gone before: seven men crammed in a tiny vessel, sailing the uncharted waters of one of the earth's last frontiers, where a fortuitous but fleeting confluence of politics, history, and geology sheltered remnants of a magnificent forest in which nameless creatures roamed for the naming. Although the van felt more like a ship of pasty-white fools adrift in a sea of dangerous green, its bug-eyed occupants and witch's brew cargo (take your pick on which was which) doing nothing to dispel the comic veneer, ours was a decidedly serious enterprise: at a time when Western biologists were jostling to be first to enter Vietnam's unexplored world of wonders, we'd slipped to the front of the line. The lure of new species was a Holy Grail to most biologists, so it was the prospect of finding a herp equivalent of Sao la that propelled us through the night jungle.

SUNRISE FOUND US in the hill station of Tam Dao, autumn's first rain pulsing along its ridges on a wind from China. One of several isolated mountaintop forests we would visit, Tam Dao was an eerie place. Wisps of fog streamed through the canopy, occasionally dissipating to reveal where forest had reclaimed the ruins of summer homes that French colonials torched during their 1954 retreat from the country to avoid ceding them to Vietnamese hands.

After a day of snoozing and hallucination-filled dreams fueled by our weekly dose of malaria meds, we snapped on headlamps and ventured into a darkness dominated by the car-alarm wails of giant tree crickets. Ilya hummed as he flicked geckos from the walls of abandoned houses with a collapsible pole. Doug vacuumed up insects attracted to the black light of a Canadian Tire bug zapper and entertained a steady stream of children shilling jars of etherized beetles, centipedes, and scorpions they'd caught in can-traps baited with human shit. Bob and Kolya disappeared up one jungle stream while I waded into the chest-deep waters of another.

When we reconvened after midnight, between us we'd turned up a dozen different frogs, various lizards and snakes, a Tam Dao Warty Newt (*Paramesotriton deloustali*, an exceedingly rare salamander found only here), several strange tadpoles, and a caecilian that was very likely a new species. Unfortunately, the evening's true prize was lost; Kolya had scooped up an enigmatic new snake only to find that the bag he'd placed it in had a hole. Loss aside, it was a promising start.

Like the desert, the jungle took getting used to. At first every animal seemed to resemble a leaf or twig; frogs, snakes, lizards, and insects found abundant and creative ways to pass themselves off as vegetative matter. Endless paradoxes beat back expectations: there were snakes that looked like worms and worms that looked like snakes and lizards that looked like both. But what really made our headlamps spin was the incredible diversity of frogs.

Tam Dao had been scoured early in the century by the French herpetologist René Bourret. Kolya, most familiar with Bourret's voluminous work, dutifully answered our taxonomic questions about frogs but seldom offered a scientific name without adding the modifier "complex," as in "Ees member of *Rana nigrovittata* complex." This I knew to be basic biologese for "I have no clue what it is." Such ambiguity emanating from an expert spoke to how little was known about Vietnam's frogs in even well-studied areas.

Biologists in the twentieth century had little opportunity to work the remote interiors of Indochina because of regional conflicts following the disintegration of French colonialism. As North Vietnam closed up under Ho Chi Minh's Communists, its forests were effectively locked away. Even after the American war, when Eastern Bloc interests flooded Vietnam, the area saw little outside biological interest. All that changed in 1992, when *Pseudoryx* sent shockwaves through the biological community: how could a large, hoofed animal have remained anonymous this long? Described only from skin and bones and yet to be seen alive by scientists, Sao la was a top hit in the media, but its true significance was often overlooked.

"Sure, large animals are newsworthy," Bob explained, "but what it *really* showed was a dire need for detailed surveys—there could be anything out there."

Dr. Bob had actually planned fieldwork in the country before the discovery of *Pseudoryx*, securing official contacts and a crucial invitation. The Russian-Canadian partnership evolved because the ROM had the means and the Russians the ways; Darevsky's godlike stature in Communist scientific circles would open doors, and the ROM would finance the expedition. Darevsky's previous finds here raised expectations that new species would pop up like mushrooms after rain. Currie also anticipated a bonanza; only a fraction of the earth's insect fauna was known, and Vietnam's claim of five thousand species was likely off by an order of magnitude.

Biodiversity may have been the buzzword of the '90s, but it still frequently begged definition. To the public, it meant saving rain forests and Giant Pandas, but to biologists it was a yardstick of ecosystem health as measured by its mix of animal and plant species. As such, biodiversity tie-ins offered a way to get research funded, earn a reputation, or keep a career alive. You had but to ring the biodiversity bell to see biologists salivate like a squadron of Pavlovian nerds. In post-*Pseudoryx* Vietnam, the number of scientific parties vying for entry spawned legions of proposals—including one by the French to round up live Sao la with a blimp—leaving the Vietnamese both starry-eyed and nervous.

The country needed some kind of traffic cop to deal with the mess, and that person was Cao Van Sung—decorated colonel of the North Vietnamese army, Moscow-trained mammalogist, friend to Darevsky, and veteran of the Russian-Vietnamese cooperation pact. A diminutive man with tiny hands and hyperdrive mind, Sung was usually found with a '50s-era phone and sheaf of papers in hand, flying around his office at the Institute for Ecology and Biological Resource [*sic*] in Hanoi, where he brokered a steady stream of foreign delegations with a typically North Vietnamese demeanor—happy, outward looking, amazingly unresentful of the traumas foisted upon his country. Sung was also eminently practical, with a keen sense of opportunity. When the biological caravans beelining to Vietnam's forests shifted from creaking Eastern Bloc carts to upscale Western wheels, they brought something Sung's institute desperately needed. At a mountaintop Buddhist shrine in Ba Vi National Park, where we lit incense and meditated (sort of), Sung made no bones about his desire to secure outside funding for Vietnamese biology, and he even had a sense of humor about it.

"You must pray for successful expedition," he'd laughed. "I pray only for money."

AFTER WEEKS OF bouncing around the countryside, we reached our ultimate goal of the North Truong Son Range. We knew it was the right 'hood in the village of Con Cuong, where wide-eyed children, mobbing the first whites they'd ever seen on the dusty main drag, led us to the horns of a young *Pseudoryx* adorning the wall of a tiny café. While we uttered exclamations of near-worship and clambered over each other to behold the fabled beast's remains, vacant stares from café patrons put our ludicrous fawning into perspective. To them, Sao la was nothing new—just another forest animal they'd hunted and eaten for generations with no less zeal than any other.

In a country of backwaters, Con Cuong stood out as a genuine frontier town. Maybe because it squatted amid the strangely detached, towering limestone eruptions that gathered slowly westward into mountains; maybe because it sat in the sun-baked open abutting cool, dense jungle; or perhaps because the convoluted border with Laos—and hence the river of conspiracy known as the Ho Chi Minh Trail—meandered through the whole mess like a centerline painted by a drunk. Certainly the place boiled with the illicit air that comes with smuggling and surreptitious military activity.

As a result, inhabitants were wary of outsiders. In the market, where Dr. Bob and I were taking in local color and cuisine, a shrewlike policeman pointed his baton at Bob's camera and held out his hand for the film. In an amazing sleight of hand, Bob pulled an unexposed roll from his pocket and peeled it from its cartridge in such a way that it appeared to spool from the back of the camera. This satisfied the petty tyrant, who'd made a show of rousting foreigners in front of a crowd. Such scenes played out for days until protracted negotiations with officials—who viewed our Hanoi documents with the kind of deep suspicion that required deep pockets to dispel—yielded permission to enter the forest.

The logging camp we landed in on the Khe Moi River proved another herpetological mother lode, where every night yielded a new frog or two. Darevsky-trained herpetologist Xiang would look at each, shake his head in bewilderment, and defer to Ilya, who inevitably commented, "Ees eenterestink, but I do not know . . . " Kolya—who'd usually caught the beast—would laugh and rub his hands gleefully, "Somethink new?"

Most new forms required laboratory analysis back in Toronto to ferret out. The Khe Moi's frogs played every morphological game going, and several "cryptic" species were difficult to distinguish from each other. Cryptic species may or may not be related but share a basic body plan, color, or pattern and often live in the same area and do similar things; nature allows this overlap because of minute differences in ecological niche (like the two *Desmognathus* in Chapter 8). On the Khe Moi, the winning fall fashion statement was medium-sized brown frog with a black eye-mask. Up to four species displaying this morphology bred in the river, distinguishable only by their different calls, egg-laying sites, belly color, or internal anatomy.

Mimicry is a special case of crypsis where the imitator derives benefit from its ruse. There were at least two such mimics among the cascade frogs that perched on the sides of stream gorges. One, a highly toxic, bullfrog-sized animal that killed anything it was put in a bag with, occurred in either a brown mottled version or a shimmering green-backed morph, and separate mimics existed for each. The mottled imitator was as large as its model, but the green-backed impersonator was much smaller than its subject—just as the Viceroy Butterfly is dwarfed by the foul-tasting Monarch it resembles. Color and pattern are the key to mimicry. Even crude approximation of a toxic species' warning coloration is enough to deter a predator. Nature's logic thus accounts for the plethora of nonvenomous imitators of deadly coral snakes, whether the ophidian artist is faithful to the original or barely pulls it off.

Cascade frogs were adept at the same-but-different game of crypsis and mimicry, but, as with one species' mottled and green morphs, also demonstrated the different-but-same vibe of polymorphism, where species benefit from occurring in different forms—the evolutionary equivalent of not putting all your eggs in one basket. The Indochinese Vine Snake (*Ahaetulla prasina*), a cat-eyed, point-nosed, sinuous wraith, was another such species. Vine snakes came in blue, yellow, green, or various combinations that made them indistinguishable from a range of drooping vegetation. The stealthy, lizard-gobbling species thus occupied a wider range of the jungle's rich catalogue of micro-habitats than could a single color variant; in practical terms this adaptation meant you couldn't make it far through the bush without being slapped in the face by what seemed innocent vine. Fortunately, it rarely bit.

IT WASN'T THE biological Club Med of a well-equipped field station in Costa Rica, but on sunny days when the river ran clear, before the water was sullied by buffalo and log-skidders wakened from bong-induced naps, Camp Khe Moi felt like a low-rent tropical resort. Birds and frogs called from giant arrowheads bobbing on improbably slender stems, and butterflies tumbled through the hot clearing where we played Frisbee, a distant trumpeting of elephants the only sign that we weren't poolside in the Bahamas.

At the same time, reminders to the contrary abounded: the camp mutt we'd been served for dinner; tarantulas the kitchen matron hand-peeled from posts in the dining area, gathering their legs above their backs like a hairy switch; the geekfest of dressing for nightly excursions in Tilley hats and floral-print leech socks we'd had made street-side in Hanoi; and a constant stream of shadowy poachers that materialized and then disappeared along the river like phantoms. The jungle also harbored many salient warnings to watch your step. And one day, walking a trail with Ilya, came another sign we weren't in Kansas anymore.

Darevsky headed the Laboratory of Ornithology and Herpetology at the Russian Academy of Sciences. His broad research interests included parthenogenesis and polyploidy in higher vertebrates, phenomena he had first uncovered in 1957 in a group of Caucasian rock lizards. That development had stimulated a rash of similar research globally—including the discovery of unisexual *Ambystoma*—making Darevsky a leader in a new branch of herpetology focused on the hybrid origins of clonal reptiles.

I had devoured his work as a graduate student, and traveling with him was unparalleled privilege. A virtual fountain of information, Darevsky approached everything with childlike wonder. On our first day together, he'd taken me to a sewer canal behind our Hanoi hotel to demonstrate how to properly wrangle angry, nonvenomous snakes. Reaching into the fetid soup, he'd pulled out a watersnake of genus *Enhydris;* grasping its tail, he whipped it back between his legs, shut them, and quickly pulled the snake through until its jawbones were between his legs, preventing it from biting; then he reached around to safely grasp the clamped head and opened his legs to release the body. *Da.*

I was nothing approaching a peer, but we would often take short walks together, during which he asked as many questions as I did. Strolling a sun-dappled trail beside the Khe Moi, I stopped to peel leeches from my bleeding foot when Ilya began gesturing wildly, finger to his lips. Ahead, in a shaft of sunlight, stretched fully four meters across the trail and draped over a boulder was the dog-lip-black body of an enormous snake.

"Ees Kink Khobra sleepink," Ilya whispered, clutching my shoulder for emphasis. "We khatch!"

Now, I'll admit to an unhealthy childhood obsession with

the serpent-deity of Asian mythology, but I'll also admit that when I was facing the real thing, stampeding cowardice swiftly flattened fantasy. We carried no snake tongs or bags, and visions of wrestling a four-meter snake packing enough venom to kill several elephants provided a powerful reality check. I suddenly had no interest in King Cobras.

"No way," I'd replied, backing down the trail. "Okay," Ilya hissed, "then you make peekchoor." He pressed the shutter of an invisible camera.

That seemed wiser—maintain respectful distance and bag the beast with a two-hundred-millimeter telephoto. But as I lined up the shot, the cobra's head suddenly shot up in panic, and I was shocked to see Ilya's seventy-year-old body, arms outstretched, fly through the viewfinder. In one quick spasm the snake heaved its massive body forward and flowed into the jungle like an oily stream of liquid death. I stared at Ilya in disbelief.

"Snake wake up but I khannot khatch," he said, shrugging as innocently as a kid who'd dropped a fly ball.

THEY SAY JUNGLES are the lungs of the earth, a metaphor for the equatorial photosynthetic machine that inhales our respiratory waste during the day and exhales life-giving oxygen at night. Spend time in one and you feel the rhythm: days can be oppressive, with little stirring; night, in contrast, reverberates with surreptitious industry. The forest comes alive, and only then do you understand its complexity—a web of suspicion where every animal fears every other in a conspiracy to climb the food chain. You gain perspective on this dynamic wading a jungle stream: malaria-dealing mosquitoes buzz in your ears; the green eyes of giant hunting spiders flash in your headlamp; hungry leeches reach from the tips of overhanging branches; camouflaged tree vipers lurk everywhere. Basically, you're glad you're not a frog.

But being human isn't always fun, either. Khe Moi was crawling with aggressively territorial King Cobras whose semaphore was an abundance of shed skins (I got the message). Worse, our bunkhouse harbored a dozen highly venomous Banded Kraits: a rat had chewed a hole in a sackful Kolya had stashed under a sleeping platform, loosing into our midst a Jekyll-and-Hyde species that feigned docility in daylight and transformed into an agitated, lashing monster at night.

This critical mass of serpents posed a certain objective hazard, but smaller organisms were taking the biggest toll. Fevers, diarrhea, and vomiting made the rounds as unfamiliar microorganisms found their way in and out of our guts. Currie developed a severely infected eye that swelled shut, oozed puss, and threatened his vision. Soil roundworms burrowed into the soles of our feet, flatworm larvae left our legs covered in swimmer's itch, and biting insects pierced exposed skin while fungus took root on any that remained covered for more than a day. Tenacious terrestrial leeches sucked merrily on weakening veins, leaving bug-attracting streams of blood running down our necks and legs. We were, quite literally, being eaten alive.

We pressed on, of course, believing that the biodiversity work was a vital contribution to the country's way forward. But any notion that Vietnam's isolation or recent signatory status to the 123-nation Convention on International Trade in Endangered Species (CITES) could protect Sao la or other fauna evaporated like dew one evening on the Khe Moi.

Wading several kilometers upriver just before dusk, I'd rounded a bend to find a clutch of men huddled around a fire on a sandbar and radiating conspiracy. Behind them sat a brace of rifles and bamboo-frame packs lashed with the dried bodies of gibbons, critically endangered primates under the highest level of protection. The gibbons' sardonic death masks were hauntingly human and particularly specter-like given that it was Halloween. Closing ranks around a tobacco-and-opium bong, the men fastidiously avoided eye contact as I waded past ludicrously pretending not to notice. If Indochina's remaining forests were an animal gold mine, then lawless, isolated outposts like the Khe Moi were places where CITES was meaningless. The miners would make their way downriver by night to Con Cuong, where their booty would be traded along a pipeline to China, the smelter into which the vast majority of the planet's illegally obtained wildlife flowed.

Despite CITES, Vietnamese markets were full of putatively protected animals, restaurants specialized in them, and even the gift shop at the Hanoi airport brimmed with animal contraband. The good news was that our presence—educating where and when we could without interfering with traditional lifestyles—would actually prove helpful. Dr. Bob eventually made a dozen forays to various parts of Vietnam, and each built on the goodwill of the last to bring increased awareness. There was no dearth of outside interest waiting in the wings to help Vietnamese conservation—both philanthropic, like the World Wildlife Fund, and symbiotic, like us, uncovering marketable scientific fodder to provide Vietnam with international leverage.

The Vietnamese were also justifiably wary and didn't want to get burned by short-term glory hogs panning for nuggets in their biological gold mine. What they wanted were real links to the world's foremost academic institutions and money to develop their own science. Without cash for implementation and enforcement, jungles and their animal citizens would continue to evaporate. It wasn't twilight on the Khe Moi just yet, however, and the forest still vibrated with possibility.

My most burning memory came one evening while returning to camp. As I followed the loggers' highest trail, something caught my eye in the dusk at the bottom of a gully. Squinting, I traced the outline of an animal; a meter at the shoulder and half-again as long, a dark form broken by bright lines around the face, black horns drawn straight back like tapered spindles. Or was it just branches, shadow play, and wishful thinking? After all, no Westerner had seen one in the wild; the beast was a zoological phantom—skin and bones in a museum drawer. Chuckling, I took a step downhill, and my stomach dropped. The Sao la turned to look for only a second, the white of its eye glowing like a pearl. Then, hooves churning through the underbrush, it charged up an invisible trail.

IN THE SUMMER of 1997 I was as lost as I'd ever been. Separated from my wife of eight years, with a young child as bewildered as her parents about what was happening, I'd given up a high-profile magazine job in California to return to Toronto.

Back home, things seemed better. I was healthy, fit, surrounded by friends, making a good living, and living near a vibrant daughter with whom I had a wonderfully close relationship. Still, all I could see was bleakness. Defeat appeared on every horizon, a malevolent sun behind red clouds of guilt. Blown marriage. Broken home. Everything in storage. Living with my parents. Mirrors reflected the image of a man who was clearly afraid. Afraid of his failures. Afraid of the future. Afraid, it seemed, of unavoidable truth. Who was I? *What* was I?

With no answers forthcoming, I'd worn my wavering sense of self like blinking neon. Maybe that's why Dr. Bob insisted I return to Vietnam with him. The scene of previous scientific and journalistic triumphs for both of us, it was also fraught with extreme difficulty and persistent danger; I wasn't sure. Dr. Bob, father to three daughters and long since divorced himself, saw things differently: when career success, good friends, and wonderful children can't override your funk, then stifling heat, leeches, malaria, amoebic dysentery, deadly snakes, Communist bureaucrats, and tribal militias will surely bitch-slap you out of it. As usual, Bob's reasoning seemed a prescription for disaster. But maybe he knew something I didn't.

When I consented to a return mission in September 1997, with an assignment to shoot a series of documentaries, my inner adventurer was once again keen and my inner worrywart not so worried. Bob had now been there six times, and the pioneering nature of that first arduous trip was surely well behind. We'd have it wired.

As it turned out, the only thing Bob had wired was how much money we would need to navigate Communist bureaucracy. As we headed south from Hanoi toward the Central Highlands, officials in town after town lightened the hefty briefcase we were schlepping full of *dong*—an anachronistic currency requiring a fistful of bills to buy a stick of gum.

In Hanoi, we'd checked in with Sung, whose job was to help smooth the way with local committees, police, and military in the countryside.

"Everything no problem," he'd chirped, pushing a pile of paperwork constellated with official stamps across his desk, a phrase I knew to mean, "You're screwed!"

In the hinterlands, our Hanoi letters were once again treated as missives from Mars—officials simply laughed. Our dealings worked better once we stuffed Sung's wad of documents into the briefcase full of dong. We drank a lot of tea and did a lot of negotiating, measuring progress south in centimeters. In one town, feverish and sick, we were even placed under house arrest for a week awaiting permission to enter the jungle, unusual even for this cloistered and heavily militarized country. Something was afoot. Then suddenly, they let us go with blessings to explore a nearby forest.

We set up camp in an abandoned sawmill abutting a small, stilt-raised village. The Banai, a colorful nomadic mountain people adept at slashing, burning, and bolting—when they weren't sipping nasty fermented rice from earthenware barrels through bamboo straws—brought creatures in from the forest that we could never hope to find: phantasmagorical frogs variously imitating moss, birdshit (honestly), or the forest floor—the last sporting horns resembling the upturned tips of dried leaves.

The Banai always knew what kind of animals they were dealing with, but the ethnic Vietnamese often did not; a King Cobra mimic they brought in, thinking it was real, fooled even Kolya to the tune of $50. Bob had learned never to trust local identifications—too many harmless snakes resembled death dealers and vice versa. Every snake was treated as if it were a menace, removed from any bag before it was pinned and handled with proper equipment. Our caution hit home in September 2001, when Joe Slowinski, a thirty-eight-year-old herpetologist from the California Academy of Sciences, lost his life after trusting a local assistant in the jungles of Myanmar. Expedition member and friend Mark Moffett recounted the incident:

> Joe's Burmese field assistant, U Htun Win, held out a snake bag. "I think it's a *Dinodon*," he was saying. Joe extended his right hand into the bag. When it reappeared, a pencil-thin, gray-banded snake swung from the base of his middle finger. "That's a fucking krait," Joe said. He pulled off the snake and kneaded the bitten area, seemingly unmarked, with a fingernail.

Other scientists have been known to cut off their finger at such a moment. Joe sat down to join the rest of us for breakfast at a long wooden school table, joking about his thick skin... Snakes of the genus *Dinodon* are harmless, but some are near-perfect mimics of the multibanded krait (*Bungarus multicinctus*), a cousin of the cobra and much more deadly.[17]

A lengthy drama ensued in which Joe, far from rescue, failed to receive any medical attention. After twenty-nine hours of desperate artificial respiration and CPR by expedition members, the krait's paralyzing neurotoxins finally did him in. Joe's body was cremated in the jungle he loved. The scene Mark described was so eerily familiar that my mind kept replacing Joe's face with each of ours. His final morning had been like every single one in our jungle camps. Mornings when each of us might for any reason have been momentarily imprudent and died just as easily.

Dangers aside, finding new species fast became a local industry with the Banai, who were happy to make more money for their efforts than they'd ever seen. The tribe celebrated its good fortune one day with a feast and procession led by a naked, one-armed war veteran and perpetual drunk. Winding through the village, they chanted and banged traditional bronze gongs, skin drums, and hollow bamboo; children sang and women in color-trimmed indigo skirts pounded grain in giant stone mortars with huge wooden pestles. We all drank nasty rice beer, and spirits were high when the first raindrops from the latest typhoon chased us back to our respective shelters.

While we waited out the deluge, word about how helpful the Banai were being in guiding us to secluded areas traveled the jungle grapevine back to town. A stone-faced army captain showed up, stepping from his jeep with a riding crop under his arm like a modern-day Rommel while a minion held an umbrella over him. Thinking this an official visit to congratulate us on our work, Bob was an hour into polite tea drinking and translating when the captain stood, thanked him, and announced we had twenty-four hours to pack up.

From the back of the dump truck they sent us packing in, we saw what they were hiding: a huge illegal logging operation. Like most prohibitions, a government clampdown had actually increased the activity tenfold. As if this weren't bad enough, we also saw endangered wildlife on sale everywhere during a fitful train ride back to Hanoi.

"Not to worry," said Sung, whose pragmatic approach to East–West scientific cooperation included salvaging expeditions. This extra service would, however, cost us. "I send you primary forest northeast of here, near China," he declared, counting out a stack of dong higher than he was. "Many new creature. OK?"

OK, we'd said, but was the army there, too? Sure, he answered, but they're nicer.

At least they weren't hiding a logging operation, as there was fuck-all left to cut on the mostly bare hills surrounding the small village we arrived in. Skeptical of any biological mother lode in this quasi-wasteland, we were pleasantly surprised to find that Sung's promised bio-bonanza was real: in pockets of forest we hiked several hours to reach, we found new species of frogs, lizards, and snakes. Kolya, who knew as much as there was to know about Asian snakes, pulled a species of *Oligodon* he'd never seen before from a hole in a blank rock face with his trusty tongs, throwing one hand up in faux exasperation as he held the snake in the other.

"I do not know thees," he declared. "Ees fantastic. *Fantastic* new snake."

We were excited, and so was Ninh, our new guide. Like others before him, Ninh was unfamiliar with the jungle. Worse, he was a botanist who knew nothing about animals; he carelessly flirted with dangerous snakes we were photographing, stepped on them in the forest, and stumbled into ponds, paddies, and mudholes. He managed to get not only us but also our native trackers lost. He got drunk one night, then fed us endangered, MSG-soaked eagle he'd had the trackers blow out of the canopy while our host, Mai, a decorated soldier and hobby taxidermist, stuffed the carcass in a back room packed with wire-stiffened squirrels and the giant, cat-sized tree rats that pounced on us nightly. Ninh was trying to kill us. He couldn't, of course, because we were too stupid too die.

"*Ninh!*" I finally screamed, nerves frazzled after a run-in with a particularly aggressive, two-meter krait he'd grabbed by the tail with frightening nonchalance. "Don't touch *anything* dangerous unless it's a plant, OK?" Minutes later he was sporting burning skin welts from some alkaloid-addled shrub he thought I wanted to see.

On our final night, the group split up. Amy Lathrop, Murphy's latest PhD student, and I took Ninh down one ridge while the others followed an adjacent one. The plan was to meet up in the intervening stream. Naturally, Ninh got us lost. Crawling on hands and knees through dense bamboo thicket trying to find our way out, we encountered a specimen of the alarmingly agile tree viper *Protobothrops mucrosquamatus*. But as the delicate brown-and-gold-banded serpent wound through the tangled brush, we were unable to maneuver our snake sticks effectively enough to catch it. Suddenly the snake dropped to the jungle floor, where, sensing no escape, it charged us with head held menacingly aloft.

With sweat dripping into her eyes, Amy managed to pin the meter-long beast to the ground. I held open a bag with shaking hands and weakening bladder while she dropped the writhing creature, translucent fangs glistening under my headlamp, into the sack with tongs no longer than chopsticks. For once Ninh kept his distance.

After the dramatic capture, Amy knotted the snake bag and dropped it into my backpack, and we continued our search for the streambed.

Like a scene from some cheesy action-adventure flick, we soon found ourselves hurtling down a slick, vine-covered slope. Sliding out of control toward the valley floor, we dodged thick, looping lianas that threatened to twist our ankles like chicken joints. The slope was studded with razor-sharp bamboo courtesy of log skidders who'd carved the flume from dense brush. Amy and I exchanged curses as we shot past, words swallowed by the rapid-fire snapping of twigs, crackling leaf litter, and cascading rock.

When we finally splashed down into the appointed gorge, the group showed little sympathy—they were well into a show-and-tell session. We quickly joined in, unbagging our nifty *Protobothrops*.

"Humph," snorted Kolya with contempt, fishing one out of his own bag ahead of an assortment of snakes topped by a hefty Banded Krait. "Now *thees* ees snake."

And this was where childhood obsessions, high-school hobbies, and decades of university education had landed us all: my sure-to-kill-you snake is better than yours. In the way of any black humor, all you could really do was laugh.

As I stood soaked in sweat, creepy bird-sized crane flies brushing my face and accidental death clutched in every surrounding hand, I wondered whether I'd splashed down in heaven or hell. One thing was sure—my divorce was as far from my mind as it could be.

Dr. Bob was right again.

· · (11) · ·

ODE TO A GARTERSNAKE

Arguably we know more about the common garter snake . . .

than any other snake in the world.

DOUGLAS A. ROSSMAN, NEIL B. FORD, and RICHARD A. SEIGEL,
The Garter Snakes: Evolution and Ecology

As I stepped from the simple muck of my boreal comfort
zone into the desert or jungle's philosophical quicksands,
one thing had become clear: most of the hard-to-deal-with stuff
didn't happen in the pastoral reaches of the Great White North.

There were some similarities—road driving, for instance—
but these were outnumbered by the many salient differences.
Given the north's sharp seasonality, we were inexorably tied to
the rhythms of the land—summer dispersal patterns and habitat usage, fall feeding binges, descents into winter hibernacula,
and explosive spring breeding aggregations. Springtime, in particular, went beyond the literary cliché of rebirth: to this day I
can't drive or ski past a frozen pond without wondering what
kind of party ice-off might bring.

The image of the polite Canadian resonates even within the
international herp community, which, until ROMMY, was given
to viewing us as their most reserved cousins: we were indeed far
more likely than our American counterparts to study pedestrian

issues like range limits, cold tolerance, and hibernation physiology. This tendency made sense given that Canada's herpetological landscape was charmingly predictable—most common names sporting the subspecific prefix "Northern," as in Northern Water Snake, Northern Green Frog, and so on.

Beyond constraints of extreme latitude and climate, however, much of the country's wilds harbored surprisingly large populations of reptiles and amphibians. And despite the paucity of venomous serpents (the now rare Massasauga Rattlesnake in Ontario and the Prairie (*Crotalus viridis*) and Pacific (*C. oreganus*) Rattlesnakes, whose northernmost ranges peter out in those respective areas), you could still get into at least some trouble. Like rubbing your eye after picking up a poisonous Rough-skinned Newt (*Taricha granulosa*) on Vancouver Island so that the eye went numb and didn't work for hours; or having a twenty-kilo snapping turtle latch onto your waders and back into deep water. Or easing down into one of Manitoba's celebrated snake pits to marvel at thousands of Red-sided Gartersnakes (*Thamnophis sirtalis parietalis*) merrily doing it in a hole the size of a hot tub, only to find you couldn't climb out because your shoes were slippery with their foul-smelling shit. Believe me, I knew.

THE WORLD-FAMOUS SNAKE pits of Narcisse, Manitoba, are truly one of the Seven Wonders of the Herpetological World. Imagine fifty thousand snakes in your living room and you get the picture. One look could kill an Italian gardener.

I'd first heard of them as a kid, maybe seen a sketchy picture in a newspaper, but I wasn't truly prepared for the spectacle. My first April at the ROM I drove to Manitoba to collect salamanders; when I stopped in Winnipeg to jaw with celebrated prairie herpetologist Bill Preston (Randy Mooi's predecessor at the

Manitoba Museum) about where the best egg-filled ditches might be, he rattled off locations that charted a northeast vector away from the city when I'd expected to be pointed southeast. Why that way? So that you can see the snake pits, he said. Ya *gotta* see the snake pits.

And I did. Not *la vraie chose,* it turned out, but a reasonable facsimile. On my way to Narcisse, when I pulled off to investigate a pond-filled quarry, snakes surged ahead of my footsteps in densities greater than the rattlers of Isla Tortuga, drawing me to a large sinkhole where hundreds of their brethren poked from holes or hung from chalky blocks of limestone, soaking up the sun. I climbed down to take a few shots of modest-sized mating balls—a dozen or so small males swarming a lone, larger female—and was shocked to have trouble extracting myself, cracking the camera and my face on the rock in attempts to scramble out. After I finally escaped the prospect of spending a night curled up in a snakeshit tomb, the day grew cold and I had no time to press on toward the Narcisse mother lode; I vowed to return one day and honor Preston's entreat.

A hearty spring aggregation of near-north snakes has a lot to say about boreal adaptation, sexual gamesmanship, and the chemosensory aspects of migration and mating, but at the time it simply added another dimension to the love-at-first-bite relationship I'd conducted with gartersnakes since that fateful day at Camp Mil-da-la-ca. I wasn't alone in this long-running affair, as several visits to the nerd-fest of *gartersnake.info* have shown me. Without any of the powers or mystique of the cobra going for it, what is it about this snake that has hold of our psyches?

To start, whether you brand it lowly, ubiquitous, or multifarious, the gartersnake is the serpent most familiar to the general public in most of North America. It lives at all but the most restrictive latitudes, in all but subzero conditions, and in virtually every terrestrial and aquatic habitat. Because North America's venomous snake species are all patterned with crossbands, longitudinal stripes readily identify garters as harmless—though this feature doesn't prevent them from being chopped to pieces by snake haters—and any pet snake permitted by a skeptical parent is usually a garter. Gartersnakes are also classic classroom critters and turn up in children's books whenever a cute, chirpy snake character is required. Even if you grow up to be terrified of giant constrictors, skulking vipers, and swaying cobras, gartersnakes may still hold a particular place in your heart as innocent scions of the landscape of youth.

Those who've forged respected careers on the gartersnake's sinuous back share this fondness. Entire books are dedicated to its biology, relationships, and myriad forms. University of Victoria professor of zoology and champion hoser herpetologist Patrick Gregory, aided over the years by a small army of collaborators and ever-keen graduate students, has helped stack the shelves of science libraries with information about this genus gleaned from dozens of fastidious studies, including several involving the Narcisse pits. Like many, Gregory was smitten early by the striped juggernaut, and it has served him well as a researcher: "Garters were the first snakes I saw in the wild, so there's always been a bit of nostalgia attached. I don't know how much we can use them as 'models' for snakes in general, but gartersnakes *are* speciose and diverse, with both generalists and specialists, so they offer opportunity to do comparative ecological and behavioral work without the confounding effects of great phylogenetic differences. More important for me is that they're abundant. I may not look for questions that *don't* involve snakes, but I still care about sample size, statistical analysis, and publishing."

I was contemplating the attraction of such qualitative and

quantitative bounty—the great gartersnake within—as I drove through Vancouver on a May morning toward the University of British Columbia Endowment Lands. One of many jewels in Vancouver's trove of urban parkland, these lands form a fourteen-square-kilometer greenbelt that buffers sprawling UBC from the sprawling city. Bisected by several major streets, the narrow, lengthy ecotones running between grassy boulevard and forest were teeming with Northwestern Gartersnakes (*Thamnophis ordinoides*).

By dint of basic character, renaissance habits, and myriad manifestations, gartersnakes are an ode to generalism in an age of specialization. In this respect, *T. sirtalis*, a consummate generalist that dwells everywhere and eats anything, lives up to its status as the group's flagship species. Nevertheless, the group includes at least some bona fide specialists—like *T. ordinoides*. A slug-and-earthworm maven with ecological preferences tied to this habitus, it's a snake of absurd abundance in certain places where people often have no idea it exists literally underfoot.

I pulled into a lot next to a small interpretive center used by school groups. Steps away was the thin, weedy strip bordering a tangle of blackberry backed by forest on one side (decidedly dark) and a paved jogging path on the other (bright light). In this gravid greenery snakes lurked coiled and undetected in broken light and shadow, prepared to disappear into grass or gloom should they be unduly disturbed. The density of snakes here was ridiculous—up to seventy in a single hundred-meter stretch—yet they were well conditioned to human traffic. You ran by, biked by, even walked by, and they didn't move. Pause in front of them, however, and they were instantly alert; make any move other than away, and they shot variously off in any direction but the path, stopping and starting in what seemed a random manner.

Why did so many snakes lurk here? Partly because they wanted to and partly because they could. "Wanted" had to do with thermoregulatory and feeding opportunity: this open patch and its nearby source of radiant heat (the trail) was a perfect place to bask and mirrored classic natural habitat for T. ordinoides, which prefers open areas near thickets, meadows, and grassy berms bordering forests associated with the coastal fog belt. Once revved up, these diurnal (daylight active) snakes cruise the local smorgasbord of slugs and worms in the damp edge habitats. The "could" part, however, had to do with safety and our old friend polymorphism.

Though patterned much like the snowboard fashionistas on the nearby slopes of Whistler, the Northwestern Gartersnake's intent is precisely the opposite—*not* to be noticed. Basic ground color ranges from buff brown to charcoal gray, with a bewildering decorative array that includes a definite-to-indefinite mid-dorsal stripe of cream, yellow, orange, red, or blue, no stripe at all, and/or a checkered-cum-spotted look that may or may not also have flecks of orange or red, the latter unlikely but effective camouflage that renders snakes coiled in pine needles at the shadowed edge of a forest almost invisible. Because of the extreme variability of *T. ordinoides*, its members have repeatedly been described as new species. *The Garter Snakes* summarizes why this polymorphism is beneficial and how it is related to behavior:

> In an elegant series of studies, Brodie . . . found that escape behavior in northwestern gartersnakes was correlated with color pattern and that behavior and color patterns were genetically correlated. Striped snakes crawled directly away from predators because it is difficult to detect motion or judge the speed of a striped object. On the other hand,

spotted or unmarked snakes suddenly changed directions
then held still when they encountered potential predators,
since a blotched pattern makes it hard for a predator to
locate a prey item with this pattern.[18]

I quickly rounded up six different-looking individuals to
photograph. Examining them more closely, I realized one was
not *T. ordinoides* but a young specimen of Puget Sound Gartersnake (*T. sirtalis pickeringii*), one of eleven subspecies of the continental superspecies *T. sirtalis*; in contrast to *ordinoides*, it sported a
more definite neck, darker ground color, three distinct longitudinal stripes, and a regular series of bright-red side blotches.

Despite a litany of lofty justification, the idea of "subspecies" turns largely on how much appetite one has for it. In much
the same manner that we broadly class people as introverts or
extroverts, taxonomists are frequently tagged as either lumpers
(leaning toward fewer taxonomic categories of greater variability) or splitters (leaning toward numerous taxonomic categories
that attempt to formally name every variant). The debate reaches
far back into history, and speciose groups like rattlesnakes and
gartersnakes that represent successful, continuing adaptive
radiations have always been battlegrounds in what is largely a
projection of personalities. The great E.D. Cope, a noted splitter
heavily invested in *Thamnophis* description and taxonomy, recognized twenty-five species and twenty-one subspecies in his
final scientific paper, published posthumously in 1900. He was
roundly excoriated by A.G. Ruthven, who tackled the genus in
a classic 1908 monograph and recognized only twelve species
and but seven subspecies.

Although the entire subspecies idea is likely biologically
unrealistic (all populations within a nominal species can still
potentially interbreed and are thus neither genetically nor

evolutionarily isolated from one another), the world's most impressive snake phenomenon nevertheless involves a putative subspecies—the star of the Manitoba snake pits, *T. sirtalis parietalis*. Regardless of this snake's taxonomic status, its sexual habits remain a spectacle worth experiencing, and we will get to this once we learn why it occurs in such an improbable place.

IN WINNIPEG A few springs back, waiting for optimal weather in order to experience Narcisse in all its supercharged splendor, I decided to kill time by tracking down another of Manitoba's herpetological highlights: populations of Western Hognose Snake (*Heterodon nasicus*) and the endangered Northern Prairie Skink (*Eumeces septentrionalis septentrionalis*) clinging to the scrunched-carpet hills and relict dunes of Spruce Woods Provincial Park two hours to the southwest. I didn't know anything of this area or whom to consult, but this was where our age of technology truly shone: thanks to the Internet, you could now travel anywhere with a virtual herpetologist, without the mess and embarrassment of the real thing. A few minutes on the computer and I was in the car drawing a bead on the mesic dune complexes of Spirit Sands, on the park's western edge.

Under a bruised sky contemptuously spitting rain, I forged west toward Brandon, conjuring the many times I'd driven this endlessly spooling stretch of the Trans-Canada Highway, thankful that this time, at least, there was no blizzard. With nothing gracing the fields but spring mud, there was little to hold my attention save the thawing carcasses of a zoo's worth of winter roadkill, draped on the shoulder like toys kids had shaken the stuffing out of and tossed from the car. I silently cheered when a sign pointed me south off the morgue.

I hiked into Spirit Sands on a well-worn trail, Internet herpetologists propelling me as I burrowed through spruce and birch into an open area dominated by ground-hugging succulents and juniper. Ahead, huge preternatural dunes sailed improbably over the treetops, one of many sandy afterthoughts of glacial Lake Agassiz. Named for our boy Louis, world's first and only herpeto-ichthyo-glaciologist, the oceanic water body that pooled at the terminus of the retreating Laurentide ice sheet was a mind-boggling 440,000 square kilometers at its greatest extent, dwarfing the combined aquatic grandeur of today's Great Lakes. These waters, which began draining 8,200 years ago when the ice dam in central Canada finally burst, influenced the climate of eastern North America for some two hundred years. Though long gone, Agassiz (the lake) still dominates Manitoba's geography, from its vast, pancake-flat bottom to the beaches thrown up around its edges; rivers flowing in and out of Agassiz played a hand in everything from creating Spirit Sands (the exposed, remaining 4 square kilometers of a 6,500-square-kilometer sand deposit) to eroding the cavernous Narcisse sinkholes.

The Hognose Snake is generally secretive, but like most animals newly emerged from hibernation and driven to restart the engines of existence, it can be less discreet in spring. Despite temperatures around 10°C, I was hoping the heat-holding sand offered an outside chance of finding one. But hours of hiking turned up nothing more eye-opening than pincushion cactus, and I had to be satisfied with mute tracings on a sand flat that *might* have been made by a passing hognose, plus a few translucent scale-rows of shed skink skin—the types of forensic evidence I'd used on the summer job where I'd seen my first hognose.

The problem that day was that neither of these reptiles is particularly cold adapted, requiring consistent solar radiation and temperatures closer to 20°C for sustained activity. This in stark contrast to other Manitobans that are perfectly happy to slip beneath the ice and breed in frigid ponds, call from reeds while snowflakes pile onto their little heads like tiny dunce caps, or wrestle a score of other suitors on a cold limestone slab in a battle for the female of their dreams. How *those* ectotherms pulled it off was a science unto itself.

Animals employ two strategies in seasonally cold climates: freeze avoidance and freeze tolerance. The two share some biochemical and physiological similarities, but freeze tolerance, in which certain tissues actually freeze for varying periods of time, is more complex and interesting. Among those amphibians and reptiles identified as particularly freeze tolerant are the Wood Frog (*Rana sylvatica*), Spring Peeper (*Pseudacris crucifer*), Painted Turtle (*Chrysemys picta*), European Common Lizard (*Lacerta vivipara*), and Common Gartersnake (*Thamnophis sirtalis*). There are others, of course, and we wouldn't be out on a limb to add the European Adder (*Vipera berus*) I encountered in Finland to the list.

The most tolerant and best-studied is the Wood Frog, which ranges to treeline in subarctic regions of North America. Ken Storey of Carleton University has done most of the work on this species and what he has found out borders on incredible.

Wood Frogs hibernate on land so that they can get busy as soon as the snow melts. But frogs can't dig into the ground, so they hibernate in damp leaf litter to keep from drying out. Whenever frost penetrates into this environment, the frogs freeze, as ice forms in their fluid compartments and encases all their internal organs. Ice crystals appear between skin and muscle layers, the eyes turn white, blood stops flowing, and up to 65 percent of total body water turns to ice. Functions such as breathing, heartbeat, and muscle movements stop, leaving the frog in a state of suspended animation.[19]

Freeze tolerance has three main components. The first is control of the freezing process itself. Lowering temperatures trigger special nucleators, or starter grains, to actively seed ice formation in the frog's body, allowing animals to begin freezing just below o°c. The second is production of cryoprotectants, high concentrations of sugars and sugar alcohols that prevent cell volume from excessively shrinking and increase the content of bound water. Like the glycols we add to our car's radiator for the same purpose, cryoprotectants keep the insides of cells from freezing. Thus, ice forms around the internal organs, drawing water from them but leaving a thick, syrupy solution inside unfrozen cells. Finally, because the blood is frozen, organs acquire an elevated ability to survive without regular delivery of oxygen or nutrients; during thawing, antioxidants resist the cellular stress produced when oxygen is suddenly reintroduced, and repair mechanisms go on high alert—for instance, the level of clotting proteins rises to staunch any bleeding from ice damage to organs.

Behavior also plays a role. As frogs freeze, they assume the "water-holding" position typically employed by animals to avoid desiccation: head down, limbs drawn in. This position reduces evaporative water loss over what can be weeks of continuous freezing. What is currently being studied is how signals for breathing, heartbeat, and brain activity are reactivated during thawing, when all organ functions miraculously reboot *within two hours.*

Though somewhat freeze tolerant, the Red-sided Gartersnake is no Wood Frog. Rather, it's tolerant by degree and with regional variation—northern populations can handle the freezing of skin and skeletal musculature but not for periods stretching beyond hours or days. Winters where subzero temperatures reach deeply into dens for extended periods still cause massive die-offs. Nevertheless, *T. sirtalis* has the longest activity season of any North American snake, often roaming the surface with body temperatures lethal to other species: I'd seen garter snakes moving through spring snowfalls in Ontario, and Pat Gregory documented snakes emerging from a den on the Alberta–Northwest Territory border with internal temperatures as low as 0.5°C, active and crawling across patches of snow.

The Finnish vipers were in good company.

THE NEXT DAY, Mother's Day, was warmer, and the remaining clouds had retreated to the edges of the sky. I was heading northeast toward Narcisse with a friend, Michelle, and her son, Skyler, but having trouble locating the famous snake pits.

If these were where one imagined they should be—somewhere in the snake-addled southern U.S.—towering billboards would hector you in from all directions for a hundred kilometers. There would be souvenir stands and cheesy motels, fireworks for sale, and roadside pecan pie stands. Instead, we saw only occasional tiny Manitoba Ministry of Transportation signs. I wasn't even sure I was going the right way until I spotted a ten-meter statue of two giant smiling, intertwined snakes—mascots known province-wide as Sammy and Samantha—at the town of Inwood. A right turn and several kilometers later, a large sign announced we'd arrived. It was the middle of nowhere, but we were clearly not alone.

Some seventy cars crowded the lot. Where I expected a handful of snake aficionados and a few trepidatious observers, there were instead *hundreds* of people—dads and moms and kids and even marauding dogs that shouldn't have been allowed anywhere near the place. Michelle informed me that a visit to Narcisse was a traditional Mother's Day outing for many Winnipeggers. Whereas this scenario might not play elsewhere on a continent where pancake breakfasts and visits to botanical gardens were the norm, here, taking Mom, beleaguered by her own reproductive spoils, to watch snakes mate was apparently OK.

A three-kilometer signed path loops past four dens. Trudging with a dozen other visitors, we were a hundred meters in when smallish snakes rushed the path ahead, startling those who weren't prepared to see them outside of the pits. The dens themselves were fenced to keep people from disturbing mating snakes, but the barriers also served to keep the overly curious from falling in. As we closed in on the first den, the ground truly sprang to life. Like grass blades fluttering flat in a strong wind, snakes fired off in waves, threads of desperate males hard on the scent of particularly pungent females, oblivious to our presence. Ahead we heard screams, groans, and all manner of exclamation as kids and adults alike made first visual contact with a three-meter deep limestone depression carpeted with thousands of wriggling snakes.

The animals were dispersed on the floor in great, Medusan clots, hanging from fissures and holes, draped over rocks and branches, smaller aggregates circling the main mass like bizarre, coalescing satellites. Snakes ringed the sinkhole, plying its edges, decidedly underfoot as they whipped over shoes and popped their bug-eyed heads from cracks in the wooden viewing platform to swivel like prairie dogs. In contrast to other biological wonders, the subject here couldn't be avoided—no distant viewing opportunity through binoculars, no chance to be anything but among and within. We were embedded in an orgy to the extent that true Zeligs felt part of the congregation, while others struggled mightily to suppress panic and maintain composure in an epic battle between rationality and deep-seated fear.

"Aiiiiiiiiiiiiiiiiii!"

"*Eeeeeeekkk!*" from another quarter, perhaps the only time outside of a comic book you could justify spelling a shriek this way.

"Ohhh, gross," moaned a woman to my right, a hand to her forehead.

"What do you think?" said her friend.

"Well . . . it looks pretty damn much like I expected it to—I was just hoping it wouldn't."

Not much chance of that. This 11,882-hectare wildlife management area contains the largest concentration of snakes *on the planet*, with a population estimated at some eighty thousand. That such a profusion occurs this far north seems all the stranger, but it really makes perfect sense.

Winters here are harsh, with surface temperatures south of −30°C for extensive periods and frost moving deep into the soil. Good hibernacula are at a premium—they must be located below frostline but above the water table and remain humid so that hibernating snakes don't desiccate. The Narcisse dens are located in deep, well-worn limestone sinkholes surrounded by natural aspen parkland punctuated by extensive fingers of marshland left by the retreating Lake Winnipeg (né Agassiz). For a generalist that inhales insects, worms, amphibians, fish, and even small mammals, it's a giant buffet.

In the not-too-distant past, dens and summer habitat were adjacent, but ever-retreating lake margins have caused the animals to make extensive migrations between the two as marshes shrink away to the north. Pat Gregory discovered snakes could travel almost twenty kilometers to summer habitat in spring, then make the return journey to den areas in early fall. Here they gather to sun and feed until autumn's cold drives them into the limestone, where they loop down through cracks and fissures. Up to twenty thousand snakes might occupy a single den. In late April and early May they reemerge, males first, followed a week or so later by females; when the ladies arrive on the surface oozing snaky sex appeal, all hell breaks loose among eager males milling at the limestone bar.

Narcisse is a giant, self-contained laboratory, where sample size is never a problem for biologists like Gregory who have studied hibernation physiology and behavioral ecology in these snakes for over thirty years. In fact, the first pheromone (an externally secreted hormone that transmits information to members of the same species) identified in a vertebrate was the "sexual attractiveness" pheromone of the Red-sided Gartersnake. A human version of this chemical would be worth billions, its power evident in the almost comic spectacle of "mating balls" observed at dens in the spring, where a single pheromone-secreting female is assailed by up to a hundred males. On second thought, writhing masses of humans would not only look ridiculous but also pose a definite traffic hazard.

Still, as aggregations of reptiles go, the Narcisse pits are second only to the spectacular and oft-referenced *arribada* ("arrival") in which up to half a million Olive Ridley Sea Turtles (*Lepidochelys olivacea*) mass off of ancestral tropical beaches to mate before females haul out to lay eggs in the surf-pounded sand. Who could imagine such a thing in Canada's frosty latitudes? Or that it was an educational tourist attraction drawing some 35,000 folks a year? According to Audrey, a Manitoba conservation interpreter I met, Narcisse hosted its own arribada as up to fifteen school buses roared in each day through late April and early May; unfortunately, this tide of interest was unregulated, a situation that could too easily turn the benevolent to malevolent.

In an aspen grove where snakes darted in every direction, Audrey, employed for the breeding season to disseminate information and keep damage to a minimum, encouraged adults and children alike to handle the animals gently and not disturb those obviously trying to mate. She acknowledged that 's hard to balance the benefits of hands-on experience and e cat on with the snakes' welfare.

"I'm overwhelmed by the lack of care people exer h these creatures. Some nights I go home praying I r 1 e another snake in a person's hands," she sighed. "But the d k, even if a few are accidentally killed it's nothing compa : \ h the toll the crows take. And at least while people are here, the crows *aren't*."

SKYLER IS A brainy, slightly sensitive eight-year-old with an extensive knowledge of and interest in snakes, paired with a healthy fear of them. Like most, he was excited when he saw his first one slither across the path. Scared to touch one but desperately wanting to, his first attempt was decidedly tentative; despite my catching a smallish snake and Michelle holding it to soften the blow, Skyler could only manage a brief brush with a finger. But after we'd let it go, he was clearly thinking hard about the experience and beginning to believe that he might be able to work up to touching a snake.

"I'm warming up my hands to hold one," he told me when I inquired why he was furiously rubbing his palms. Brilliant kid reasoning.

We steered back to the first den, where snakes abounded in surrounding native grass, and I quickly caught a forty-centimeter male. It was more nervous than most I'd picked up and trying harder to get away—possibly it had the scent of a female—but Skyler sucked up his courage and held the determined snake for several heart-thumping minutes, following my directions for hand-over-handing as it moved forward. Michelle snapped a picture. When Skyler lowered it to the grass to rejoin the fray, he was beaming—the kind of breakthrough the conservation people hope for.

When I returned alone a couple of days later, the crowds had set sail, and only a handful of vehicles were adrift in the parking lot. One belonged to Wendell, another seasonal worker who farmed not five kilometers away.

"I've been trying to get a job here for years," he said proudly, pointing to his name tag. "This is my first spring."

He'd worked Mother's Day with Audrey, so naturally we got to talking about crowds, mishandling, and other problems plaguing the dens.

"Yeah, Mother's Day is busy," Wendell began, "but nowhere near busiest. I've seen the parking lot full in April, cars lined up along the highway on both sides. That's *really* crazy."

Did he think crowds were a problem?

"Sometimes. Especially when it's *all* schoolkids and there ain't enough goddamn teachers to control 'em. An' some people don't realize what they're dealing with." His voice suddenly ascends. "I had a woman get *pissed* because I was trying to show her two-year-old how to hold a snake properly. The kid was squeezing the life out of it, and Mom was going, 'Well, the man's getting a little bossy now dear so we better go . . .' And I'm all, 'Lady, your kid is *killing a fucking snake*. If you don't want her to know how to hold it properly don't let her pick it up.' "

He had a point, although minor mortality from grab-happy kids was likely compensated by the provincial prohibition on the devastating commercial collecting that used to occur here, as well as by a new fencing system installed along the highway that funnels snakes through passes under the road, allowing them to avoid the treacherous pavement crossing.

"We were losin' up to twenty-five thousand snakes a year before they put that fence in," said Wendell. "They reckon it's down around two thousand now."

The road toll was actually greater in fall than spring (one estimate suggests some ten thousand die in that season alone), as animals made their way back to den sites and drivers were less inclined to watch for them. But there were dozens of dens in the vicinity, and you couldn't set up fence-and-funnel systems everywhere: on my return drive to Winnipeg I saw many flattened snakes, and it was all I could do to avoid the live ones darting with regularity from the shoulder.

A species adapted over millennia to take advantage of every opportunity to enhance its existence is no match for even an isolated rural road. When the needless deaths of some two thousand harmless, ecologically essential organisms is seen as a vastly improved state of affairs, you're living in callous times.

MULLING OVER MY experiences in Finland and Narcisse later that summer, I asked Pat Gregory what life-history characteristics the most northerly ranging snakes in Europe, Asia, and North America shared, given that these were represented by *Vipera* on the first two continents and the phylogenetically distant *Thamnophis* on the last.

"I'd say the only thing that really unites them is live birth, the fact that females probably don't mate every year, and the need to pass the winter in hibernation."

Fair enough. But given that nothing remotely close to the Narcisse pits was known in all of Eurasia, did he feel the Manitoba aggregation was an underappreciated natural phenomenon?

"Sometimes when places to hibernate are in limited supply, we get communal hibernation," he started, with the metric of a scientist wishing to tap out empirical facts in logical sequence. "Sometimes when communal sites are far from summer habitat, we get long-distance migration. Because communal denning and migration are spectacular, we tend to treat them as characteristic of northern reptiles. But whether they are or not remains to be seen . . . we *can* say Narcisse is spectacular in degree though not necessarily in kind."

He paused for a second.

"But underappreciated? I don't know—isn't it being appreciated to *death*?"

12

GEEKS LIKE US

Learn to live like the lotus—

untouched by the filthy water it grows in.

KRISHNA in the *Bhagavad Gita*

"FIRST OF ALL," said Dr. Robert A. Thomas, director of Loyola University's Center for Environmental Communications and the man at the lectern in the cavernous convention center, "let me say that the Cottonmouths are winning. They sit there and eat everything that comes by and when they've eaten everything else... well, they eat each other."

In New Orleans, where everyone and everything suffered from 2005's back-to-back hurricanes Katrina and Rita, cannibalism seemed a logical step along the postdisaster road of natural and human anarchy.

When Katrina's ten-meter storm surge had rushed into town the previous August, nothing had time to run away. Much of the city's human population was gravely affected, but animals had been vanquished as well. Up to fifteen species of amphibian and reptile once occurred in the city and its lush outskirts, but the storm had ripped the bark and leaves off most cypress trees, a centerpiece of local ecology. When the levees broke, the naked woodlands were inundated with a stew of salt water, mud, and toxic waste from oil refineries. The forests now stood stone silent.

Wetlands were also devoid of animals; some languished under seawater for up to two weeks after Katrina, only to be inundated again by Rita. An aerial panorama of the 500,000-hectare Sabine National Wildlife Refuge revealed expanses of dead brown water sewn together by a ten-kilometer debris thread of barrels, refrigerators, upside-down boats, trucks, trailers, ship containers, and pieces of homes and buildings.

Humans and animals alike were in a pitched battle to overcome the disaster, but the scrappy Cottonmouth (aka Water Moccasin)—stout, truculent, venomous icon of southern U.S. swamps—was demonstrating best how to ruthlessly overcome adversity. At least the Gulf of Mexico's beleaguered sea turtles weren't affected, said Thomas; they'd hung out offshore with a few friends they hadn't seen in about 250 million years—alligators that had been washed out to sea. Although somewhat salt-tolerant (they've turned up at oil platforms sixty kilometers out), alligators wouldn't pat together their vegetation-mound nests in saline situations or during drought. The best breeding seasons ever for Louisiana's alligators were 2004 and 2005; in 2005 there were some forty thousand nests. In 2006 that number dropped by 50 percent—was it hurricane, drought, or both? The population hadn't declined: more alligators than ever lurked everywhere—many had headed inland after the storm surge, and hundreds more had escaped from farming operations.

Mirroring the struggle of the city's displaced humanity, Thomas meandered back and forth between hope and horror in the final talk of the plenary session for the Joint Meeting of Ichthyologists and Herpetologists in July 2006, which—as excruciatingly detailed in the official program—comprised the eighty-sixth annual meeting of the American Society of Ichthyologists and Herpetologists (ASIH), sixty-fourth for the Herpetologists' League (HL), and forty-ninth involving the Society for the Study of Amphibians and Reptiles (SSAR).

Plenary sessions were usually somniferous affairs, sporadically attended with so many comings and goings that taking a chair near the door was like manning a turnstile. First up that morning was the outgoing ASIH president, a fish systematist who titled her talk "A Sense of Scale" (such cutesy clever puns were rampant). Next was the HL Distinguished Herpetologist lecture by Dr. H. Carl Gerhardt, a specialist on frog calls. "Evolution and Mechanisms of Acoustic Communication in Frogs and Toads" was part cool engineering and part sound physics. Interesting as this all was, however, most only stuck it out to hear the inevitable local courtesy talk—Thomas's "How Do Severe Storms Affect the Herpetofauna? Louisiana is Alive and Croaking."

I was pretty sure the pun was unintended.

EVER OPTIMISTIC, THE beleaguered folk of New Orleans had thought the worst over. They thought they'd seen the last of unruly crowds, Salvation Army clothing, and the slimy, ill-tempered creatures that invaded the city in the wake of Katrina's pernicious floods. But just when the recovery was gathering momentum, disaster struck again. The joint meetings had descended on the Big Easy spreading noise, irreverence, and bad fashion. Resilient and mindful that the situation couldn't get any worse, the good citizens had welcomed the latest foul and loathsome tide with open arms and a shocking display of hospitality. They may have been rehearsing for an upcoming investment bankers' convention, but I'm not that cynical. The scientists responded in kind by spending a day helping with reconstruction efforts in the devastated Lower Ninth Ward. Doubtless some secretly hoped to collect a few Cottonmouths for their efforts.

I had attended many such meetings, but this one had been my first solely as an observer. I'd come to see old friends and catch up on the latest research. I'll also admit that I enjoyed listening to people talk unselfconsciously about frogs and snakes and looked forward to the bounty of accompanying schadenfreude. Watching students slither offstage after a disastrous talk while their disappointed professors writhed in a snake pit of glowering peers would help me recall the stress and dread of exposing my own nascent work to the harshest of critics.

Like the stab of fear Canadians felt approaching the U.S. border—as if they'd be labeled a drug smuggler, terrorist, or illegal alien when all they really wanted was a pair of cheap running shoes—I'd always felt a mountebank when delivering a scientific paper, convinced I would be outed as a charlatan when, in fact, my work was no less a mix of hard work, empirical data, faulty analysis, and wishful speculation than the next person's.

In either scenario, intimidation overrode legitimacy. The difference was that border guards had only seconds to make a decision, whereas scientists had the stated full-time job of policing each other. If you told the right story at the border, you were in. Among scientific peers, however, passing muster with one gatekeeper did not guarantee you would stride freely into the domain; hundreds waited in the wings to savage your work, some for no other reason than it wasn't *their* work. No matter how much respectability and street cred you amassed over a lifetime of celebrated endeavor, factions—entire scholastic ecosystems even—subsisted on opinion contrary to yours.

This tilt was unlike a sporting event, where you ultimately shook hands with your nemesis over a battle well fought; some scientists despised each other so thoroughly they conversed only obliquely, through the various organs of publication and presentation. Given the glacial pace of science, arguments could be drawn out over decades. Many researchers thus found themselves in dogfights with the same individuals over their entire careers.

This kind of animosity was nothing new, of course. Among biologists, heated debate went back to the initial acrimony over Darwin's *On the Origin of Species* and the historical exchange between creationist and critic Bishop Wilberforce and natural selection defender Thomas Huxley. Still, few scientific pissing contests were as supercharged as the one I witnessed in the first session on systematics.

"The Amphibian Tree of Life," a newly published, 371-page American Museum of Natural History monograph by some nineteen international collaborators, has problems, stated David "Catfish" Cannatella of the University of Texas when he took the stage to critique the newly theorized relationships resulting from this integration of morphological and molecular data that had been years in the making, the first major overhaul of Class Amphibia since the 1930s. Catfish itemized issues with missing taxa, poor gene choices, and DNA sequence alignments. Why didn't some toad taxa cluster with toads? Were these simply bad reads by an automated sequencer? Apparently not. If you aligned these sequences against others in GenBank (an annotated log of publicly available DNA sequences), they actually fell out with parasitic worms. This result suggested contamination, i.e., parasitic worms embedded in toad tissue samples. If this heavy charge weren't egregious enough, said Catfish, then the mess the authors made of the complex analysis alone justified the paper being trashed, not to mention all the name changes now required by the study's scarifying conclusions. This statement stirred the audience. A lumper versus splitter vibe was burbling when Darrel Frost, the paper's senior author, leapt up.

"I don't even know *how* to respond to this Karl Rove version of our work," he sputtered before pointedly asking Cannatella if he intended to use some of his several million dollars in grant money to publish his own overdue work on the subject.

"Publish?" teased Catfish from the lectern, calmly sipping water while Frost wound up.

"Yes or no?" pressed Frost.

"Oh, you mean *this* stuff?" said Catfish, waving off the litany of criticism and barely suppressing a smile. "Sure."

Another of the authors asked Cannatella if he saw *anything* good in the paper. "Hmmm . . . well, let's see . . . there *is* a lot of data," offered Catfish, in the way one might admit that an ugly mansion was at least really big.

Shortcomings notwithstanding, the paper was a long-overdue taxonomic dam-breaker, and this criticism was clearly territorial, likely also political, and very, very personal.

It was still a systematic jungle out there.

I STRUGGLED THROUGH a sea of earnestness and shuffling chairs toward the crush of coffee break. More *plus ça change, plus c'est la même chose.* Familiar faces abounded, many grouped in the very clusters I recalled from a decade ago; I felt like an escapee. It was déjà vu all over again when I realized these groups were also executing familiar fashion-suicide pacts. Herpetologists thought cargo pants, with all their loops and sagging pockets, were invented for *them,* and they'd long ago taken ownership with gusto. But their almost comical devotion to khaki was more CRAP than GAP; the official uniform of established herpetologists was cargo shorts, Hawaiian shirt, white tube socks, and running shoes that had never been run in.

Unfortunately this style had also been adopted by young ichthyologists, though their button-up shirts tended toward Escheresque prints of interlocking fish, and they were more inclined to sandals—as if in any instant they might need to step into water. T-shirts from past meetings were also legion: maybe a stylized pike on the fish guys, snakes on the herpers. At joint meetings like these, however, the T-shirt logo was often an ectotherm gumbo of reptiles, amphibians, fish, and sharks, in which case you couldn't be sure who you were looking at. But I had a way to tell them apart: whether from habit or the courtesy of experience, herpetologists reflexively wiped their hands on their pants before shaking yours. Don't think too hard about that one.

Beyond dress details, the meeting could have been any other conference or convention as folks chatted around cookies and java urns. Until you realized these conversations didn't concern sales projections, office politics, or last night's baseball game. Instead, they were about how so-and-so's wife was doing since losing half a calf muscle to a Black-tailed Rattlesnake bite. Oh yeah, stated someone authoritatively—that *Crotalus molossus* venom is nasty shit. (Jeezuz—what venom *wasn't*?) Or how much money the U.S. Army was doling out to fund gopher tortoise research on their firing ranges. Or how a tiny fungus no one had heard of a decade ago was poised to wipe half the world's amphibians from the face of the earth.

While a comforting air of menace hovered over the herpetologists, uptown ichthyologists maintained their usual banter about wine, women, and song. There *were* poisonous fishes to worry about, I surmised, but none that would go after you and all of which, save in the rarest circumstance (looking your way, Steve Irwin), were easy to avoid. That thought was scrubbed midstream by a passing pair of graduate students, khakied to the hilt.

"Can you believe that shit?"

"Yeah—someone just threw everything in the same bag without telling anyone and he just reached in and *wham!*"

I caught myself scribbling notes about these people the way I would about critters in the field.

Student 1: "There's a rumor next year's meeting will be podcast."

Student 2: "Wow. That kind of takes all the fun out of it."

Legendary herper Wild Bill Duellman: "But just think, you'll be able to watch a presentation and drink at the same time."

I bumped into another former ROM buddy, Nick Mandrak, freshwater ichthyologist and geographical modeler based at Fisheries and Oceans in Burlington, Ontario, handily distant from any reeking ocean. He told me that he now worked on species at risk and also policed exotic fish introductions from live-animal Asian markets and the bait trade. I said I was writing a book about herpetology.

"That'll be a snoozefest," he chortled.

"Well . . . I am trying to make it funny," I countered, missing the sarcasm.

"Oh—not much material there," he added, then recalled an anecdote even I hadn't heard.

We were all at a meeting once at the California Academy of Sciences in San Francisco, and the Grateful Dead were playing in nearby Berkeley (weren't the Dead *always* playing in Berkeley?). Some of the guys wanted to go, but I had to leave the conference early to return to Toronto. Everyone ended up in Dave Morafka's Toyota 4Runner for the forty-five-minute drive, poor lumbering Nick stuffed in the backseat. Given the context and potential for indulgence in reality enhancement, I can only imagine how what happened next went down. Without thinking, Nick found himself toying with "a pillowcase with a knot in it" sitting on the seat beside him. He'd casually flipped it around a bit when it dawned on him that the guy driving the truck was a herpetologist. Who collected rattlesnakes. Nick had freaked.

"Don't worry," Morafka had insisted over his shoulder, "there aren't any snakes in *that* bag . . . just scorpions."

"They're crazy. All of them," Nick stated flatly. "Good luck."

Right.

And then suddenly the morning grew dark. Rain fell sideways in great, gravid sheets, dense enough to obscure the still boarded-up windows on surrounding high-rises. Lightning tore a hole in the sky, backed by tom-tom thunder and a banshee wind. With delegates shuffling between talks, the maelstrom drew everyone to the floor-to-ceiling windows, each with the same thought: is *this* what it was like during Katrina?

Affirmative evidence had traced the ride in from the airport—diarrhea-brown water marks painted six meters high in places as if they had been made last week.

The rain stopped. The crowd dispersed. I went back to my program.

Now I *could* have gone to the third ASIH Workshop on Gonadal Histology of Fishes, where I would have found out why you can learn more by viewing colorfully stained, ultra-thin slices of fish ovaries and testes under a microscope than cradling the real thing . . . or I could have pushed pins through my eyeballs. After dismissing several such options, I slid into a smallish room where Dr. Aaron Bauer, exotic lizard aficionado extraordinaire, was presenting the travelogue "Herps and Herping in India and Sri Lanka."

Because "herp" is not a word (I, like most, have lapsed into using it as a designation of convenience), I found myself wondering when "herping" became a verb. Especially given Bauer's predilections; when the portly man talked about "the work I've done in India," I suspected it did not refer to "work" in any presently understood context but was bio-code for "the fun I had collecting and eating in India."

The talk was nevertheless interesting. Along with South America, Africa, Australia, and Antarctica, India is part of the Gondwanan assemblage of continents—which Bauer admitted to particular affinity for—and the 200-million-year-old jigsaw traced some interesting biogeography. He talked about the Western Ghats, where new species of primitive snakes were found every year, and the Eastern Ghats, where a large, colorful leaf-toed gecko last seen in 1890 had been rediscovered in 1985, common and vociferous, directing loud clicks and other sounds into amplifying boulder chambers on the outskirts of a village where it was *the* noisiest organism in the evening air.

As pictures of geckos flashed across the screen, Bauer waxed Ditmars-esque about their ornamental beauty and diversity. Suddenly, the scaly stream was interrupted by a frog and caecilian.

"I threw in some pictures of amphibians . . . for people who like such things," chuffed Bauer to an audience of mostly lizard groupies.

His comment revealed, it seemed, an even further class divide (now *that's* a clever pun, dammit!) at play. As one graduate student observed to me about her first herpetological gathering: "Even the reptile people are different than the amphibian people. They're a whole other level of weird."

The social event that night was held at the Aquarium of the

Americas. It was a decidedly fishy affair, but a few token herps kept the rest of the crowd happy: softshell, Red-eared Slider, and snapping turtles; a five-meter anaconda, glistening like a massive, wet sausage after shedding its skin; and, for a touch of surrealism—as if more were required—a gargantuan, bone-white alligator. It's not albino, insisted a sign, but leucistic (pronounced loo-*sis*-tic)—a condition wherein the eyes aren't red and occasional blots of pigment are scattered like birthmarks.

Perfect.

THE JOE SLOWINSKI Symposium paid tribute to a man whose passion for the world's deadliest snakes knew no bounds—right up until one killed him. But his contribution to snake systematics wasn't his only legacy. Presenter after presenter spoke of Joe's dedication, single-mindedness, lust for life, and the fine, feverish mind, which, like any good iconoclastic organ, applied new methods to old questions while continually posing new ones. The speakers presented many excellent studies, but when "Phylogeny and Toxinology of Kraits (Elapidae: *Bungarus*): Taxonomic and Medical Implications" began, the talk cut a little close to the heart. Although Joe would surely have approved, friends shifted uncomfortably in their seats.

Like mountain climbing, herpetology is a game of ghosts that honors its fallen, forcing you to confront the paper-thin line between loss of a colleague and your own mortality. Many skilled and careful climbers have died as a result of unpredictable rockfall, avalanches, equipment failure, or the mistakes of others—simply victims of an accumulating numbers game. Stuff happens in the mountains. Spend all your time there and you'd have your share of close calls.

Likewise when you spent all your time among the objective hazard and unpredictability of venomous snakes. Shockingly high numbers of amateur and professional herpetologists had been bitten. Some—like a few Aussie snake men, venom collector Bill Haast, or nut-job Cobraman—had made a career of it. Others simply perished in an unguarded moment—like a usually vigilant peasant in a rice paddy who one day failed to watch his step.

No hagiography was underway for Slowinski—herpetologists are too realistic for that—and sitting in a sterile auditorium listening to the plaudits, I couldn't help but feel an inevitability to it all. His buddy Mark Moffett had said as much while putting the risk into the kind of perspective even a climber could appreciate:

> Joe was careful with snakes; he'd chased them since he was a boy in Kansas City, Missouri. He was also famous for close calls . . . On a previous trip to Burma, a spitting cobra had struck through the bag Joe put it in, stabbing his finger. He waited calmly for the venom to take effect. Luck of the draw, he would say, telling the story: Sometimes a snake bites without injecting its toxins. On a later Burma trip, a cobra squirted venom into his eyes. After a few hours the excruciating pain passed. Joe never paused much over these incidents. He seemed to embody the understanding that a fully natural world includes the possibility that nature can kill us—and afterward glide freely away into the wet grass it came from. That love in any form involves an element of risk.[20]

Beyond the Slowinski Symposium, a dozen other sessions on snakes, lizards, turtles, frogs, and salamanders could get you excited for fifteen minutes about something totally esoteric. On it went for four days, an eclectic mix of significant knowledge, experiment, and practicum merging the known world with the decidedly unknown. I attended as many talks by friends and colleagues as possible. Pat Gregory gave a paper on death feigning as a predator-escape mechanism; although it seems maladaptive to place yourself limply into a predator's clutches, studies show death feigners are more likely than nonfeigners to survive such encounters. Elsewhere, serious odes to dedication and tenacity were on offer: long-term studies like David Green's quarter-century look at a population of Fowler's Toad and the work of Dr. Jacqueline Litzgus of Laurentian University on the Spotted Turtle (*Clemmys guttata*)—data gathered over a twenty-four-year period suggested that females might live an astounding 110 years.

True to their beer-loving form, Canucks of all taxonomic stripes hung together at social events—like the comically inordinate number who'd signed up for a brewery tour (organizers should have seen that one coming). We were enjoying each other's company so much that we'd even met at a swampy-smelling French Quarter dive to try and revive the moribund Association Canadienne des Herpétologistes. After ordering drinks we rose around the table one by one to say who we were and what we did. Another herpeholics confessional.

When my turn came I announced my name and residence, then closed with "I used to be a herpetologist—now I just study herpetologists."

I think I was the only one who found it funny.

THAT EVENING BUSES disgorged everyone outside the New Orleans zoo's swamp exhibit, which, given the surrounding swampland, seemed charmingly redundant. Elevated boardwalks radiated through electrified enclosures containing begging raccoons, sleeping gators, a somnolent puma, and black bears panting in the heat. Juggling tiny plates, the crowd fanned out along the walkways, lodging themselves into small groups to talk, inevitably, about their work—the fate of this species or that, a population decline here, various conservation initiatives there—with no apparent sense of the irony cast by their surroundings. I'd found myself staring fondly at the green-speckled surface of what could have been any pond of my youth save for what it contained: as cicadas screamed from drooping cypress in the glomming dusk, my eyes followed the scalloped trail etched in duckweed marking the sinuous passage of an invisible alligator.

Dinner at the aquarium several days earlier had featured excruciatingly long lineups for nano-samples of Cajun rice, andouille sausage, filé gumbo, grits, and cornbread muffins served amid tanks filled with better-fed lower vertebrates. Beers, however, had been served whole and liberally, and the last thing I remember was seeing a four-meter white alligator—a good night out by anyone's standards.

At the zoo, dinner involved excruciatingly long lineups for micro-samples (a slight improvement) of Cajun rice, andouille sausage, filé gumbo, grits, and cornbread muffins among tanks filled with better-fed lower vertebrates. An excellent zydeco band was playing, and the herpetologists drank like fish. Others danced. It wasn't a pretty sight, and I had immediately recognized the spasmodic twitching of a certain ichthyologist, always first on the dance floor at such events, whom we used to call the Pithed Guy.

Those not up for shucking and jiving simply wandered. In an unabashed stroke of commercial genius, the zoo's layout made you pass through the gift shop and its trove of melodramatic paraphernalia to get to the *really* interesting animals: a giant male alligator (they reach six meters, and this one was close), a handful of turtles, and some snakes. The shop, however, wasn't entirely without merit. Wading through bins of stuffed animals toward the far wall, I'd found a display case containing skulls of representative crocodilians: American Alligator (*Alligator mississippiensis*), Nile Crocodile (*Crocodylus niloticus*), and the needle-nosed, fish-eating Indian Gharial (*Gavialis gangeticus*—think swordfish meets anorexic croc). But the star was a two-meter skull cast of *Parasaurus brasiliensis*, an ancient land crocodilian with the approximate length and bulk of an eighteen-wheeler. It was the largest carnivore to ever live, heavier and considerably nastier even than T-rex, favored fossil *enfant terrible*.

I was making notes in front of this display when shouting erupted from the center of the shop.

"They've frozen the little shits and lacquered them and stuck them on a bunch of rotting crap that looks like an alligator nest," screamed a drunken, indignant herpetologist who stood in front of an interactive nest display that was indeed crowned with stuffed, varnished juvenile alligators.

"Look what they've done to the little fuckers. It's *bullshit!*"

As the woman at the cashier's desk quietly called security, he went on, voice alternating between melancholia and the kind of maniacal laughter that usually accompanied tears.

"They've fucking *painted* them! At least they're not shooting them like in Florida. They're shooting them there for eating fat fucking golfers and joggers. Fuck, I say *that's* natural selection, baby! Let them eat flesh cake!"

They *were* shooting nuisance gators in Florida, and in unprecedented numbers. The latest fatal attack, in early May 2006, had been on a fit, pretty young university student. She'd disappeared while jogging near a canal in Fort Lauderdale, and her arms were later found in the belly of a three-meter, one-eyed male gator; the only selection going on there was against wearing an iPod while jogging.

Security arrived. The drunk continued to rage, hurling abuse even as he was being dragged out.

"Look at these poor little fuckers! Are you *fucking* kidding me? What kind of conservation exhibit is this? Fuckers . . . "

On the other side of the gift shop I'd found a fairly decent live collection of local nasties: Eastern Coral Snake (*Micrurus fulvius*), Copperhead (*Agkistrodon contortrix*), Cottonmouth (*A. piscivorus*), Canebrake Rattlesnake (*Crotalus horridus atricaudatus*), and Pygmy Rattlesnake (*Sistrurus miliarius*), the species that once nailed Pat Gregory when he'd picked one up on a road, inattentive from a long day of traveling. I also saw harmless varieties: Speckled Kingsnake (*Lampropeltis getula holbrooki*), colorful Louisiana Milk Snake (*Lampropeltis triangulum amaura*, a coral snake mimic), ratsnakes, racers, ribbons, hognose, and a motley collection of watersnakes. The surprising crown jewel of the collection, however, was another leucistic alligator, sibling to the one housed at Aquarium of the Americas.

In 1987 a hunter had found seventeen white baby gators paddling through a swamp. Since then they'd been celebrated and sent around the known world (which in Louisiana meant several other states and Mexico). At the time of discovery they'd received tons of press, including their own Top-Ten List of White Alligator Peeves on *Late Night with David Letterman*.

The problem was that we had all once again ended an evening of copious drinking by seeing a four-meter white alligator. Possible? Coincidence? Flashback? Or did organizers *really* need to rethink whether Canadians should be allowed to attend these meetings?

THE BIGGEST DISASTER discussed in the conference corridors, however, was not group hallucination or small food portions. It was not hurricanes. It wasn't even Joe Slowinski's untimely death in the Myanmar jungle. Rather, it was the microscopic meteorite plowing into the world's amphibian species and incinerating everything in its path.

The symposium on amphibian declines was the most populous metasession of the meetings, comprising an entire day in a standing-room-only theater. In contrast to declining-amphibian gatherings of my past, almost every paper presented in N'Orleans was related to the global spread of the deadly chytrid fungus *Batrachochytrium dendrobatidis* and the fact that amphibians' vulnerability to it had been accelerated both by climate change and other anthropogenic factors.

The statistics were staggering. Of approximately 6,000 species of amphibians, 120 had *fully disappeared* since 1980, and some *30 to 50 percent* were nearing extinction. Ecosystem-level extinctions were occurring in Central America, a wave of disaster moving south at around twenty-eight kilometers a year that could be tracked back to the Golden Toad debacle of the mid-'80s in Costa Rica's Monteverde cloud forest.

We heard about chytridiomycosis catastrophes in dozens of tropical American frog species that had disappeared or been displaced from high elevation. We heard of the multicountry conservation initiative in the Andes concerning genus *Atelopus*: of 110 species, a third had disappeared, and the rest were at risk. Other frog populations had seen a 95 percent drop in as little as six months.

Researchers presented models demonstrating how climate change might be an accelerator. Compelling but as-yet-unsubstantiated stories implicating global warming were trotted out: hot and dry conditions meant frogs couldn't rehy-drate properly; water stress caused them to huddle together where chytrid spores easily spread. Climate change could also mess with water temperature, breeding phenology (cycles of male and female departure and arrival), spatial distribution, and rates of parasitism—all of which affected interaction with, and resistance to, chytrid fungus.

The immediate effects of this disaster were further reaching than a pile of dead frogs; a 75 percent loss of amphibians at some sites was affecting energy transfer from aquatic to terrestrial habitat and between trophic levels in terrestrial ecosystems. For example, amphibian declines caused a decrease in snake preda-tors, but the remaining snakes didn't leave the area; they simply started preying on lizards. Lizards then sharply declined, and the effect on populations of their invertebrate prey was unknown.

This mess detailed an ecological house of cards fluttering quickly to a chaotic demise. Interestingly, the chytrid prob-lem may derive from an undetected introduction by a for-eign vector—the African Clawed Frog (*Xenopus laevis*), widely exported around the globe for use in pregnancy tests in the mid-twentieth century. *Xenopus* carries chytrid in wild and lab pop-ulations but isn't always affected by it and thus, in theory, had decades of opportunity to cross-contaminate native species in labs, through the pet trade, and via escapees now established in the wild. Intra- and international trade in amphibians would have further helped this emergent pathogen spread. At least one report from the Centers for Disease Control concludes that the origin of chytrid *was* Africa and that international trade in *X. laevis* was the means of dissemination.

Involved early on during my stint at McGill, I'd assumed an objective scientist's view of the declining amphibian crisis, but hours of doom-and-gloom talks in which speaker after speaker decried the disappearance of anurans from areas of pristine wilderness around the globe landed a visceral blow. I felt tears welling.

You could have fun making fun of these folks all you wanted, but when the animals that delivered to you an understanding of your own existence evaporated before your eyes, you could only react as one in kind.

13

RIESLING AND RATTLESNAKES

If you see one rattlesnake, you've already

walked by nine and didn't even know it.

MIKE SARELL, herpetologist

I WAS STARING at the rings of Saturn and seeing stars in broad daylight.

Jack Newton had just topped up my afternoon glass of merlot, but it was he and not the grape treating me to close-up views of the sun and other marvels courtesy of a hydrogen filter mounted aside his computer-driven, sixteen-inch telescope, centerpiece of an impressive hand-built observatory.

As proprietor of the Observatory B&B, located high on a mountain overlooking Osoyoos, British Columbia, Jack took pleasure in dragging guests along on his continual scouring of the visible universe. Jack's was one of several observatories dotting mountaintops in an area of notoriously clear skies and comparatively low urban glow.

But astronomy wasn't the only science intersecting with the fruits of local commerce. Shifting my gaze downward and across the valley revealed a different kind of universe—the terrestrial mosaic of vineyard, orchard, pine forest, and sage desert of the southern Okanagan Valley. Officially known as the Bunchgrass Biogeoclimatic Zone, this is one of North America's most fragile and fastest-disappearing ecosystems. Agricultural and developmental pressure are consuming habitat at an alarming rate, bringing people into increasing contact with creatures that depend on it. The semiarid land responsible for the explosive success of both British Columbia's and Washington State's wine industry is also home to many species of plants and animals at risk—including cute-as-a-puppy Burrowing Owls and the not-quite-so-cuddly but no less important Northern Pacific Rattlesnake.

How burgeoning agribusiness handles conservation issues will determine whether the desert ecosystem survives, and the plight of the much-maligned rattlesnake—rodent-hunter extraordinaire, icon of the Wild West, bogeyman of every Boy Scout campfire—is a signpost of that struggle.

"I've seen plenty," said Jack, who wintered at another home observatory in Arizona and was no stranger to the buzzkill of a rattler's buzz. "Almost stepped on a few, too . . . but of course, I'm used to looking up, not down."

Around the Okanagan, winemakers and other land-gobblers were similarly trying to come to grips with serpents underfoot, raising an all-too-common question: could humans and snakes coexist? I figured this unlikely intersection of herpetology, desert ecology, and dessert oenology made a good story. And so, in the waning warmth of early October, with snakes curling into winter dens and gourmands crawling the Okanagan during its annual wine festival, I had set out to explore what I'd rather cleverly pitched to a magazine editor as "a dalliance of decadent and deadly." Seemed I was still coming up with cutesy talk titles.

As usual when it came to "work," I had other reasons to make the trip: I'd lived on the dark, dank coast of British Columbia for five years and had yet to experience its warmer, drier heart; and I liked wine; but mostly I craved the thrill of photographing rattlesnakes up close again.

I had also spent enough time around both rattlers and herpetologists to understand the nanosecond the latter took to make a painful mistake, so I would have one rule: snake chasing could precede wine tasting but never vice versa.

THE TRAIL BEGAN at the waterfront Okanagan Nature Centre in Kelowna's City Park. Inside, kids clambered over each other to peer into aquaria housing fauna like the endangered Great Basin Spadefoot Toad (*Spea intermontana*), Western Skink (*Eumeces skiltonianus*), Alligator Lizard (*Elgaria coerulea*), handsomely blotched Gophersnake (*Pituophis catenifer*), nervous Western Racer (*Coluber constrictor*), Plasticine-like Rubber Boa (*Charina bottae*), and, of course, rattlesnakes. The tiered cages and prepubescent crowd were reminiscent of Marty's long-ago camp nature hut, the excited chatter not unlike what I'd recently heard from herpetologists trolling the tanks at the New Orleans Zoo—except the kids weren't drunk and wouldn't need to be removed.

Scott Alexander, an award-winning educator, conservationist, and resident naturalist dressed in Ranger Rick garb, proved a fountain of arcane information on everything from waterbombers to wasps and, of course, rattlers. Scott explained that the center opened in 2004 on funds raised by the Okanagan Nature Centre Society after a conservative-minded provincial government pulled all support for environment and parks initiatives, a ludicrous move given that Kelowna's annual population growth was approaching 10 percent.

"Habitat is evaporating overnight around here, but agriculture is only part of the problem," explained Scott. "Housing and roads do *far* more damage to rattlesnake populations."

The issue, at the northern edge of the rattlesnakes' range, was that their dens, located in the rocky scree of hillsides, were separated from lower foraging habitat by all manner of development. Acreage in vineyards alone tripled from 1990 to 2000 and came with a huge spike in population and visitation. In the summer of 2007, newspapers brimmed with reports of increasing encounters between humans and rattlers driven from their hillside homes by construction and cultivation. By June the problem had resulted in four bites—100 percent above the annual average. Granted, the victims were all morons who ventured to pick up snakes, but with the breakneck development the problem was only going to get worse: colonization by more morons was inevitable.

Modern vintners take a more enlightened approach to rattlers traversing vineyards en route to and from dens—in fall and spring, respectively—than orchardists of yore, who simply did them in on sight. Still, local enmity toward rattlers runs deep in some quarters. That there's a church on every corner doesn't help.

As we drove north to check out a den near Oyama, Scott related the tale of Vernon's rabid Reverend Mackie. In the 1930s, promulgating a literalist biblical view of subduing the earth, the good reverend launched a personal campaign to eradicate the serpent scourge. He spent twenty years clubbing snakes, dynamiting dens, and perpetuating the poor animals' satanic image to a god-fearing populace.

It was unfortunate that many gullible farmers got on Mackie's bandwagon, because rodents are what damage crops, and snakes are far more efficient rodent predators than other animals—not only consuming adults but locating nests and wolfing down young.

Rattlesnakes are also among the most reasonable forms of dangerous wildlife: their first line of defense is to remain motionless; if you surprise them or cut off their retreat, they offer an audio warning; if you get too close, they head for cover. Venom is intended for prey, so they're reluctant to bite, and 25 to 50 percent of all bites are dry—no venom is injected (of the four bites mentioned above, three were dry).

Scott pulled off the highway, a shimmering lake to our right and the dry pine-juniper woodland we were headed into on our left. With wan afternoon light filtering through rapidly yellowing leaves, we climbed a steep, rutted hill. At its crest sat a low pile of rocks that marked the den structure. Flanked by several smaller, more colorful coils, a dusty, meter-long rattler lay wedged in its entrance. Its bulging body was as thick as my arm, with strongly keeled scales that resembled glaucous beads. The tail, banded in black-and-white, sported a long, drooping rattle. Looking safely through my trusty telephoto, I counted sixteen segments.

Despite our stealthy approach, the smaller rattlers had melted quickly into the closest cracks while the larger snake slowly uncoiled into the dark vacuity. I took a couple of shots as it slipped away. But as I maneuvered for a final photo, a Western Racer sprang from nowhere across the broken rock, and without thinking I shot a practiced arm out to grab it, two bolts of lightning colliding in the sun. With its clean lines and lithe look, it was clearly built for speed. Scott pointed out that the harmless constrictor's presence demonstrated how several species often hibernated together and how destruction of one den could spell doom for all. This snake's den was in an ecological preserve, but most in the Okanagan weren't that lucky.

"I've seen dens used by four or five different species bulldozed for a mall parking lot," he'd said. "That's enough to drive you to drink."

Later, as the sun dipped over Lake Okanagan, we sipped a dazzling riesling on the terrace of Gray Monk Estate Winery and chatted about Ogopogo, the lake's version of Nessie, commonly spotted plying the steely waters from just such lofty, lubricated vantages. An entrepreneur had once built an Ogopogo amusement park near the beast's supposed home on tiny Rattlesnake Island. Before building commenced, Reverend Mackie's acolytes had hacked up resident rattlers with shovels and tossed their bodies into the lake. Nobody caught the irony of vanquishing one of humanity's "monsters" to make way for another. The amusement park lasted but a few years; the island reclaimed the ruins, and snakes occasionally made their way back across the short channel. Reality: 1; Fantasy: 0.

"Rattlesnakes," gurgled Scott in a clumsy toast, "you gotta love 'em."

NK'MIP CELLARS IS North America's first Aboriginal-owned and -operated winery. Situated on a long bench overlooking Osoyoos Lake, the winery boasts row upon row of emerald vines, which contrast with the adjacent tract of natural desert.

Beside the winery sits a heritage center promoting the Osoyoos band's program to restore habitat and reintroduce species at risk. Roads posted with "Brake for Snakes" warnings and interpretive signs pointing out plant life and describing the history of the Osoyoos people offer counterpoint to the typically dry (pun intended) winery tours that troop through the region. But the highlight for most here is the rattlesnake-tracking program. Visitors to the center could watch snakes being tagged with the same kind of under-skin microchips used for dog and cat identification and hear a spiel about the multiyear project being conducted in conjunction with the Canadian Wildlife Service. The program enabled Nk'Mip and wildlife managers to monitor populations and work out protection strategies.

This approach seemed both more enlightened and hands-on than pure PR programs—like the token dollars some wineries threw at off-site studies of the doomed Burrowing Owl whilst simultaneously tearing up its habitat for new vines.

At Nk'Mip I joined Jeff Brown, a master's student from the University of Guelph, on his final day of tracking before he headed back to Ontario for the winter. Osoyoos band member Roger Hall was assisting him with the telemetry study. Telemetry involves surgically implanting microtransmitters in animals and then tracking them, an increasingly popular method as hardware shrinks in both size and price. The study's focus was on identifying movement patterns and critical habitat usage in order to better manage rattlesnakes.

"It isn't easy to convince people not to kill rattlers on their property or even on someone else's property like a golf course, but people around here are pretty reasonable compared with other areas where rattlers occur," said the sanguine Jeff, who also worked on Massasauga Rattlesnake conservation in Ontario's cottage country, where convincing Bay Street bond-traders not to hack up the rattlers that their million-dollar retreats were displacing was like banging your head against the limestone walls of the Toronto Stock Exchange.

As a result of education and outreach programs, most local vintners and campground and golf-course keepers in the Okanagan were adept at safely removing or diverting snakes as recommended by fish and wildlife officers. Tinhorn Creek Vineyards, for instance, had constructed a pilot-project fencing system with gates that remained open while rattlers were migrating but were shut during the prime growing season so that vines could be attended worry free. (Many of British Columbia's farmworkers are originally from the Punjab, where venomous snakes are far more of a danger; because agriculture and poverty have brought together high densities of snakes and people, India continues to lead the world in snakebite deaths with an astounding twenty thousand annually.)

The rattlers were on their way back to den sites now, and after tracking twenty all summer Jeff was following up on their autumn denouement. He zigzagged up a steep incline at a slow run, dodging sagebrush and skirting rocks, raising puffs of dust from the scarified soil as he swept a telemetry antenna ahead of him.

"Following this guy is like following a squirrel," grunted Roger from behind.

With sweat stinging my eyes, I was thinking that he was more like a mountain goat, when Jeff abruptly pulled up at a large sage wrapped haphazardly around some shattered rock.

"It's not here," he announced, flat static emanating from his transceiver. "The snake I'm tracking stopped here yesterday, but it's gone now."

"It's funny," smiled Roger, poking the ground and arching an eyebrow, "but several snakes have stopped in this *exact* spot on their way up to the den."

I'd peered at the stark, rocky substrate for any clue as to why this particular clump of mangled brush was a popular roadside attraction for migrating rattlers but couldn't see anything obvious. That alone offered a compelling reason to gather the basic biological and ecological data telemetry focused on.

As we approached the den, high on the steepest part of the hillside, Jeff's transceiver clicked sporadically, and we peered under every rock jutting from the slope. "I don't think it's the one I'm tracking," said Jeff finally, pointing to a tight space underneath a large flake, "but there's a snake here."

I could just make out the coil of a small rattler, barely visible through the netherworld of shadow and grasses. Drawing its head briefly from the depths and holding its tongue out in a steady flicker, it gathered whatever information was pouring off me and, finding nothing good, wedged itself farther into the shadows.

The retreat was an apt metaphor for the Okanagan's beleaguered snakes, and I didn't blame the animal one bit. As I drove back toward the Pacific Coast and home, I realized that the next time I visited the Okanagan, many of the animals I'd seen would be gone.

HERPETOLOGISTS HAVE A way of finding each other. Meeting Stuart in Fiji had seemed unlikely, but then, I'd been waving a rare snake around on a tropical island. I never imagined anything similar happening in Whistler, the mountain town I live in on the British Columbia coast, where if you weren't talking skiing, mountain biking, or how to make a fortune off weed or the Olympics, you were just another tourist. But there I was one June morning, minding my own business in a coffee shop, when I was beamed into the belly of a spacecraft full of herpetologists.

I was parked in an easy chair reading Ron Altig's essay on tadpole evolution in the journal *Herpetologica* when a woman walked by, did a double take, and then cleared her throat.

"Excuse me," she prodded, "is that *Herpetologica* you're reading?"

The words sounded nonsensical in the context of our surroundings and echoed wetly off the walls. Outside, trees swayed like question marks; there was only *one* reason anyone would *ever* ask such a question, but even dogs sniffing each other's butts had a protocol.

"Yes—why?"

Elke Wind turned out to be a herpetologist from Vancouver Island working on a local amphibian biodiversity project, and she immediately invited me to join the group she was leading. One minute I was innocently sipping coffee and trying to decide whether Altig was off his nut to say that "tadpoles evolved and frogs are the default," and the next I was wallowing in a mucky pond, net in hand, with people I'd never seen or heard of, chatting about Northwestern Salamanders (*Ambystoma gracile*), Rough-skinned Newts (*Taricha granulosa*), and Coastal Tailed Frogs (*Ascaphus truei*).

Granted, I'd once again flaunted a powerful semiotic, but it wasn't like herpetologists were streaming through ski-resort coffee shops every day. The encounter was either cosmic kismet of epic proportions or more evidence of a curse I'd never shake. Was I really snakebit?

Besides its literal meaning, the term "snakebitten" had a figurative connotation in the arcane slang of the southern United States, where it denoted someone either specifically predisposed to bad luck or, more generally, cursed in a way that alluded to an insidious lifelong burden. It seemed an apt metaphor for the weird and obsessive worlds of the herpetologists I'd been tracking and, by dint of association, my own life: bitten by a harmless snake as a child, I too was drawn irretrievably into this secretive world. I could leave herpetology, it seemed, but it would never leave me. I was marked.

Having the sign meant occasionally being able to read it, too. On my trip to the Okanagan I'd been introduced to "a local naturalist" named Mike Sarell. But from the second we shook hands I knew the truth: he was a snake guy.

Sarell and I had immediately headed off in search of a rattle-snake den, hiking and climbing through the Skaha Bluffs, a Dr. Seuss–like land of sheer, rocky faces above the Naramata Bench outside of Penticton, home to half a dozen famed wineries. After several false turns in the labyrinthine landscape, he'd finally located the den, improbably high on a scarily narrow shelf that fell away over a twenty-meter cliff. A few snakes were wedged in the tight cracks, and Sarell, lying on his belly with a long stick, had even teased a junior rattler into the light for a photo.

I had found Sarell's quiet sense of humor and field style to my liking, and we'd kept in touch about rattlesnakes and the Okanagan's many other species at risk. A guy like Sarell puts you on a quick learning curve, and my interest had been piqued, so early the following summer I returned to the Okanagan to join him in a search for one of Canada's rarest reptiles: the Desert Night Snake.

Yanking his truck into the parking lot in Okanagan Falls where we'd arranged to meet, Mike looked exactly like he did the last time I'd seen him: water-repellant cargo pants, blue eyes burning under sandy, tightly curled hair, cigarette in hand, mountain-man spring in his step.

"Let's go," he said by way of hello.

We headed east, winding up a logging road into the wilderness of the Vaseux Protected Area. When the road disintegrated into a track, we swerved around deadfalls and snapped branches out of the way. There was plenty of downed and soon-to-be-downed wood. The rugged parkland forest dominated by Ponderosa Pine had burned in the great Vaseux fire of 2003; most large trees survived, but smaller trees and dead snags went up like torches and were just now starting to topple. We had been chatting about Rubber Boas and alligator lizards, but as we neared our first search spot, talk turned to our current quest.

As its name suggests, the Desert Night Snake is a rarely seen nocturnal species. Small, inconspicuous, and cryptic, it hunts its primarily reptilian prey deep in rocky rubble and, other than road driving in the right locations (as when I'd found one in Death Valley), was maddeningly difficult to locate. Which is maybe why the first record in the Okanagan dates only as far back as when you were playing The Clash's *London Calling* on your Walkman. The first recorded specimen had been found by Howard Lacey in 1980 near Kaleden, B.C., several hundred kilometers beyond its known northerly limit in Washington State. By 1996, when the information was published by Lacey, Sarell, Pat Gregory, and others, only thirteen additional specimens were known from the area, all caught in hot, dry, near-desert shrub-steppe.

A decade later the total stood at only a couple dozen, and Mike Sarell had seen and caught more of those than anyone. In fact, Mike had bagged nine so far that spring in five locations, further filling in its range in the Lower Okanagan. What had he gleaned from these captures? For one thing, small rattlesnakes were on the menu—a specimen barfed up a tail with its button rattle in 1992. And snakes were primarily found on rocky slopes, underneath rocks. They preferred large rocks embedded in soil, advised Mike, holding his arms in a fingertip-to-fingertip circle.

"What's really cool," he said, "is that the ones I *have* found are always under rocks I knew were going to have something. I was like 'This is the rock.'"

If I couldn't find this phantom snake with a guy like Sarell, it would be a long, fruitless, rock-turning time until I found one on my own.

At our first stop, we flipped plenty of rocks but found no snakes. It was backbreaking, hand-scouring work, made more uncomfortable by uncharacteristically muggy heat; it had rained, more clouds threatened, and mist hung over the usually sere landscape. Back in the truck, contouring the mountain toward the south, we bumped over diminishing double-track. We didn't want to lose altitude, so when the faint trail bucked downward, we stopped in a meadow, ready for a stiff hike to the talus above.

Five steps from the truck, Mike yelled, "Rattlesnake!" It was a big one.

The rattler buzzed unenthusiastically, then coiled into a cleft in a large boulder. There it sat, backed by the rock, tongue pushing out slowly to hang for a second, its forked tip vibrating before being retracted and tucked into Jacobson's organ, a sensitive chemosensory structure on the roof of the mouth (Jacobson was the Danish physician of the 1800s who, without fully understanding the structure's capability, first described its relationship to the olfactory area of the brain). Alert but not overly disturbed, the rattler signaled with the S-shape of the latter third of its body that it was nevertheless ready for business at a moment's notice. We snapped a few pictures, made GPS notations, and moved on. Two minutes later another, almost as large, surprised me by buzzing furiously when I was only a step away. It slunk across rain-flattened grass and slid under a rock. Mike stepped over to find a deer mouse quivering in the grass; figuring the snake was after it, he tossed the rodent under the rock, doing what he could to apologize for the interruption.

We spent the rest of the morning hiking difficult terrain and turning difficult rocks. Like most snake hunting, it was hot, physical work. When we finally retreated, I was bruised and bleeding from a dozen places. On the track out we passed a magnificent Golden Eagle perched atop a burned larch. Shining in the ether formed by mist and weak light that glowed from a bladder of clouds, it seemed like a symbol; protected areas should remain so.

Our next stop, on the lower mountain, was a place Mike figured Desert Night Snakes *should* be; he had found them on an adjacent rocky knob, and Western Skinks—a primary food source—were in the area.

· Warm haze now alternated with heavy showers. We searched the rock-littered hillside for about an hour, finding no snakes but dozens of bright, blue-tailed skinks and one suspicious shed that was almost certainly *Hypsiglena*—again recalling my long-ago summer job: you couldn't always be in the right place at an optimal time to see a species per se, but you could infer its likely or possible presence from the evidence at hand. Proximity of another population of the same species, a good food source, suitable habitat, and a shed skin said plenty. *Hypsiglena* was probably here somewhere.

Maybe it was the rain, or maybe we were just too late (*Hypsiglena* was almost never found during the summer when heat drove them to near invisibility), but our huge effort had turned up nothing. I wasn't too disappointed, though—I'd had fun looking. Besides, I reasoned aloud, it *was* a rare snake.

Mike didn't agree. "I think there are scads of them out there," he explained. "There *has* to be for us to have found the few we have; and they don't move around much, so populations are quite localized. I wouldn't say they're the rarest snake here—more like the hardest to find."

LIKE THE PREVIOUS time I'd hung with him, I'd learned plenty from Mike Sarell. Born and bred in the south Okanagan, Mike started in the nature game when a talk at a local park got him going on his first bug collection. That was age six—the year he killed his first rattlesnake with a group of other kids, "'cause that's what you were supposed to do."

Like many who grew up here and embraced nature, he remained indifferent to rattlers until, around 1980, he was asked to skin one a friend had killed.

"I thought about it for a minute and said no," recalled Mike of what would prove an epiphany. "I said, 'I'm not going to do that.' I don't know why, but that was it. Since then I've worked to save them."

Mike took to park interpretive work. He went to university and learned what he could, keeping aware of and involved in local issues. He knew as much as any ten men about the area's animals and plants and the ecological ties that bound them. Like other herpetologists I knew, he was also a freak for bats. Because they conjured images of miniature, furry pterodactyls? No. More that they were another poorly understood animal people didn't like.

Soaked to the skin, we were winding down with a few brews at a century-old Okanagan Falls hangout when a jabbering drunk asked Mike to explain a bizarre snake sighting: it was thick like a boa, with no tapering of the body and a stubby tail; unlike a boa it had a wide, arrow-shaped head like a venomous snake and longitudinal stripes like a garter—essentially a chimera of every snake in the valley. Without dismissing him outright, Mike encouraged the man to get a picture next time, casting me a sidelong glance that clearly said, "This happens all the time."

When the drunk cleared off, we ordered another round and talked up another Okanagan phantom, the Pygmy Short-horned Lizard (*Phrynosoma douglasii*). The only two specimens were collected near Osoyoos in 1910. Sarell himself had searched high and low, even traveling to the States, where they're abundant, to hone his search image. No luck. Currently, the species is considered extirpated in British Columbia—first victim of the wine-crazed Okanagan.

It's all about grapes here, and although development may sometimes be slowed by endangered or threatened species, agribusiness trumps all. The grasslands are almost gone, and what remains is weeded over. Open land dominated by Antelope Brush is the most valuable to wine companies and therefore most threatened. Mike related an overheard conversation in which a well-known agri-land developer boasted about "specializing in turning mountains into vineyards." The company used huge pulverizers to turn rock into soil, bypassing the thousands of years of weathering and microbial breakdown usually required. The conceit fairly boggled.

Research shows that a functioning ecosystem requires 40 percent of its original components; in the south Okanagan, these have already dropped to 30 percent, so recovery is unlikely. Wetlands are down to 10 to 15 percent—in the range of hopeless. The concern is not about species at risk anymore but *ecosystems* at risk and *all* species being threatened. So the Burrowing Owl, Spadefoot Toad, Pygmy Short-horned Lizard, Northern Pacific Rattlesnake, Gopher Snake, and possibly the Desert Night Snake are pretty much toast. As I listed them aloud so that Mike could offer long-term prognoses, he referred to each case as "bleak," detouring only when we came to the rattler. Here, he leveled me with a sad half-grin and said, "*Very* bleak."

Few knew that the Northern Hemisphere was courting a biodiversity crisis as acute as that of tropic regions—perhaps more so because of the slower regenerative capacity of northern ecosystems. Although the Okanagan community and government are aware, they have brought little concerted effort or regulatory clout to ameliorate the situation.

"Lots of people are aware, and a few say they care, but where does caring start? With an opinion?" said Mike, sounding suddenly tired.

We both agreed that opinion fell short: true caring starts with action. "Doesn't your own work give you satisfaction?" I asked.

"It actually depresses the hell out of me," Mike said. "I'm the person doing environmental impact assessments for the next big development disasters."

He had a point. His work was like censusing a city before someone dropped an atomic bomb on it. And rattlesnakes bore the brunt of most land-use bombs. As building reached higher onto the benches above the lakes, the more snake immigration-emigration was interrupted. Public education appeared to be having some effect because persecution was declining, but much of that decline had occurred because snakes had been made scarce by rabid development.

Mike summarized by putting our day into perspective: "I know people who've lived here their whole lives and have *never* seen a rattlesnake. We saw more in one day than the average person sees in a lifetime. And they're arguing over whether there should be more protected areas and parks."

People, pressure, politics—the perfect storm for a snake.

14

SAVING THE WORLD REDUX

Snakes are to the animal world what toadstools

are to the vegetable world—wonderful things,

beautiful things, but fearsome things.

ERNEST THOMPSON SETON, *The Birch Bark Roll*

I FOUND MY first Armenian Viper a hundred meters from camp.

High on a windswept col, I had been searching the area around a crumbled shepherd's hut. Only a couple of stone walls stood intact. Inside, thistles and pugnacious burdock thrust up through the rusted springs of abandoned beds; their combined vegetative hydraulic had even levitated a child's cot from the ground. Twisted pieces of cheap Soviet sheet metal used for everything from wallboard to windbreak lay scattered about. As did an abundance of the corrugated, asbestos-composite roof tile diagnostic of all former Soviet states in Asia—as if some Moscow functionary once decreed that every dwelling in the southern empire adopt the same dull, gray pallor to promote unity. The assessment likely wasn't far off the mark, except that the tile more likely promoted asbestosis; predictably, it was an inferior material with a short shelf life that went brittle in the sun and readily disintegrated.

Not finding anything, I'd headed back toward the tents. Walking past a pile of haphazardly stacked roofing, I'd absently flipped a large piece to expose nothing but scurrying earwigs. Under the second slab was the viper.

It lay tightly coiled atop another piece of tile, an orange-spotted chocolate band hovering like a Magritte illusion over bland gray, as if it, too, were fighting the soulless rule of Communism. The perfect juxtaposition of natural and unnatural. I'd felt the familiar electricity of uncovering treasure, what seemed in the same instant both privilege and deserved reward.

Once again I had found one of nature's stealthiest vehicles, whose every design feature revolved around staying off the radar. As with the Finnish vipers in their snowy crib, for a moment my reverence knew no bounds: the snake was the most beautiful thing I'd ever seen.

Then it moved.

DR. BOB HAD said the Armenia trip would be "fun." I'd signed on even though I knew what that meant.

On a hot July night, I had exited the ghetto airport of Armenia's capital, Yerevan, and scanned the crowd. I didn't have to look far to spot the Geek King, face hidden by a massive camera, taking pictures of me ... looking for him. Kolya stood to Bob's side, hands in pockets, feigning dissociation.

"Bop," he shrugged, head shaking in mock disgust, his peculiar truncated pronunciation chopping the vowel in half.

His meaty hand engulfed mine as we half-hugged, shoulder-to-shoulder, L.A.-gang style. Bob took another shot and turned the display to show us, like a third-world beach vulture hawking vacation photos. Kolya rolled his eyes. I hadn't seen these two together in a decade, but it may as well have been last week. *Plus ça change.*

In Kolya's considerable shadow lurked Aram Aghasyan, our Armenian host. He was dark and diminutive, with a cigarette permanently on the go. When I shook his hand, he exuded the kind of mute reverence you offered someone of importance. Didn't he know I was an interloper? *What did Bob tell him?* Jeezuz.

Aram lived in a Stalin-esque cluster of high-rises in northern Yerevan; bleak towers of disintegrating concrete with garbage chutes that fired waste to the ground outside where an army of dogs distributed it in all directions. My bags had barely hit the floor in his cramped three-bedroom before a king's banquet of roast chicken, sliced cucumber, tomato, pepper, sour cheese, and bread appeared. Aram's wife, Margo, and son, Levon, ushered us toward the table. I was embarrassed, thinking they'd waited dinner for me, but they hadn't, which doubled my discomposure: it was all for me. But you couldn't fight tradition. When someone arrives after a long journey—the only kind anyone could make in Asia Minor—you put out food and drink for the traveler.

I dug in while the others picked over a plate of watermelon. Except Aram, who between cigarettes was dissecting a bucket of extra-large, boiled-red Sevan crayfish fetched from the eponymous lake that pooled in the country's midsection. He had as great an appetite for these organisms as he did for cigarettes.

A full stomach and indeterminate number of vodka toasts later, and I was stretched out on a church-bench of a sofa that was, inevitably, a head too short. I would gladly have slept on the floor, but I'd already seen a swarm of light-scattering cockroaches in the phone booth–sized bathroom. So I toughed it out, drifting off in hazy recall of the far-sketchier places I'd bunked down with Bob—stretched out in the fetid back of Morafka's truck somewhere in the searing desert, curled fetuslike on a pool table at 40°C and 90 percent humidity in a banana warehouse in northern Vietnam, sweat stains spreading like blood across the green felt, and worse.

Thirty minutes later an entire country's worth of ownerless dogs cranked up, and the torturous squeals of fighting and fucking continued until dawn, when the hounds handed things off to the birds for an hour before rejoining the cacophony in a triumphant coda that heralded the end of any hope for sleep.

Still, I'd been fed, fêted, and laid down within hours of arrival. No shakedown in customs, no hovering government official, no side-trip to any ministry, no one to pay off, and, so far, no radical change of plans. All things considered, it was the best start to one of Bob's field trips ever.

TEN DAYS LATER not much had changed. Bleary-eyed breakfast again consisted of all the food and vodka we hadn't consumed the night before and strong coffee brewed Turkish-style (Aram insisted this was actually Armenian-style), the thick residue clotting the bottom of the diminutive cup reminding me that I'd soon be as hopped-up as everyone else in the country. As usual, Dr. Bob downed three before he could function.

Aram hovered in a cloud of smoke, aiming a spray-bottle into the portals of a ceiling-high wooden hutch where stacked, glass-fronted cages variously contained an odiferous hedgehog named Hitchcock, a large green iguana that subsisted on table scraps, a somnolent python that may or may not have been alive, and various indigenous vipers. Aram worked at the Department of Protected Areas Management in the Agency for Bioresources

Management of the Ministry of Nature Protection (I didn't make this up) and also headed Armenia's CITES committee, working closely with NGOs like the World Wildlife Fund Critical Ecosystem Partnership. This was but his official mantle; his vocation was herpetology, which he'd studied under Ilya Darevsky in Russia, where the two became fast friends. Following in Aram's footsteps as if herping were a family business, twenty-six-year-old Levon was a herpetologist-cum–conservation biologist. Among other roles, he headed the campaign to save the almost-cute Darevsky's Viper (*Pelias darevskii*), a diminutive, cold-tolerant mountain dweller found only on the short Javakheti Ridge, which formed part of the northern border with Georgia. The ridge amounted to a microscopic fold in the vast, geologic laundry pile of the Caucasus, the snake an integral part of its fabric.

So far we'd traversed Armenia's basaltic plains to collect snakes in various surrounding ranges. We'd searched unsuccessfully for several species on Mount Aragats, Armenia's highest peak at 4,100 meters; collected pregnant Meadow Vipers (*P. eriwanensis*) outside Yerevan to check for sperm storage and paternity; camped below Javakheti Ridge to take harmless scale clips for DNA analysis from endangered *P. darevskii*; and chased dozens of lizards over the sun-blasted rocks and ruins of this hostile land. It had given me a feel for a place I'd read plenty about but could never quite visualize, and a history I was just now learning.

Surrounding a fold-down couch on which Kolya slept in Aram's guest room was the accumulated debris of inspiration and a lifetime's worth of study. Glass-door bookshelves were crammed with hundreds of volumes in Russian and Armenian, their titles incomprehensible even if you were able to translate the strange scripts (an ancient Indo-European language, written

Armenian resembles rudimentary Sanskrit). There were rolled maps, long-forgotten boxes, and an old-fashioned counterweight balance; small artifacts and mementos like a Turkish lantern and Iranian etched brass vase; and hand-built, sliding-glass shelves with a smattering of faded photos offsetting the monotony of sun-grayed book spines.

There were the usual shots—Aram and Margo alone or with friends, relatives, and colleagues—and a professional-looking family portrait that Dr. Bob had taken on the second of two previous visits. On his first, in 1992, to collect Caucasus rock lizards with Darevsky, he'd put together a decent collection of tissues. When he departed, however, Aeroflot—in inexplicable airline fashion—routed his precious liquid-nitrogen canister, complete with frozen samples, to Sweden. The container arrived back in Toronto two weeks after he'd left Armenia. The liquid nitrogen had long since evaporated, and the hard-won tissues thawed, spoiled, and exploded from their tubes into a reeking, deathlike soup. An insurance claim from the loss paid for another trip in '93. I had read Dr. Bob's subsequent paper describing unexpected genetic variability in putatively clonal *Lacerta armeniaca* (nowadays *Darevskia armeniaca*) collected during that trip, but connecting this erudite work to the slapstick backstory allowed me to take comfort in the fact that folly also followed Bob when I wasn't around.

What really drew my attention, however, was a pair of dusty snapshots sandwiching a large, out-of-focus print of two mating vipers. In one, a much younger Aram, serious as ever, coal eyes burning under jet-black mop, sat on the sofa beside an equally youthful Kolya, arms crossed as usual, hint of a smile and redder-faced than I'd ever seen him, sporting only the slightest splash of gray on his chin. In the other, a grinning Darevsky, hair an

Eraserhead tangle, sat with Margo and a child-aged Levon, while Aram, in the days before red-eye reduction, looked askance through a smoky clutter of vodka bottles.

There was something comforting in those bleached moments that stirred a sense of continuity. Brothers in arms. Friends for life. Colleagues. Family. All in the name of a few "eenterestink" snakes. Fifteen years later, I was in those pictures.

WE WERE AIMING toward the axial of Armenia's reluctant intersection with Turkey, Iran, and Azerbaijan when the familiar road-trip-with-Bob sensation had set in—a disconnectedness born of the battle between my desire to control my own fate and the inevitability of ceding it to others. I well remembered the feeling from Baja and Vietnam—trapped in the back of some vehicle, staring into unfamiliar countryside through a miasma of foreign voices laced with uncertainty, as if hope, deliverance, answers lay somewhere in the landscape. They very much had, of course, though it was hard to remember that fact in moments of rising panic.

Like an anxious child, I found not knowing what was going on more nerve-wracking than any physical affliction. How many times had I battled through a shuddering cold sweat or clutched a violently cramping stomach as I stumbled over bags of deadly snakes on my way to vomit, shit explosively, or both, only to succumb later, in otherwise perfect health, to a "What am I doing here?" haze of unease?

We had, as usual, been hours late in leaving. Bob was told we'd have two four-wheel-drive vehicles, perfect for five of us and our mountain of luggage. But another driver—also named Aram—was required for the second car, a WWF vehicle. Tall, red-faced, chain-smoking, and robed in a smart gray tracksuit, the soft-spoken man we dubbed #2 looked to be moonlighting from the Russian mafia. That assessment wasn't far off; for years he had piloted trucks between Yerevan and Moscow, paid in cash on delivery, never knowing his employers or what he carried. Creeping regulation ruined that bonanza, so now he drove cheap-assed scientists around. Given the deadly cargo he'd soon be schlepping, it was arguable which gig was more dangerous.

Three in each four-person vehicle would be tight but tolerable, but we also apparently needed a snake-wrangling field hand named Alek. He showed up in military fatigues with a jarhead haircut and a look that suggested he'd snap your neck if need be, though he turned out to be more of a gentle giant—just like Jingo, Aram #1's bone-white, sixty-five-kilo American bulldog, who usurped the final seat and any chance of elbow room. With a head the size of a watermelon, furrowed forehead, slobbering jowls, and enormous testicles bulging horizontally behind him in a tight, pink scrotum, Jingo was the ugliest dog I'd ever seen. It didn't stop there: his left eye was both skewed and bicolored, its top half in the same soft brown as his right, while the lower half glowed icy blue. It was perfect bilateral schizophrenia: sad, doe-eyed puppy on the right; leering, satanic murderer on the left. Far outweighing his slight owner, Jingo inspired disbelief in all who glimpsed him; even gas-station attendants stared dumbfounded.

"Surreal," offered Bob as we crept out of town, smug in the knowledge that he had once again assembled a rolling Dali painting.

Yerevan slid by like an unfinished basement, stark and depressing, another broke-down, post-Communist disaster of disintegrating Soviet crap. The new regime was building atop the old master's mess, creating pockets of corruption-fueled opulence amid questionable construction and general mediocrity, the interstices liberally piled with twisted iron, concrete pipes, ageless garbage, and a choke of invasive, fast-growing plants. A plague of rodents rustled through it all, and well . . . let's just say that when you destroy an animal's habitat and create an abundant food source nearby, certain things are inevitable.

Snakes had apparently been taking up residence in Yerevan. An occupational hazard for those working in the countryside, city residents increasingly encountered venomous serpents as forests and fields surrounding the capital were buried under new houses. One man had even caught a deadly Levantine Viper in his apartment—four stories up. The Agency for Extreme Situations (honestly, I am *not* making this up) had recorded a spike in emergency calls involving snakes. From 1995 to 1999, the annual average had been thirty incidents, with almost no cases in Yerevan. In 2004, however, sixty-seven Armenians suffered snakebite and three died. According to the Department for Acute Intoxication (I swear), Yerevan's medical center dealt with twenty-three of those cases, and by early 2005 they'd already seen twelve more. One tragedy involved a young boy who died after being bitten by a Levantine Viper. The Russia-produced antivenin Antigyurzin wasn't registered in Armenia, couldn't be sold in pharmacies, and was only available in medical centers that most bite victims couldn't realistically reach within the critical first hour following a bite.

Of course it wasn't realistic. But did we—those voted most likely to be bitten a bazillion kilometers from anywhere—carry Antigyurzin or anything similar? Of course not. That kind of foresight was unrealistic, not because herpetologists were disorganized and cheap but because carrying antivenin was an admission of incompetence and waning machismo. Like putting out your cigarette before pumping gas.

Like Yerevan's invading snakes, we crawled through a city filled with skinny, chain-smoking men dressed in smart shirts and pressed slacks—none of the casualness we were used to in the West. In contrast to our deconstructive dress, looking sharp was still the measure of the man here; at 45°C, only kids and herpetologists wore shorts.

The convoy pulled into a petrol station. Both #1 and #2 rolled down their windows, cigarettes bobbing. An attendant interrupted his card game to slouch over, smoke curling from his hand, and bargain over gas. Money changed hands, the tanks filled amid constant argument. Cigarettes burned. Jerry cans were topped up. Trapped in the backseat of a two-door, Bob and I had contemplated the possibility of incineration.

"Surreal," he said again, quite unnecessarily.

We'd finally escaped Yerevan, and the highway flashed south across a plain with all 5,500 meters of historic Mount Ararat hovering to the right. A national symbol in Armenia, everything from yogurt to banks to cognac bore the name, despite the entire massif being contained within archenemy Turkey (the Soviets handed it to them in the 1921 Treaty of Kars). Clearly, this was a perennial sore point. As we drew abreast of the behemoth that cast its considerable shadow over the borderland, our cell phones glowed "Welcome to Turkey!" The Armenians went ballistic.

WE WERE HEADING for a state forest reserve somewhere on the Iranian frontier, but after six cramped hours in the vehicles we needed a break.

We stopped at a roadside market where a dozen vendors sat behind a dozen identical watermelon pyramids, boxes of peaches, baskets of tomatoes, and palisades of peppers, eggplant, and cucumber. Somewhere in this relentless leitmotif, a woman lodged beside a dust-covered pot fashioned traditional wraps with mystery meat, onion, and a mix of fresh cilantro, basil, and dill wrapped in a sheet of *lavash*, the local unleavened flatbread baked on rods hung in underground ovens and vended in great bales rolled like bolts of cloth. They were delicious and didn't last nearly long enough.

We left the highway, and time unwound down every valley. When we finally pulled off to camp in a canyon hemmed by crenulated thousand-meter towers, animals roamed untended, beekeepers slept in meadows with their bees, and haymakers out of a Brughuel painting wandered the road with hand-hewn tools.

Once we threw up the tents, Bob and Kolya rushed off with #2 to check out a ruined church. Alek and Levon were readying for a hike, so I fell in with them. I'd come a long, difficult way to see an Armenian Viper and jumped at this first chance to make it happen. Alek had collected them on the ridge above camp in May, and although it was now too hot to find them at such low altitude, even a remote prospect was motivation enough. Alek spent considerable time busting out a Rambo outfit that included head scarf, black wristbands, army boots, binoculars, and a tool belt dangling snake tongs, knife, and compass. Levon's preparation consisted of lighting another smoke.

The heat was oppressive and footing impossible. The steep basaltic talus we scrambled up ranged from fist-sized gravel to dinner-plate slabs; unanchored by the sparse, semidesert vegetation, it behaved precisely like sand, albeit a painful form that battered ankles as you sank in on each proverbial one-step-back. Side-hilling to lessen the angle of attack proved even more challenging—like walking diagonally across a sloping roof whose tiles occasionally shot out from under your feet.

Eventually we gained the ridge with views down to camp—a multihued dot in a copse of walnut trees—and across the dizzying main valley, where angled cliff bands, stacked like a tilted wedding cake, arched upward into the icing of afternoon thermals. Atop these lay the summer habitat of the threatened Armenian Viper (*Montivipera raddei*).

Of the many species of animals named for the prolific eighteenth-century zoologist Gustav Radde, *M. raddei* was likely the most handsome. Its delicate beauty and submeter length were vaguely reminiscent of small, montane species of rattlesnake. It was, however, more ornate, possessing prominently horn-rimmed eyes and offset rows of rust-orange spots along the midline of its brown body (a comeliness that, unfortunately, made it a favorite of the international pet trade). Although one imagines it as conspicuous, in the orange lichen–spattered rubble of its high-altitude home, the creature virtually disappeared.

The snake had a much-fragmented distribution in Armenia and adjacent countries. It had been assigned to genus *Montivipera* based on morphology, but some scientists still believed only molecular data. Dr. Bob's aim was to validate (or invalidate) the proposed taxonomy as well as to understand how these isolated, mountaintop populations maintained gene flow—particularly in the face of the overgrazing threatening the snake's habitat.

Alek decided to rest on the rocky ridge. Grateful for any respite, Levon and I dove for pockets of shade afforded by the largest boulders. I greedily downed water while Levon lit another smoke. Alek sipped contemplatively from his canteen, mopped his brow, then methodically broke out a mat and put his back to a rock. Pulling binoculars to his face, he seemed to be scanning for enemy combatants but was actually searching for bears—he'd seen a young male that spring on the opposite slope, turning stones in search of food. Herpetologists weren't the only large mammal aware of the potential bounty beneath the rocks.

Despite scrutinizing the entire range with Google Earth precision, Alek saw nothing, eliciting stoic disappointment. Resignedly, he'd packed up, and we headed across a gully where a spring-fed trickle offered enough moisture for a tangle of ground-hugging vegetation and the fastidious taproots of walnut. Suddenly Alek leaned down to pluck up something and then turned to reveal his thumb and forefinger pinching the thorax of a gangly, hand-sized spider. As he extended it toward me so that I could get a closer look, I expected to see a tarantula, but instead of eight beady little eyes embedded in a hairy head, I saw the multifaceted orbs and frantic, akimbo antennae of a smooth-faced... *grasshopper?* Where there should have been nasty, fanglike chelicerae were instead sharp, chitinous mandibles hanging open like wire cutters beckoning toward a set of maxillae that opened and closed furiously.

"*Saga pedo*," smiled Rambo triumphantly, presciently answering my next question, "Orthoptera. Sometime eet lizard."

Now we were getting somewhere: a giant, carnivorous branch of grasshopperdom that looked for all the world like a large ground spider and hunted like one, too. This explained its common name of Predatory Bush Cricket, but the stranger-than-truth *Saga pedo* had another secret: also known as the Matriarchal Katydid, it was an obligate parthenogen for which only a single male had ever been found.

Gingerly, I took the beast to inspect it closely. I had little doubt that if I held it improperly it would bite and that the bite would be painful. It seemed that anytime I cared to ask, nature had something mind-blowing to show me. In this case something unlikely to be seen again: sadly, the amazing *Saga pedo* was on its last spine-addled legs; unchecked grazing has left it Red-Listed the world over. The reasons for widespread extirpation of *Saga pedo* were the same as those responsible for steep declines in Armenia's threatened vipers, and I wondered if conservation efforts here were the same sad salvage operation as in British Columbia's Okanagan. For the time being, however, I was hot, tired, hungry, and, despite the serendipity of *Saga pedo,* disappointed not to have found a snake.

THE NEXT DAY'S first stop was the shell of a sixth-century church that a clutch of large pigs had to themselves. Bop and Kolya had wanted to "make photo" of the primitive structure and strange inscriptions, but our real reason for combing the rubble was reptilian. Small, salt-and-pepper lizards of genus *Darevskia* and large, lime-green *Lacerta* flitted more commonly around such ruins than anywhere else. If you wanted to collect a ton of lizards in Armenia, you couldn't avoid going to church.

Armenia was long known, even among biologists, for little more than churches until an unknown Russian herpetologist named Ilya Darevsky discovered populations of rock lizards consisting entirely of females. His findings, published in 1958, were the first known example of an all-female vertebrate "species." Armenia was suddenly on the herpetological map with its own mecca: Darevsky's Wall, a road cut famous for unisexual lizards.

So we combed the walls of ancient churches, swiping at *Lacerta* and *Darevskia,* arms afire from the stinging nettles the creatures inevitably ran for cover in. The churches were interesting—like an extravagant twelfth-century structure wrapped around a simple, Lego-like sixth-century nucleus—but nothing compared with what we found atop a windswept, rock-strewn plateau in what's called the Sisian region. Here we chased flattened, heat-hoarding Trans-Caucasian Agama (*Agama caucasia*) over the remains of 7,500-year-old Carahunge—an observatory constructed some 3,500 years before Stonehenge but similarly replete with a ring of large stones levered into position. (*Car* means stone and *hunge*, voice or sound; there's likely a connection with Stonehenge, since the latter is younger, the names are similar, and *henge* has no meaning in English.)

After a fruitless hour, I finally pinned a spiky, toad-headed *Agama* against a toppled monolith. And I thought this: when these stones were first erected by Neolithic pagans, *Agama* were likely running around here. Observatories, churches, and humans came and went, and the same damn lizards happily occupied the aftermath. Biologically speaking, not much had happened here in 7,500 years. Not much at all.

THE ROOM SMELLED like fresh blood. It might have been the hindquarter of pork that #1 had been chopping on the floor. Or it could have been the exsanguinations of a dogfight that just sent crimson arcing across the walls and pretty much everything else.

We'd finally arrived in Shikahogh State Preserve and had unloaded our vehicles into abandoned barracks that looked far more military than utilitary. The Arams had been prepping food for a giant banquet planned for the director's house when #1, for reasons unknown, unleashed Jingo from the heavy chain he was always kept on. Sitting across the room, I'd had a front-row seat to what happened when the park director strolled through the door with arms outstretched to welcome his friend, Aram. The scrappy black mutt at his side had immediately seen the back end of Jingo, an obvious intruder and, with lips curled, lunged through the air. I'd yet to see Jingo do anything more aggressive than lick his balls, but in a lightning ninja move, as if he'd seen it coming, the bulldog had simply spun 180 degrees and opened his vast maw, into which the attacking dog's neck was vacuumed. Jingo's jaws snapped shut to a wrenching animal cry that made the agony of mating raccoons sound like the murmuring of mice and transformed the room into a chaotic tumble of dogs, bodies, equipment, meat, and produce. Jingo held tight, shaking the other dog like a cheerleader's pom-pom. With teams pulling at the bleeding pets from both ends and beating them hard with heavy sticks, the mess took five snarling minutes to disentangle.

All's fair when it comes to dogs, and the tussle was quickly forgotten as we got down to the business of banqueting. Though this banquet would be the biggest, we'd had several thus far, all unfolding similarly: Bob funneled money to #1, who purchased food and booze; the host gathered womenfolk to prepare breads, sour cheeses, dried meat, and pickles while the men smoked and fired up the barbecue pit to roast eggplant, tomatoes, banana peppers, and any available meat on long, heavy skewers that would be shish kababs elsewhere but were here called *khorovatz*; the men continued smoking and grilling after handing the charred vegetables to the women, who painstakingly peeled the burnt parts away and made various dishes with the mashed remains; the meat was finished and the table loaded—filling it was key—with plates stacked atop each other, wads of fresh lavash at every place and any empty spaces filled with bottles of vodka, beer, and wine; the women then evaporated to parts unknown while the men chowed down; food was eaten slowly, liberally sprinkled with toasts to anything anyone could think of (and you *had* to think of something as you were expected to toast until you were toast); while the men got cross-eyed, the women cleaned, rearranging the remaining food for a post-meal meal; as things wound down and blindness overtook the men, someone produced a bottle of homemade hooch and total destruction was achieved.

Aram #1, guarding his lavash with his life (he once smuggled fifteen kilos of it on a trip to the United States because he was afraid he wouldn't be able to find any there; maids were not impressed when he'd strung it up in his hotel room) and with a bag of Sevan crayfish by his side (where did *that* come from?), rose to steer the toasts. Despite his slight stature, #1 had an incredible capacity for alcohol. He fired off three toasts in a row, each a mini-opera and each followed by a shot. The subjects, as far as I could tell, were snakes for being snakes, Bob for being Bob (fair symmetry), and Aram's thirty-year association with Kolya.

Then everything went black.

WE WERE HIGH on a ridge in the Shikahogh forest preserve, about a hundred meters above treeline. We'd driven up here in a parade of camouflaged, four-wheeling park vans. They seemed a lot like military vehicles, but hey, what did I know? Perhaps they had something to do with the "Warning: Land Mines" signs we'd passed along the way. Or the stacks of rocket-propelled grenades and unexploded artillery lying around, reams of expended Kalashnikov shells crunching underfoot, and the fact that the reserve abutted Azerbaijan, the archenemy Armenia had recently concluded a war with. Call me old fashioned, but it just didn't seem fair to shell your enemies from, or in, a forest reserve.

Sidestepping the abundant ordnance, I'd found the first Armenian Viper of the trip, and the boys had since bagged several more. Giant Caucasus bumblebees—the world's largest—bounced off me like woodchips as we waded through swaying grasses, towering weeds, and dried opium pods sprouting in what was left of a small village that I was pretty sure belonged to Azerbaijani shepherds. I was also pretty sure they were killed on impact: sheet metal, wood, and roof tile from obliterated buildings adorned the ground. It was perfect habitat for rodents and perfect cover for snakes, and there were plenty of both: Rambo slung a pillowcase bulging with serpents surprised from their afternoon snooze; Bob too; Kolya, stoic as always, tongs in hand and toothpick in mouth, surveyed the scene, the wedge-shaped head of a meter-long Levantine Viper pinched between thumb and forefinger.

As always, I found his casualness disarming. The Levantine is a *very* dangerous snake, up to two meters long with a nasty disposition, lengthy fangs, and high volumes of tissue-destroying venom. Darevsky lost part of his finger to one, and many more had died from its bite. And yet this one hung from Kolya's hand like a rope he didn't know what to do with. I helped him bag it, then kept flipping through the mountain junkyard. Vipers aside, the excursion was little different than scrambling through the wasteland of Toronto's industrial parks.

Back at camp a park warden had slaughtered a sheep. Guts were everywhere, its stomachs bulging and intestines uncoiling over the ground like spilled spaghetti; fecal contents oozed from several tears. It seemed sloppy, but what did I know? Besides, we were hungry and another full-on feast was brewing.

After next morning's breakfast of leftover meat and vodka, we tromped up the road to a rock formation that caught early sun to "make photo." First up were the Armenian Vipers, gorgeous and velvety in the morning light. They cooperated, coiling into perfectly natural sit-and-wait poses on the lichen-spackled rock. Even the nasty-ass Levantines were charmingly photogenic. Not so the next species.

Schmidt's Racer (*Hierophis schmidti*) is a large, shiny red colubrid reminiscent of North American coachwhip snakes of the genus *Masticophus*—like the one that chewed on me in Baja. Rambo, Levon, and I had been trying to tire out a live-wire, 1.5-meter specimen by chasing it up and down the road, but the snake, striking continuously for almost an hour, showed no signs of staying still; getting it to coil for a photo was like stuffing a jack-in-the-box into a beer mug. Furthermore, it had nailed Rambo on the left index finger, drawing blood and ire.

While shooting, Bob and Nikolai communicated in a truncated but well-rehearsed way. As they posed an animal, it often adopted a defensive posture or tried to make a break. Watching the prodding and positioning closely, Bob would say, "Hmmm"—which meant, "The snake is trying to get away." Kolya might then answer, "Uh hmm"—which meant, "I see that." The dialogue didn't shift in accordance with the gravity of the situation. "Hmmm" could just as easily mean, "That cobra is spitting at you." While Kolya's "Uh hmm," as he wiped venom from his camera lens, would still mean, "I see that."

NIKOLAI "KOLYA" ORLOV grew up in St. Petersburg (Leningrad at the time), where he first became interested in amphibians and reptiles in middle school. Each day after class he would trot over to the zoological institute, where mentor Darevsky would introduce him to other scientists as a colleague. These days his encyclopedic knowledge of the world's herpetofauna and his legendary fieldwork placed him in high demand as a scientific expedition leader. By the time he landed in Armenia, he'd already traveled that year to China, Nepal, and Vietnam—twice.

Kolya embodied the turn-of-the-century explorer-naturalist-collector whose passion was embedded in a broad fascination for foreign lands and all things living. He'd described over a hundred new species of frog, lizard, and snake, and at least that number languished in his office awaiting description. As a measure of his importance, when we'd first visited Vietnam in 1994, the country had some eighty species of amphibians on the books. Today that number is over two hundred and rising fast enough to double in the next few years.

Kolya had an uncanny ability to intuit where animals would be and to find them where they might be overlooked by others. In short, he was a collecting machine, a label that carried negative connotations as by necessity it led to pickled animals and frozen tissues. But scientists knew what the public couldn't see: conservation wasn't always pretty, and preventing extinctions sometimes required sacrificing a few individuals. The advent of nondestructive methods like blood collection, scale clipping, and digital photography notwithstanding, voucher specimens of new species were usually required. Considering that he had single-handedly increased biodiversity indices in parts of Asia as much as threefold, conservation organizations, instead of calling Kolya's vocation into question, should have been lining up to give him a medal.

In Armenia, however, the man we called The Bear had been slowing down. Perhaps he was simply tired. At fifty-five, Kolya couldn't possibly keep up his current traveling and collecting pace. His invincibility seemed to be flagging as well; although I'd never seen him sick before, in Armenia he was struck down hard.

It happened after the photo session. He and Bop had trudged back to camp with grumbling stomachs that just didn't feel right. A sign of impending doom. Within an hour, Bob was at my tent.

"Got any toilet paper?" he'd said. "I'm right out and just shitting water." He looked pale and wasted. Kolya was in the same straits. An afternoon of violent vomiting and voiding left them crawling on hands and knees. I thought I'd dodged the bullet, but it hit me that night, around the time the toilet paper ran out. I wasn't quite as ill but was bad enough. It was probably the unsanitary sheep slaughter, but that's the way it went in the field. Kolya and I both got sick a couple more times over the coming weeks, and each time it wore on him far worse than it did on me. Maybe he just needed a break from all this craziness. I sure did.

THE FINAL WEEK had been desperately long and maddeningly hot. We'd returned from a final outing with bagfuls of new specimens, only to find that the animals we'd processed and fixed before leaving were decomposing in the sun on Aram's balcony. He'd left the sealed tray full of specimens there to avoid filling his apartment with the caustic miasma of fixative, but the formalin he'd fetched at the ministry turned out to be bad. I would be surprised if it had contained even 1 percent formaldehyde—the tray had become a fetid soup of rotted flesh and quasi-intact skeletons dangling conspicuous ROM field tags. Fortunately, although the animals were lost, tissue and scale samples were safely stored in tubes of ethanol, a reversal of Bob's last Armenian disaster. He could still conduct DNA analyses, and he would know which individual and putative species each sample was from, but his only record of most animals would be photographic. It could have been worse.

Actually, it was worse. Some overheated, hopped-up frogs had knocked the lid off their container and escaped to become crispy critters in the nether reaches of #1's apartment. And a couple of snakes had died, rotting too quickly in the heat to save any tissue.

So we'd spent the past couple of days salvaging what we could and fastidiously processing everything else. The apartment was a disaster, with blood and venom and ethanol everywhere.

On our final day, we'd slumped around the living room, a noisy, jerry-rigged fan blowing pathetically warm air. On TV a Russian documentary played, interrupted every few minutes by commercials for an energy drink in incomprehensible Armenian. Recumbent on the bench I'd occupied for three weeks, I noted through fluttering eyelids that Kolya sat close to the set next to Margo, both staring intently at the black-and-white footage of hollow-eyed, great-coated soldiers marching through mud and snow, a requirement, it seemed, of every Russian documentary, regardless of its subject. Bob hunched over his computer, working on photos. Levon was on his cell phone and smoking, as was Aram, between peeling flesh from his latest potload of the crayfish he was most certainly propelling to extinction. The smell was enough to make me vomit.

I pulled the visor of my hat down, remaining aware of everyone—their position in the room, their position in the universe. I loved these guys, these generous, open-hearted people trying to save the world from an inauspicious command post. But I had to get the fuck out of there. I couldn't take the heat, or the waiting, or the smoking, or the stomach cramps, or the vodka, or the disasters anymore. Soon I would be in my own spacious bed in the cool forests of British Columbia, and all would be right with the world . . . soon . . .

I'd opened my eyes to a nearby commotion. Chairs scraped aside as everyone scuffled around the room. Aram, somewhere near my feet, was trying to sweep an overlooked baby viper into a dustpan. It had been lurking around the warm wires leading to the television set and, when chased, had dashed toward the sofa where I slept, which it immediately climbed. A normal person—perhaps myself a few months back—would have pulled up his feet or jumped in alarm. But sudden movements were never a good thing, were they? The herpetologists would take care of things, I knew. They were the best there were. And if not? Well, there wasn't much to be done.

I pulled my hat back down and drifted off thinking about wide open spaces and our second-last day in Shikahogh.

While Bob and Kolya had been barfing their guts out and shitting themselves silly, before my own bowels had followed foul suit, I'd spent the afternoon climbing to the highest peak in the area, looking for nothing more than to get away from the plague that had felled them. Based on the view from camp, I'd expected no more than a brisk walk, but in the illusory way of mountains, wavering grasses petered quickly out and the rock slope jacked up like a rogue wave, turning the enterprise into a scramble—somewhere beyond hike, somewhat short of scaling cliffs.

At the top, I'd sat on a rock pinnacle, legs hanging in space. I seemed to have drawn even with the sun, which cast everything in stark relief, and the scope of what I could see was mesmerizing. Behind, our primary-color tents looked to have been painted on the landscape. Below, the shimmering green of treed slopes and canyons seemed completely out of step with the brown wasted plains of Azerbaijan to the east. Southward through the mountain haze was northern Iran, timeless villages cradled in terraced valleys and accessed by zigzag roads that seemed to climb forever. No wonder the wars that broke out over the millennia with Hindus, Arabs, Persians, Turks, and others had raged along this ridge. You could see anything and anywhere from up here. Into the centuries. Into the geological past and biological present. Into the uncertain future of a dozen different species. A true crossroads in every conceivable sense.

The perspective was both broadening and grounding—the kind I would never have been privy to had I not been running with this particular pack of lunatics. While my feet dangled in the shadow creeping down the peak's far side, I had thought hard on that.

I owed a lot to herpetologists. Ultimately, they'd delivered me an understanding that no type of blind faith could ever serve up. Most importantly, I'd learned how to question and why ("when" had never been an issue: always). They had also given me laughter, absurdity, knowledge, deep time, discovery, healthy fear, and sheer terror. But if herpetologists like Jim Bogart and Dr. Bob had taught me how to *look* at the world, then snakes had shown me how to *see* it. From within and never without. As part and not apart. Snakes had led the way to a lifetime of natural appreciation. They'd also brought a sense of mystery, reverence, and true beauty. So I was indebted to them, too. In particular, a small gartersnake that once escaped the clutches of a grubby six-year-old but remained forever in the grip of a curious mind.

As fiery alpenglow lit the peaks and a cold wind rushed in, I had recalled the trip to Finland months before that kicked off my voyage of reconnection and rediscovery. My search for the roots of this strange affliction had driven me to many musty dens—those of snakes *and* herpetologists—so I was obliged to both groups of coldhearted little bastards. After all, a love of snakes, nature, and the outdoors had ultimately led me to skiing and even writing; skiing, writing, and Finnish vipers had then led me here, to this aerie, closing a long, looping circle.

A strange connection, perhaps. But then, what in herpetology wasn't?

IN FINLAND, I'D hung around the den well past the time the second viper had methodically uncoiled into the damp warmth of subterranean refuge. Fascinated by the bizarre juxtaposition of serpent and snow, I'd sat on a rock to breathe in the air of continued mystery.

There's a way light swims through the long Arctic evening, unprojected from any one point but traded by a glut of celestial bodies. While the clear sky purpled on one horizon and flamed over another, a range of hues flowed over the snow like spilled paint. They were fleeting and tonal like the myriad serpents of my youth—ruby and gold where sunlight ebbed over the drifts; onyx and mercury in a thin shaft of moonlight; turquoise and topaz under eddies of incandescence thrown by light from the village. As night's inevitable cold descended, winter reasserted its rule over Viperworld, entombing the heat seekers once again.

Refrozen snow around the den had crunched underfoot as I walked away. How would anyone guess that in only a few hours, venomous snakes would be basking on this very spot? It was surely one of nature's most arcane wonders, though only one of many I'd been privy to. If life was a long, slow dissolve to solving the riddle of your potential, and chasing snakes had been such a big part of my solution, I reckoned I'd best pay more attention.

A few million years. A few thousand species. A few hundred secrets. So much to know and so little time before much of it was gone forever. Nothing to do but keep turning rocks and learn what you could.

I was snakebit all right—and thankful there was no known cure.

NOTES

. . .

CHAPTER 1
1 S.A. Minton, Jr., *Life, Love, and Reptiles: An Autobiography of Sherman A. Minton, Jr., M.D.*
   (Malabar, Florida: Krieger, 2001), 3.
2 S.A. Minton, Jr., *Life, Love, and Reptiles: An Autobiography of Sherman A. Minton, Jr., M.D.*
   (Malabar, Florida: Krieger, 2001), 5.
3 D.G. Wheeler, *Tales from the Golden Age of Rattlesnake Hunting* (Lansing: ECO Publishing,
   2001), 59.

CHAPTER 2
4 R.L. Ditmars, *Confessions of a Scientist, by Raymond L. Ditmars* (New York: The Macmillan
   company, 1934), 117.
5 R.L. Ditmars, *Snakes of the World by Raymond L. Ditmars, with Illustrations from Life*
   (New York: The Macmillan company, 1931), 1.
6 R.L. Ditmars, *Snakes of the World by Raymond L. Ditmars, with Illustrations from Life*
   (New York: The Macmillan company, 1931), frontispiece.
7 J. Seal, *The Snakebite Survivors' Club: Travels among Serpents* (New York: Harcourt, 1999), 9.
8 R.L. Ditmars, *Snakes of the World.* Reprint (Delhi: Komal, 2000), foreword.
9 J. Cann, *Snakes Alive! Snake Experts & Antidote Sellers of Australia* (Kenthurst, Australia:
   Kangaroo Press, 1986; Lansing: ECO Publishing, 2001), 57. Citation is to the
   ECO Publishing edition.
10 S. Orlean, *The Orchid Thief* (New York: Ballantine Books, 2000).

CHAPTER 5
11 R. Hofrichter, ed., *The Encyclopedia of Amphibians* (Toronto: Key Porter, 2002), 124.

CHAPTER 6
12 S. Orlean, *The Orchid Thief* (New York: Ballantine Books, 2000), 33.

CHAPTER 7
13 D. Quammen, *The Song of the Dodo: Island Biogeography in an Age of Extinction* (New York:
   Scribner, 1996), 18.
14 E.R. Pianka and L.J. Vitt, *Lizards: Windows to the Evolution of Diversity* (Berkeley:
   University of California Press, 2003), 2.

CHAPTER 8
15 W. Souder, *A Plague of Frogs: The Horrifying True Story* (New York: Hyperion, 20c

CHAPTER 9
16 A.S. Romer, *The Vertebrate Story*, 4th ed. (Chicago: University of Chicago Press, 1954), 1.

CHAPTER 10
17 M. Moffett, "Bit," *Outside* magazine, April 2002.

CHAPTER 11
18. D.A. Rossman, N.B. Ford, and R.A. Seigel, *The Garter Snakes: Evolution and Ecology* (Norman: University of Oklahoma Press, 1996), 222.
19 Paraphrased from www.naturenorth.com.

CHAPTER 12
20 M. Moffett, "Bit," *Outside* magazine, April 2002.

Epigraphs for chapters 1 and 9 are from the album *Don Juan's Reckless Daughter* (New York: Asylum Records, 1977).

Epigraph for chapter 14 is from E.T. Seton, "Snakes Good and Bad," *The Birch Barck Roll of the Woodcraft League of America Inc.*, 1902. http://www.inquiry.net/outdoor/skills/seton/snakes.htm.